This is the work of an unusually awesome intellect and flawless scholarship. As Ato himself may agree, if our scholars and writers have to do their work using the English language, then we of the neo-colonies are doing that language a whole lot of good. If the book was about nothing else than Professor Sekyi-Otu's merciless dissection of the wretched story of the life and career of Kwasi Kwarteng, an arch-conservative member of the British Conservative Party, that alone makes the book a compelling read.
— The late, **Ama Ata Aidoo**,
author, poet, playwright and academic, author of
Changes: A Love Story and *Dilemma of a Ghost*

More precious, untimely observations from the most important black political philosopher writing in English. Read, learn, savor, be provoked, read again, repeat.
— **Paul Gilroy**,
author *The Black Atlantic*

The echoes of Fanon pervade this incisive analysis that spares no one, refuses any postulation of idyllic longings, and interrogates our responsibilities in every aspect of the histories that live within us. This work offers a powerful and incisive reflection on human freedom and responsibility in an affirmation of dignity that can only fully emerge upon recognition of the cruelty of the inhumanities that pervades our histories and their geographies. It is an existential call to lay bare so that we might understand the biting complexity of indignity and reach through its morass to discover the depths of our humanity no matter how deeply that humanity is assaulted. *Homestead, Homeland, Home* charts this journey with biting clarity and takes irony as a "vital organ of truth and justice" to the apogee of its power.
—**Jacqueline M Martinez**, Professor of Communication,
College of Integrative Sciences and Arts
Arizona State University,
Vice-President, Caribbean Philosophical Association

I lost count of the number of times I laughed out loud reading this book and the number of times I had to put it down in chest-tightening anguish. Ato Sekyi-Otu long ago demonstrated that he was a first-rate scholar. With these meditations, though, these 'peeves' as he hilariously describes them, he reveals himself a member of an even more remarkable group - those who dare attempt to rouse a world lost in shadow gazing. *Homestead, Homeland, Home* dissects global society and reveals a malignant inhumanity. It is a challenge and resource for those who can be shaken and a damning indictment on those who will not. It is bracing, severe, funny, heartbreaking, brilliant and very, very cool.'

—**Bryan Mukandi**, Senior Research Fellow, School of Languages and Cultures, Faculty of Humanities and Social Sciences, University of Queensland, Australia

This is a book of peeves well worth peeving about. It is testimony from a great elder of political thought whose heartfelt commitments to dignity, freedom, justice, and humane existence irritate his soul as a witness to the continued cruelty, degradation, and double standards unleashed against the Damned of the Earth; it is erudite outrage at so many ignored opportunities to make good on political responsibility to build a better world, a world otherwise. Every sentence, every paragraph, every page, every chapter is a Sankofic demand against historic amnesia and an encomium to re-member and, in doing so, courageously embrace our shared responsibility to build institutions for the urgent repair of nothing short of humanity's homestead in which we are, in Sekyi-Otu's words, "compelled to recognize that only we can save ourselves."

—**Lewis R. Gordon**, author of *Freedom, Justice, and Decolonization* and *Fear of Black Consciousness*

Homestead Homeland Home: Critical Reflections is political-philosophic tour de force by Ghana's leading public intellectual Ato Sekyi-Otu. Each chapter brims with insight, irony (humorous and often indecent, like the George W. Bush highway in Accra), and analytical precision as he subjects the homesteads, Canada and the USA and the homeland, Ghana, to his partisan universalist critique. He weaves his reflections with the thoughts of philosophers, thinkers, and sages of the human condition and the poets, songwriters, and dreamers of human liberation.

— **Nigel Gibson**, author of *Fanon: The Postcolonial Imagination*

Raging against the solitary confinement of despair into compartmentalized finitudes and possessive particularisms, Ato Sekyi-Otu continues in these epigrammatic reflections to put his unmistakable mixture of resentment and fury at the service of a new principle of hope. In search of a place to call home, untethered to any exclusionary metaphysics of difference, he makes short shrift of the willful amnesia surrounding the criminal junction of capitalism, slavery, colonialism, and anti-black racism, with their interlocking systems of subjugation; refuses the preaching of collective guilt and abject misanthropy alike; and instills in the reader a concrete utopian belief in freedom from the dominion of race, egalitarian self-determination, and partisan universalism as common sense. These fragments of a vision of humanity unbound will leave no one untouched by their relentless tarrying with the world's prose and intermittent poetry.
—**Bruno Bosteels**, author of *The Actuality of Communism*

For those familiar with Sekyi-Otu's work, *Homestead, Homeland, Home* is another instalment of what are gift offerings of his extraordinary mind and intellect. And for those not familiar, they better start reading these reflections right now, and don't stop until you are fully done with them. Here is something to arouse the consciousness with beauty, poise, and quiet brilliance.
— **Ato Quayson**, Jean G. and Morris M. Doyle Professor of Interdisciplinary Studies, Stanford University

Homestead, Homeland, Home

Critical Reflections

Ato Sekyi-Otu

Daraja Press

2023

Published by
Daraja Press
https://darajapress.com
Wakefield, Québec, Canada

© 2023 Ato Sekyi-Otu
All rights reserved

ISBN 9781990263545

Cover design: Kate McDonnell

Library and Archives Canada Cataloguing in Publication

Title: Homestead, homeland, home : critical reflections / Ato Sekyi-Otu.
Names: Sekyi-Otu, Ato, author.
Identifiers: Canadiana 20230175732 | ISBN 9781990263545 (softcover)
Subjects: LCSH: National characteristics—Philosophy. | LCSH: Ethnopsychology. | LCSH: Home— Philosophy.
Classification: LCC BF753 .S45 2023 | DDC 155.8—dc23

*IN MEMORY OF
ANANI AND AMA ATA*

CONTENTS

	The Argument	i
I	Forgetting to Re-Member	1
II	Songs of Sankofa	8
III	One Reason for the Journey Back	17
IV	The Black Professor's Burden	26
V	Human Things, Black Kinds?	38
VI	Property Rites	42
VII	Observations on USA	53
VIII	Homeland is Not Yet Home	84
IX	Strange Things of the World	147
X	Kwarteng's Tale	172
XI	Peeves and Dreams, at Large	196
XII	Persistent Polemics, Countervailing Musings	242
	Epilogue: When I am Still Old Enough to Dream	252
	About the author	254

Once they have grasped themselves and established what is theirs, without expropriation and alienation, in real democracy, there arises in the world something which shines into the childhood of all and in which no one has yet been: home.

—Ernst Bloch, *The Principle of Hope*

THE ARGUMENT

I am a seething cauldron of peeves. The other day the town criers summoned us to a festival meant to bear joyful witness to the end of a millennium and the radiant dawn of a new one. I did not show up. Why? Because as I surveyed the earth, I saw one incandescent pyre of lacerated bodies and souls and oaths – this is the hardest of all to behold –, oaths sworn at hallowed moments of that lamentable millennium to end immemorial iniquities. Was it not in that epoch that, among other noteworthy testaments to the efflorescence of civilization, multitudes of African peoples, captured and sold with the complicity of our villainous chieftains and merchants, were transported to demonic destinations, there to endure the terror of servitude and degradation, a holocaust second to none in the execrable record of historical crimes? Yes, in my picture of the world, I confess to being a loyal member of the congregation of miscreants whom one of the anointed sages of our time, in his oblivious contentment, spitefully called the "school of resentment." In these epigrams, I voice some, but only some, of the myriad things that incite in me a withering resentment. I take perverse pleasure in ferreting noxious deceptions, toxic motives and censored truths behind the cherished verities and pieties of our world. Time has tamed the ire of souls more prudent than mine. My rage has aged well, refusing to heed the call to obsequious maturity, the counsel of acquiescent sobriety. Yet I am a steadfast votary of what those enamoured of things as they are disdainfully call utopia. Indeed, the two impulses are here united: wrathful resentment and the call of utopia. Utopia not as beatific idyll and final destination, but rather as the lodestar which illumines the radical insufficiency of our present attainments, discloses the ills and failings of every homestead we have ever found or built or dwelt in, especially the land of our birth, and so goads us unremittingly towards ever-expanding horizons in a restless striving after a place we might call home. This is as it should be. Like black-eyed peas, the grains of matter from which these raw emanations of the irate mind sprout tell a tangled tale. Cultivated in circumstances of dire necessity, they are blessed with the most life-enhancing of nature's energies, seedlings of renewal for body and soul. So it is with the provenance and purpose of the peeves here assembled. My numberless resentments are provoked by the foolish notion that humanity's prospects are not and cannot possibly be exhausted by what we are now trained to discern on our pitifully shrunken horizon; they are roused by remembrance of things not yet done. An unrepentant member of the community of those unwilling to grovel before a despotic divinity of our own invention, I have no gods to exalt, no shrines to worship in, no comforting hymns of exultation to chant. Yet I am no wayward wanderer without belief. Here is the family of things to which I pledge ardent devotion and those for which I swear sacred hatred: Even as I reverence every person's right to shape her destiny, to follow the special path of her chi, I share Frantz Fanon's revulsion with life lived in the service of the depraved creed according to which "each-one-shits-for-himself, the godless way of salvation," while our common homestead is in ruins; the call to savage self-interest as the sovereign principle of human conduct, the triumphal tenet of the favoured few, no less than the desperate temptation of the damned of the earth. I adhere to the educated hope of those who proclaim, in the simple words of the revolt against the global despoliation of the many by the few: "Another world is possible." Awed by the immense possibilities of our earthly powers, I resent the picayune realism that says that this is all there is to be; that, in a malign version of a famous quip by a hilarious jester of days gone by, "what you see is what you get." There are, there must be, other ways of dwelling on this earth and being with one another. There must be other truths beyond those that are made to command our obeisance at the behest of the rulers. That is why I resent the artless parade of transient habits and provincial peculiarities in the masquerade of timeless necessities. With equal passion, I resent the unthinking refusal of shareable human dreams in the name of the fight against empire and the duty to

THE ARGUMENT

protect what is our own from the marauders. We cannot, with justice, fight the evil that empire has done by accepting, as if it is a corollary of that duty, all practices of our particular communities, however wicked they are, and by renouncing what is demonstrably best for our native humanity. Above all, I resent the illicit power that the ordinance of race has contrived to foist upon all our attachments and allegiances, all of life's questions and quests, even as I recognize the contingent foundation of that power. Thanks to this predicament, I cannot survey the world through a stainless lens. Rather, I do so in the manner of Ama Ata's "blackeyed squint," the wry vision given to an eye bruised by history yet enabled by that very wound to descry glimmers of a transfigured world. That way, these reflections relive the pain visited upon body and spirit and, at the same time, imagine the redemptory resources wrested from that pain. I hear that conspiracy of agony and aspiration in the philosopher's protesting portrait of life made hostage to forcible finitudes: "this narrow world strewn with prohibitions." I hear that utterance as a call that all captive ways of living our human condition must fall. Say, then, that these epigrams are contrapuntal variations on the philosopher's searing imprecation and visionary invocation: unfinished ode, resounding with intermittent fury, to the dawn of human existence set free from all tyrannizing enclosures.

I

FORGETTING TO RE-MEMBER

OBAMA AT THE DOOR OF NO RETURN

It is Holocaust Remembrance Day. That horrendous event must never be forgotten. Nor should its baneful uniqueness be obscured by transforming it into a parable of all human iniquity. I wish and hope that every Nazi war criminal will be found and duly punished. I wish and hope that anyone who denies the truth of that terror will be sent, as Ayi Kwei's avenging griots demand, "hurrying to face the wrath of ancestors." I wish and hope that every Holocaust Remembrance Day re-enacts a universal oath never again to let such iniquity stalk this earth.

But who will remember *our* holocaust, the unspeakable evil of the enslavement and damnation of Africans? If you doubt the horror of that holocaust, visit THE DOOR OF NO RETURN: the door out of which, after their sojourn in the bowels of the infernal dungeons, the captives emerged bound for an unknown destination and an unfathomable fate. Technically speaking, that fate, unlike the Nazi holocaust, was not the product of hate. It had everything to do with love, the wicked love of African labour. Where I ask, are the terrible dates engraved in the public memory of the world that insist on keeping knowledge of this history alive? Where are the solemn acts of atonement, where the vows never again to allow such a ghastly thing to blight the face of humanity? I mean *public* acts of remembrance and expiation and resolve. For there is no dearth of scholarly attention to the details of the slave trade and the experience of slavery. Was slavery utterly debilitating? Did it turn its victims into perpetual infants completely bereft of the will to freedom? Or did slaves attest to an irrepressible desire for liberty by fleeing from bondage at the first opportunity? And did they succeed, while in bondage and in spite of bondage, in fashioning binding human associations and enduring communities of meaning? From Elkins to Orlando Patterson and beyond, these and other debates have continued unabated in the scholarship on slavery. But that's just it: These are debates in the halls of the academy rather than matters of public discourse. The voice of the academy, however earnest, is no substitute for the peoples' work of remembrance. The consequences of that wilful failure to remember are evident in public culture. Consider the radically different responses to *Schindler's List* on the one hand and to *Amistad* and *Beloved* on the other, the malign neglect to which the latter two were condemned. *Our* "fearful holocaust" has not received due public rites of recognition, to say nothing of atonement and reparation. To the original crime of brutal enslavement must be added this criminal act of oblivion, this sinful silence. To it can be accredited the utter incomprehension with which the slave-owners' descendants greet the complaints and demands of those who live Black lives and keep on reaping the bitter fruits of a cruel and unatoned past. As Robin Blackburn reminds the masters' progeny: "We have yet to slough off all the ideologies and institutions produced in the era of racial slavery."

What provokes my peeve? Shoah envy? Avenging justice for unredeemed ancestors? Or an ethic of connectedness? For the beginnings of an answer, listen to the following two testimonies. The first is by Elie Wiesel, remembering Auschwitz at the Klaus Barbie trial in 1987:

> An order rang out: "Line up by family." That's good, I thought, we will stay together. Only for a few minutes, however: "Men to the right, women to the left." The blows rained down on all sides. I was not able to say goodbye to my mother. Nor to my grandmother. I could not kiss my little sister...This was a separation that cut my life in half. I rarely speak of it, almost never. I cannot recall my mother or my little sister. With my eyes, I still look for

them. I will always look for them. And yet I know...
My gaze stops at the threshold of the gas chambers.
Even in thought, I refuse to violate the privacy of
the victims at the moment of death.

The second testimony is that of Olaudah Equiano, writing in 1789 and recounting his fearful journey along the Slave Coast, a sudden reunion with his captured sister, to be followed by an equally sudden separation:

> In this manner I had been travelling for a considerable time, when one evening, to my great surprise, whom should I see brought to the house where I was but my dear sister! As soon as she saw me she gave a loud shriek and ran into my arms,1 was quite overpowered: neither of us could speak, but for a considerable time clung to each other in mutual embraces, unable to do anything but weep...When [the traders] knew we were brother and sister they indulged us to be together, and the man to whom I supposed we belonged lay with us, he in the middle while she and I held one another by the hands across his breast all night; and thus for a while we forgot our misfortunes in the joy of being together: but even this small comfort was soon to have an end, for scarcely had the fatal morning appeared when she was again torn from me forever! I was now more miserable, if possible, than before. The small relief which her presence gave me was gone, and the wretchedness of my situation was redoubled by my anxiety after her fate and my apprehensions lest her sufferings should be greater than mine, when I could not be with her to alleviate them. Yes, thou dear partner of my childhood sports! thou sharer of my joys and sorrows! happy should I have ever esteemed myself to encounter every misery for you, and to procure your freedom by the sacrifice of my own. Though

you were early forced from my arms, your image has been always riveted in my heart, from which neither time nor fortune have been able to remove it...To that Heaven which protects the weak from the strong I commit the care of your innocence and virtues, if they have not already received their full reward and if your youth and delicacy have not long fallen victims to the violence of the African trader, the pestilential stench of the Guinea ship, the seasoning in the European colonies, or the lash and lust of a brutal and unrelenting overseer.

Twin tales. Each tells an unspeakable story of the violent separation of dear ones doomed for degradation and suffering. Twin horrors, they have been accorded separate and unequal treatments in the narrative institutions of the world's public cultures. But as grievous as the separate and unequal treatments accorded these kindred events, indeed what enables their differing registrations is the very manner in which the organization of memory has contrived to reorder their respective places in historical time, and therewith in the macabre calculus of moral gravity. In that mnemonic scheme, the Nazi holocaust comes first. It is as though the train to Buchenwald, rather than the slave ship, has a claim not only to temporal priority but also to a privileged status as a template of terror, a pernicious archetype to which the forcible journey of kidnapped women and men across unknown seas to demonic destinations is related as a subsequent event. Dear reader, I, too, have complied with this reordering of the prior and the posterior, of archetype and analogy, by presenting to you Elie Wiesel's testimony before that of Olaudah Equiano. I am not alone. On 11 July 2009, standing in the slave dungeon at Oguaa – commonly called "Cape Coast Castle" in an act of matchless obscenity – Barak Obama, the first African American President of the United States of America, said of the sight that it reminded him of "the same feeling I got when I went to Buchenwald with Elie Wiesel." It was as though Buchenwald were the primal crime for which the slave dungeon – and the succession of unspeakable woes that awaited the captives

– serves as supplement to our inaugural knowledge of historical iniquity. No, I do not share Frank Wilderson's animus against analogy, "the ruse of analogy." I am only inveighing against the not insignificant matter of the temporal order in which we place the things of which we discern kinships. I mean this practice of misplacing in time the objects of analogy. Pointless quibble? A masochistic exercise in what Herbert Marcuse used to call "the calculus of suffering," "oppression Olympics" in today's sardonic idiom? I am all too aware that any suggestion of affinities between the Nazi holocaust and other holocausts of this past grievous millennium, to say nothing of a call to rearrange their place in our moral reckoning, may be suborned by trained haters intent on denying, for their own heinous purposes, the specific gravity of this or that instance of inhumanity. But to still our tongues when they insist on cursing kindred forms of radical evil for fear of the hijacker's inevitable misuse of our utterances – our dangerous talk of pernicious resemblances *and* odious singularities among experiences of historical iniquity – that would indeed give the perpetrators occasion for raucous and triumphant laughter for work well done. The great bard, Aimé Césaire, called the successful result of that work "the solitary confinement of despair." But it may assume another shape, indeed its macabre double. And that is a strange pride in the absolute uniqueness of your particular experience of evil, the unwillingness, as a consequence, to hear other voices shrieking with nameless anguish from other chambers of horror in this haunted house we call history. Cowering solitude or prideful singularity, the result is the same and exactly what the poet feared: the utter incapacity of violated persons and peoples, distinct yet mutually recognizable individuals and communities of suffering, to fashion a "common sense," a redemptory covenant of the "furious we."

TU QUOQUE
For Janine and Alok

But who is blameless in this matter of forgetting to re-member shareable things – terrible things – unjustly sundered? How many in my community of people of African descent have made the history and the condition of vanquished First Nations Peoples of Canada and other lands the object of pressing concern, to say nothing of taking up their cause? It was only quite late in my life in Canada that I, for one, discovered fragments of their searing history and visions of the world wrenched from their dispossession and abjection. Discovered, I said? What a lie. Like other famous discoveries, the subject of this one was quite alive before a way of seeing impaired by a trained failure to re-member lighted upon it. And as in the case of other famous acts of discovery, I was led to this one by eyes trained otherwise.

It is astonishing, is it not, the aping apartheids we contrive to erect between our worlds and within our souls, aiding and abetting in so doing the oppressors' fine work? Was that not Bessie Head's terrifying testimony? And was it not a measure of her sheer chutzpah that she saw this and more without sinking into abject misanthropy and despair, exhorting us instead "to look at life with a visionary eye"?

OGUAA'S OBLIVION

Who, indeed, is blameless? The most criminal oblivion of all: In my hometown, Oguaa (Cape Coast), sits one of the most notorious of the infernal slave dungeons. It begins with the name, the outrageous obscenity of the name: "Cape Coast Castle." No wonder our people misrecognize its very presence and disremember the gravity of its significance in the story of the African condition. They walk by it every day, and go about their business in its environs with sublime indifference. Of the "castle" and its place in our existence and our psyche, Kwadwo Opoku-Agyemang's laconic words cannot be matched: "We kneel because it stands." Thaddeus Ulzen, doctor of the soul and scion of Elmina – home to another marvel of the enslavers' carceral architecture – is less poetic, though no less truthful, in his diagnosis. To my lament that we have forgotten to remember this cardinal catastrophe, to my lament that we have managed to erase the traumatic memory that would make this site our Wailing Wall, Dr Ulzen replied with clinical precision: "It is our pissing wall." So, Saidiya, I understand the fury and the sorrow that welled up in your guts as you journeyed along the slave coast, relived the horror of enchained ancestors and witnessed the cruel failure of the living to remember. I really do. You see, as Abena Busia explains: "We too have been taught forgetting." I do not think Abena intends that to be an exculpation, still less an expiation. A consistent partisan, with Olúfémi Táíwò, of our inalienable agency, our African human agency, I would only recast the passive voice in Abena's sentence into an active voice, an emphatic active voice: *We have chosen to forget to re-member.* Oh, we have indeed been pricked in recent times from the deepest recesses of our sinful sleep. But see how at the behest of our bedecked chieftains and cunning merchants, we have elected to rekindle memory of our crowning calamity. Consider what strange rites of remembrance we have been performing. Listen to how we have of late undertaken to mourn our captured dead and sing the sorrow songs.

II

SONGS OF SANKOFA

THE JOSEPH PROJECT

The word that names the retrieval of things lost and so captures the mission of the sisters and brothers of the African diaspora coming to the motherland, specifically to Ghana, is *Sankofa*, the Akan word that means "to go and take it back." (The word would be made world famous by the film of that name made by Shirikiana Aina and Haile Gerima in 1997.) For as the elders say: "to go back to retrieve that which you forgot is no vice." In 2007, as part of the celebrations marking the fiftieth anniversary of Ghana's independence, the first official version of the *Sankofa* saga was launched: *The Joseph Project* named, naturally, after the biblical Joseph who, according to the story in Genesis, was sold by his brothers into slavery but would end up "becoming governor over all the land of Egypt." Ghana's Minister of Tourism at the time, J.O. Obetsebi-Lamptey explained: "Those of us who believe in the promise of God to Africa, take our hope from the story of Joseph in the Bible. For we believe that God loved Joseph and yet saw him cast into the hell of slavery and brought him out in triumph, to magnify the scale of his favour." Under the auspices of this biblical parable, Ghana, "The Gateway to the Homeland," would welcome people of the African diaspora, in particular, those exceptional Josephs "who have risen above their captivity and are shining examples of the human spirit and of what men can do." Clearly, the Ghanaian government hoped that such exemplary children of Africa would magnify not only the scale of God's favour but, rather more tangibly, the volume of investments in this "emerging market" society. Entirely laudable was the grand ambition impelling the project: It was "to make the 21st century the African century" by gathering and harnessing into a common enterprise scattered resources of intellect and wealth. And unquestionably praiseworthy was the recognition that a necessary condition for this enterprise of regeneration was healing, consisting in an "act of expiation and forgiveness" on the part of descendants of those who were accomplices in the original crime or are burdened with the guilt of being spared. Accordingly, there would be a "ceremony of rapprochement" in July 2007.

Who is the killjoy who looks askance at this festival of homecoming, this vision of daybreak upon the motherland after a long infernal night? What is there not to like? And, in the first place, what is in a name; I mean "The *Joseph* Project"? The answer: it is significant. The most obvious is the choice of a Judeo-Christian trope in place of an indigenous African one. You need not be a votary of Romantic Afrocentric nationalism to observe, even in these fashionably post-nativist times, the irony of a symbolism of homecoming renouncing the most elementary testimony to that which purports to be one's own. A rite of return naming itself in the poetry of the absconders' creed, however, naturalized by long usage that creed might be said to be. It is as if the very ceremony of roots has been wilfully uprooted from proverbs of existence and history native to what Wole Soyinka once provocatively called "this separate earth." It is as though we were embracing with masochistic glee a prime instrument of what Leon Damas, a major poet of the diaspora, called our *déracinement*. Might as well thank our stars, might as well, what else, thank god for the coming of the enslavers and the conquerors as indeed Obetsebi-Lamptey's statement all but implies. From radical evil, from the emblematic catastrophe of the African experience, a joyful theodicy is here wrested. And indeed, that visceral need for theodicy pervades everyday life and language, the idioms of social despair and hope alike. It is expressed in an obsessive biblicalism replete with a repertoire of scriptural citations, each one reduced to a parable unencumbered by arcane, esoteric meaning and, thanks to the healthy utilitarianism of needy votaries, mimed for the most serviceable moral lesson it contains. In its self-description and organizing idioms, the Joseph Project embodied the generic features of today's obsessional social biblicalism. But here is a legitimate question: What right do I have to sneer at the appropriation of the Joseph story for African purposes because of its allegedly alien origin? What right do I have when the words of my very own peeves assembled in these pages betray the recognizable accents of an African Cicero, if I may own up to just one figure in the shamelessly promiscuous baggage of intellectual antecedents, debts and affinities I carry on my back? Still, all petty peeves apart, The Joseph Project signalled a notable change in the existential psychology of a people in this phase of our tormented history.

In the foundational story of *Sankofa*, Africa is lost mother rediscovered. Into her joyful bosom fell the absconded child, half transfixed by the tears of remembrance, half supplicant burdened with a nameless guilt, seeking absolution for a sin not of her own making, the strange sin of unwilled separation – mass kidnapping – and enforced oblivion. But there is no mistaking the relative moral status of mother and child, protagonists in this drama of return and recognition. There is more than a hint of the receiving mother's natural primacy and the returning one's subordinate status, given his obligation to relearn at her bosom stories of the world he has lost and regain certificates of belonging and authenticity. No matter her material circumstances, in the foundational rhetoric of *Sankofa*, mother Africa retained the aura of supremacy of the spirit. No longer. A motherland rendered abysmally penurious, in desperate need of succour, reduced to abject mendicancy as macroeconomic policy, cannot sustain for long this serene separation of matter and spirit, this fiction of a perdurable spirit in proud possession, despite being housed in a prostrate body, of inviolate eternal essences. Accordingly, the Joseph Project revises the original narrative. From the fraught drama of recognition in which mother Africa reigns as source, origin, plenitude assaulted and regained, we have come to this: the prose of the returning one as moneybags, long lost and happily found progeny bringing the cargo to salvage the destitute, kith and kin as privileged investor to be royally courted; erstwhile penitent now transfigured into dispenser of grace in the shape of worldly goods. For it is clear that the figure of Joseph is but the sacral shell of the crassest materialism, the quest for investments by the avid hustlers of an "emergent market" society. If there is something redeeming in this reversal of roles, it does not quite reside in the new mission conferred on our Black Joseph, this transformation of the beseeching child into saviour as affluent investor and of nurturing mother into a dependent being. Rather, it consists of the revision of the story of the slave "trade" as a moral fable, the emblematic moral fable of the African condition. It consists of the reassignment of responsibility for the original sin of Joseph's enslavement. Africa is no longer innocent victim but collusive participant in the primal crime against our people. Such is the archetypal and abiding truth of the story of Joseph's betrayal by his siblings. In appropriating the biblical story – albeit for profane purposes – the Ghanaian revisionists are unwittingly heeding the call to unsparing critical introspection as a necessary condition of our claim to moral autonomy, a call which some of our most searching and iconoclastic thinkers have been issuing for some time. That is the good and daring news. But missing from this altogether salutary confession of African accountability is the specific responsibility of the *class* of African predators and collaborators who were part and parcel of the infernal business. In its class-blindness, the revised moral fable trades an account that exculpates *all* Africans without exception for one that, with equal indeterminacy, convicts all Africans of complicity in the nefarious trade. Such a socially-unindexed indictment condemns us to the pathos of collective guilt or, worse, abject misanthropy, the paralyzing idea of a common human sinfulness from which, predictably, only god can save us. With a class-analytic version of the moral fable, we have the means with which we can begin to understand the pedigree of our continued subjugation and recurring calamities: the historical bonds of complicity forged by social power and particular interests which have always been the enabling condition of our woes. More than that, we are compelled to recognize that only we can save ourselves.

THE YEAR OF RETURN

But here comes the most flamboyant chapter in the Sankofa saga: "The Year of Return" proclaimed in 2019 to mark the four-hundredth anniversary of the forced arrival of the first enslaved Africans in Jamestown Virginia. This new iteration constitutes a notable change in the ethics of memory as collective self-interrogation. Significantly, it has dropped the painful confessional work, such as it was, of the Joseph Project. The introspective question of indigenous African responsibility – more specifically, *class* complicity and culpability – is excised, and enslavement is recast into a story of African glory intercepted and regained. A redemptory dramatic narrative – call it a salvific racial entelechy – is thereby fashioned: from THE GATE OF NO RETURN, presumably erected in a unilateral act of singular iniquity by the interlopers, to THE EVENT OF RETURN, the groans of unavenged ancestors transformed into the joyous romance of homecoming. If in this new edition of the saga, the returning descendants are still permitted to rail, yell and holler, they will do so not against betraying kith and kin, but solely against the wicked alien agents who rudely interrupted the glory that was once theirs; not against the collaboration of villainous chieftains and merchants but against the loss of the regal status and the splendour they imagine they enjoyed before the Fall. So it is that after a traumatizing visit to "Cape Coast Castle," American TV celebrity Steve Harvey, mightily pissed off with the fate endured by his enslaved forebears and their progeny in the land of the free, had this to say: "I was just angry at what they did to us. How dare you create such an evil scheme to strip people of who they are and take us to this land, far from where we were hated even more. Standing in the dungeon, where they took us from, what they stripped us of, our land and our heritage, where we were kings, chiefs, queens and landowners." Glory *interruptus*, the glory that was royalty, property and power! "*Where we were kings, chiefs, queens and landowners*" No, you were not, brother. And incidentally, kings, chiefs, queens and landowners were and still are the bane, not the blessing, principal agents of "the cause of all our woes" – but not "with loss of Eden" as the author of

Paradise Lost has it, but the loss, quite simply but crucially, of our self-determination, our native freedom to contend with native demons and our homegrown capacity to imagine human things. That is the cruel and tangled truth the brother should learn. But a conspiracy of wilful amnesia and mystification would hear none of it. Among the events to close the Year of Return was the "African Royalty Night: The Gala." Our "fearful holocaust" consecrated with the title of its principal native agents, the sick royalism of homeland tyrants and obsequious cretins now visited upon its hapless returning historical victims. One happy returning brother has contrived to have himself enstooled chief of some rustic principality and is mightily proud of it. Far from weeping and puking uncontrollably at the very thought of royalty, he has become a learned griot of African dynasties from their majestic Kemetic antiquity to today's neocolonial kleptocratic chieftains busy selling to the highest bidder lands placed in their hands not as individual proprietors but as trustees and custodians of the immemorial and inalienable commons. The brother is deeply outraged by the anti-monarchism of a thinker such as Ayi Kwei Armah, who is insufficiently enamoured of the Kemet of autocratic pharaohs, preferring an earlier time of an egalitarian social order and envisioning the reinvention of such an order in a world to come. What a strange idea, incomprehensible to royals and power-idolizing returning scholars alike, an idea encapsulated in this inference by negation proffered in *The Healers*: "no kings, no tribes, no slaves." Descendant of enslaved ancestors, our royalist brother's indignation at the very thought of a form of human association and a polity devoid of despots and plutocrats is palpable. Irony, vital organ of truth and justice, wilfully gouged from the mind's eye. The sad imbecility of it all. The brother should be pleased with the next instalment of the Sankofa saga.

THE BEAUTIFUL CITY

And now comes *Beyond the Return*. The plot, as they say, thickens yet again. Some might say that it becomes truly grotesque. No doubt, the authors of the most recent chapter of the epic saga see it as Sankofa's consummation and moment of consecration. Launched in November 2020 is the magnificent multi-billion-dollar project of *Wakanda City of Return*. What could be more fitting than the name of the fictional country of Wakanda in the 2018 blockbuster film "Black Panther"? Fiction become fact. Art materialized. Idea made flesh. Apart from the little matter of luxurious 5-Star hotels lining the radiant coastline (the hood and the crisis of affordable housing in the Bronx miraculously undone in the motherland), the City will feature a Heritage Walk whose holiest of holies – immortal gods! – will be "THE ROYAL DOOR OF RETURN." The primal site of traumatic terror and separation cancelled. The unspeakable dread of enchained slaves doomed for demonic destinations transfigured into the majestic gait and entrance of exiled monarchs come to reclaim their rightful thrones. Is my talk of "our *crowning* calamity" a Freudian slip? Listen to the breathless words of the project's Chairman, a certain Dr Kojo Benjamin Taylor, his mind and soul, just like our returning royalist brother's, utterly voided of irony, that nagging organ of truth and justice: "Our ancestors are (sic) warriors conquering and taking over territories. So, we took the inspiration from all of this. We will have a village within the Wakanda Return City called 'Edzikanfo' which simply means our forefathers who have gone before us." There we have it. Predation and conquest – the sport not indeed of *all* "our ancestors" but the power-crazy class among them – as inspiring archetype for welcoming back descendants of the victims of predation and conquest. The fevered dream of Césaire's Henri Christophe fulfilled, the beautiful city as "a perfect replica in black" of segregated life. Frantz Fanon should be living at this hour: "A world divided into compartments" freely rebuilt. The spanking splendour that will be the city of the returning ones and the obdurate decay that Oguaa (Cape Coast) will still be. But keep hope alive. Oguaa's wayward youth will be idle no more. They can look forward to leaving their decrepit homesteads, the "natives' quarters," at dawn to enter the city of light, there to perform slave labour – no doubt rebranded with an appropriate neoliberal name – for the new aristocracy of brothers and sisters from afar. Such is our political leaders' and the new private-sector-corporate-hustlers' idea of "Exodus, Movement of Jah People." Bob Marley must be wailing and thundering in the abode of the ancestors. The vampiric "Babylon System" upon which the Rastaman bestowed searing songs of imprecation now redesigned with love and pride by our very own kith and kin, today's reincarnations of the rapacious "factors," those efficient enablers of the slave "trade."

SO ARE YOU GOING BACK TO LIVE THERE?

That is the question I was often asked by well-meaning Canadian acquaintances nurtured on "their shitholes" iconography of Africa (and more or less benign versions of the famous trope) whenever I broached my plan to return? Are you going back to live there? Trust me, it was not for the things that troubled and still trouble me that my Canadian friends asked that question, if you know what I am saying. But yes, is this the land to which I yearned to return for so long? This nation whose leaders' notion of redemptory remembrance, of how to memorialize the defining evil in our history, is to lure and suborn descendants of the victims with the promise of a city set apart for them, a sequestered life of luxury and extravagance? Are you going back to a people so lost in wilful amnesia – among its multiple scleroses – that our rulers have elected to defang the rites of memory of all avenging and cleansing rage, determined instead to fashion a festivity out of our long and bitter Nakba, a veritable *dance macabre*? A people so forgetful of that defining violence and its continual reiteration in succeeding systems of subjugation? "All good men and women try to forget. They have forgotten": that is Anowa's rebuke in Ama Ata Aidoo's play *Anowa*. They, we, have indeed forgotten. That is why the emblematic incident of colonial violence ritually invoked in the nation's epic rollcall at Independence Day celebrations on the sixth of March is that of the killing by colonial police officers of three army veterans on their way to presenting a petition to the Governor of the Gold Coast on 28 February 1948. That is our Holocaust Remembrance. That is our Sharpeville Massacre and our Soweto Uprising conjoined. That is our iconic event of martyrdom, the substance and sum total of the nation's traumatic memory. Such was the prodigious travail it took to found the nation: the shooting to death of but *three* soldiers on one discrete day in the course of an act that, far from being some cataclysmic insurrectionary deed, was perfectly obedient to the civil protocols of colonial law and order. *Tantae molis erat* … It is not inapposite, then, to echo Virgil's evocation of the gravity of the founding enterprise, since our very own undisputed Founder, the great Pan-Africanist Osagyefo Dr. Kwame Nkrumah, rather fancied the Latin appellation *Civitatis Ghanaiensis Conditor* – instead of, say, an iconic name of the ancestors – and had it engraved on the first post-independence Ghana pound, marvellous prefiguration of our coming wealth and abundance and self-determination.

So is this the homeland I am returning to, its congenital illusions and inaugural acts of forgetting still in place, its people and chieftains utterly oblivious of past wounds and so unable to attend to the rifts and torments of today? Hardly a place I can call home. So spare me the saccharine rhapsody of homecoming. Give me one elementary yet compelling reason for wishing to abandon this familiar homestead that is Canada and the alluring aroma of the colossus next door, one reason for saying farewell to all that and going back to the homeland such as it is. I am speaking of vital necessity here. I am asking for a basic reason, one spurred by the casual vexations and assaults upon the spirit that come with living life as Black life, even here in the land of the Maple Leaf. To say nothing of those emanating in their aggravated, quintessential forms as an unavoidable contagion from across the border. What am I saying? I am talking of the desire to go back provoked by the accumulated afflictions of being-in-the-world-as-existence-in-black.

III

ONE REASON FOR THE JOURNEY BACK

THE LORE OF RACE

From the 1999 Columbine High School massacre to the February 2010 Littleton sequel to the more recent horrors, the Parkland Florida school shooting in February 2018, the package bombings of March 2018 by Mark Conditt in Austin Texas, and the August 2019 shootings in El Paso Florida and Dayton Ohio, the cry of incomprehension pierces the air. Always. How could this happen here, here in this decent god-fearing community? I vividly recall Christie Blatchford writing for Canada's *National Post* at the time of the Columbine mayhem, a journalist not previously known for her motherly solicitude in her reports on "black crime," acquiring an instantaneous enlightenment tinged with a tragic sense of the human condition. She awakened to the ghastly reality beneath the myth of the angelic innocence of the young (and white). It need not have been so, this disconcerting epiphany. How many times must one be surprised by recurring events? How long will you hold on to your trained expectation of the provenance of good and evil against persistent evidence? You see, you live by a metaphysics – I choose the word advisedly – according to which evil cannot be white. And so, each time white boys and men go on a killing spree, you are utterly incredulous. You never imagined *they* could do such a thing. And we know who they are *not*. It was Jean-Paul Sartre who taught the good people of Europe that anti-Semitism is a form of escape from the human condition, the human condition of freedom and the responsibility it demands of us. So it is with every species of racism, every racist vision of the world. But anti-black racism is special. It exempts you *radically* from the labour of self-scrutiny that comes with that freedom and responsibility; it offers you a visible physiognomy of vice and virtue. Empowered by that absolute knowledge, you do not have to own up to your human, all-too-human reality. Self-deluding power. Obscuring knowledge. Bitter fruit of what philosopher Charles Mills called "white ignorance."

OF CRIME AND PUNISHMENT

When black kids commit a crime, it is due to their racial character made manifest in "inner city" life. And so they bring in ferocious lawmen, deregulated private-enterprise prisons, the Giulianis of this world, Margaret Wente, Philip Rushton, the Police Association and all the great experts in the occult science of race and crime. Here innate racial nature and culpable culture fatefully coincide. When white kids commit a horrible crime, it is because of *human* nature, human nature gone terribly awry. And so, naturally, they bring in mental health specialists, discerning experts on the moral crisis of our postmodern world, grief counsellors and all those in tune with the unfathomable possibilities of human existence. Here culture is human nature taking an inexplicably gruesome and tragic turn. Did anybody ever ask, as M. NourbeSe Philip once wondered, about the racial and ethnic origins of Karla Homolka and Paul Bernardo, Toronto's murderous couple of the 1990s? Does the race of Mark Conditt, perpetrator of the 2018 Austin package bombings, matter? Is it an accident that two of his victims were black? Was it an anomaly that in 1989 Charles Stuart killed his pregnant wife Carol, and blamed the crime on a black male, leading to the frenzied hounding of the entire black community in Boston, especially young black men, and the wrongful arrest of William Bennett? Wasn't it perfectly normal that in 1994 Suzan Smith killed her two children and claimed that she had been carjacked and her children abducted by a black man? A black man, any black man, will do. Who says justice demands a uniform view of such intricate matters? Who says individualism, the tribal religion of this society, has to be race-neutral? Whose is the impertinent voice that asks if that creed is not radically subverted by the lore of race? Congenitally vitiated. Some may even say "constitutively" vitiated, that is to say, that the lore of race is not just coeval with that creed but is, in fact, the thing that birthed the creed in the first place, perversely defined who is entitled to its blessings, caused its genetic deformities from the beginning.

SUE BIRD'S REPRIEVE

Here is Sue Bird, basketball superstar, mulling the (shareable) fate of Breonna Taylor, the woman shot to death in her apartment on 13 March 2020 in Louisville, Kentucky, by three police officers allegedly looking for drug dealers; here is Sue graphically capturing the regular lethal indifference of antiblack racist culture to the individual, more precisely, how the individual as an individual is extinguished in the common law of race: "When I take my jersey off, I could be Breonna Taylor." There but for the grace of her jersey... Someone will no doubt retort: Hey Sue, but you have that jersey. Count your blessings. At least you enjoy that episodic freedom from the unseeing violence of the racist eye. Call it Sue's reprieve. Better still, Bird's fortunate flight from the general terror. I bet the ensuing laughter provoked by this witticism will be muted and short-lived.

MY BROTHER'S KEEPER

From the people who regularly bring you vociferous denunciations of this or that public policy for being "race-based" and so offensive to liberal political morality and its colour-blind principles of justice comes this curious notion. Simply because the colour of my skin is black, I am responsible for a crime committed by *any* black person, of necessity complicit. What else could the endless talk of "black crime" and hectoring invitations to "the black community" and "its leaders" to do something about it possibly mean? The moral individualism of these hectoring voices is entirely selective, their sophistry breathtaking.

Sadly, a vicious cycle sets in, one that makes me complicit in this pernicious ascription of collective responsibility. The first knee-jerk question I ask on hearing of some terrible crime in the news is whether the perpetrator is black or white. What a relief when I learn that he is *not* black. What a diminution of my humanity, my relief purchased with the price of wilful indifference to the human victim of the crime. No, I did not invent the occult science Karen, and Barbara Fields have named "racecraft." But am I not an accomplice in the reproduction of its toxic consequences? Racial thinking corrupts even when it comes in the form of a desperate desire for the refutation of racist judgement, hence for collective absolution. "Racial thinking": that is *not* an oxymoron as I understand it – a curious paradox, perhaps even a benign paradox. That is a howling contradiction. What the noun means to say is nullified by the qualifying prefix. Get me out of here.

ZIMMERMAN SYNDROME

Of the *individual* called Trayvon Martin walking home that fateful night, of *who* that particular person might be and the specific thing he was doing or intended to do, George Zimmerman, in truth, knew nothing. Of the category of people to which Trayvon Martin of necessity belonged and the kind of activities, they are by nature and habituation bound to engage in, Zimmerman had inerrant knowledge – foreknowledge and, by entailment, predictive knowledge: "Fucking punks…These assholes. They always get away." "They," the accusatory plural. No, George Zimmerman did not murder *Trayvon Martin*. George Zimmerman murdered a young black male. You see, Trayvon Martin was a young Black male. All the recent house break-ins in the neighbourhood were committed by young Black males. Therefore, Trayvon Martin was a criminal. It was not unreasonable for Zimmerman, so said his defence attorney, to think that Trayvon Martin, being *what* he was, was up to no good, that he had no business being in that neighbourhood except the business of burglary. Nothing personal, literally. Such are the intricacies of what Cornel West – bless his generous soul – calls "racial reasoning." Such is the banality of evil as a consequence of a brutal syllogism. Syllogism as lethal weapon. And that weapon is no less normal and no less lethal just because Zimmerman, it turns out, is not "really" "white." Racial profiling is the work of white supremacy. That doesn't mean that it is exclusively a white thing.

JIVANI'S ANSWER AND SARTRE'S WAGER

The day after George Zimmerman was acquitted of murdering Trayvon Martin, there appeared in the *Toronto Star* of 14 July 2013 a profile written by Nicholas Keung – an enabling profile this time – of one Jamil Jivani, recent graduate of Yale Law School. Born and raised in Toronto, prime exhibit of an adolescence and a "background" destined for catastrophe, he would be schooled in the regular experience of racial profiling, that is to say, the experience of going-about-your-normal-business-while-black, from the streets of Toronto to, naturally, the elysian fields of Yale University. This is what Jivani had to say in his hour of triumph over daunting impediments and toxic expectations: "Who you are at the age of 16 or 17 is not all you can be. Many of us don't find direction or purpose in our lives until after high school... It takes time to find the best version of ourselves. You can always surprise yourself and surprise society with what you are capable of." Those magnificent words reminded me of a once persuasive and still compelling image central to the early Sartre's existentialism: the liberating and exacting vision of a self without a Self, a self not made captive to a scripted destiny, its world an open sea of willed possibilities. Jivani's story of who you are as a (self-)surprising achievement, akin to the early Sartre's doctrine of a subject that is able to play "the circuit of self-ness," a "self" that, according to one paraphrase, "has nothing to be and everything to do": it is such stuff that dreams are made of. And the mission statement of antiblack racist culture? Intercept this dream. Arrest its premise of possibility. Interdict the presumption, not indeed of innocence, but of that release from tyrannical fate upon which Sartre's wager is predicated. Say to the dreamer in the accursed incarnation of a young Black male: Oh no, you don't. Implant into his very "pelvic constitution" the injunction – as the famous grandfather in Césaire's *Cahier* said to himself – "Thou Shall Not."

Happy the conspiracy of circumstance, guidance and resolve that enabled Jivani to tear up that racist script and its noxious bill of interdictions. But here is the question, the question, I am afraid, that wrecks the romance of the happy ending: Will "racial reasoning" persist in seeing Jivani and anyone like him as the exception, the tell-tale exception, the exception that confirms the rule, the exception that keeps intact the dominion of the racist inference.

VARIATIONS ON RACIST INFERENCE

That last question is not at all far-fetched but touches on the deep and stubborn malignancy of racist judgment, as pernicious when it spews indiscriminate bile as when it brings gifts, speaks in praise of the exceptional black. Consider these fine specimens, variations on racist inference, from eighteenth-century Konigsberg to Toronto in the second decade of this millennium, bookends of the age of reason: "This fellow was quite black from head to foot, a clear proof that what he said was stupid." That is Immanuel Kant, among Enlightenment's most revered progenitors, voicing the racist inference, unadulterated version, in 1764. And here is an accolade bestowed upon Jacobus Elisa Johannes Capitein, African-born Christian intellectual, in a poem by an adoring contemporary, a certain Braudijin Ryser, in the Netherlands circa 1740: "His skin is black, but white is his soul." Nice emendation of the brutal absolutism of Kant's inferential judgment, don't you think? This is the real Enlightenment on display, Enlightenment self-rectified, isn't it? No, it is not. This is a poisoned chalice forged from the same pernicious metal as Kant's antiblackness without exception. And here is an echo of that perverse praise from the mouth of a fellow I heard at my gym in Toronto, one fine Sunday morning in the year 2010, delivering this resounding tribute to his doctor: "My doctor, he is black but he is very good." Or did he say, "He is very good, but he is black"? Either way, I was, and I am still certain that the idiot wanted me to overhear his words – words of admiration by exemption – as proof of his decency. This came after the ineffable ecstasy of a spinning class and the sublime inspiration of perspiration (pardon my rap-rhyme). The thrill was gone, instantly. I almost said irretrievably, but that would mean quitting the resistance. Hell no.

(Hush, hush: But wasn't Braudijin Ryser's praise of Capitein, racist premise and all, spot on? Here is the subject of Capitein's dissertation: "Political-Theological Dissertation on Slavery, as Being Not in Conflict with Christian freedom." A Black man's apology for enslavement employing the master's doctrinal tools: You may be physically in chains but spiritually free in your Christian faith. Outer physical freedom is not a necessary condition of membership in the community of faith. What could be more "white" than adherence to this body-soul apartheid metaphysics? And who embodies that teaching better than Capitein himself, black skin, white soul (the hybrid entity Ryser admired and Biko would disdain), walking incarnation of doctrinal truth, the canonical separation of matter and spirit? But I digress.)

ON THE VERY TALK OF "BLACK-ON-BLACK VIOLENCE"

A habitual way of evading the radical evil of the Zimmerman syndrome is to invoke as the real issue plaguing the African American community "black-on-black-violence." That violence and its root cause – the alleged pathology of the black family – according to Newt Gingrich, Bill O'Reilly, the usual cohort of deluded black askaris and all those newfound friends of black lives, is what really needs to be addressed with urgency. Never mind the disingenuous tactic of changing the subject or even the contestable nature of the causal attribution it proffers. Something more insane can be heard in this talk of "black-on-black" violence. And that is the macabre but inescapable inference that it will have to be accounted a mark of progress, palpable evidence or augury of postracial justice if black youth, after integrated schooling in target practice, put an end to this bizarre habit of exclusively killing one another and turned their guns on white people from time to time. Would good white people then be freed from their caring anxiety over the waste of black lives and sleep well? Would something like black-on-white-violence, or at least its exacerbation, signal the dawn of distributive justice? Oh, one more question: Is there such a thing as white-on-white crime?

Here is the Rapper's Cadenza: So white youth don't copulate, don't fornicate, don't abdicate? How is that for an irate old dude's rap cadenza to the "black-on-black-violence-and-it's-all-because-of-the-absent-black-father" cacophonous chant? Blame Cornel West, bemused reader, for setting the awful example of an intellectual wandering off the grove of academia and venturing into the abode of the people's bards. But comic relief from this deadly serious business of race is badly needed.

OF CRIME WITHOUT METAPHYSICS

What does crime without metaphysics – the everyday metaphysics of race – look like? There is crime all over the place in the homeland. As in every known corner of this forced-to-be-free-for-the-free-market-world, this world under the pathogenic occupation of neoliberalism, this world littered with the ostentatious opulence of the few and the abject destitution of the many, crime is on the rise. I should know; I have been subjected to its terror since my return. So too, to their shock and sorrow, have sisters and brothers from the diaspora who have come to live here, thinking to escape the Zimmerman syndrome and its regular enforcement by "law enforcement officers." There is indeed an exponential growth in crime, perhaps the only industry to be so blessed in this land. But there is no *black* crime, no *black-on-black violence*, just crime and violence. And there are no *black* leaders to be hectored and conscripted into mandatory reparative service. It is gloriously liberating, bracingly humanizing. Trust me. Good enough reason for wanting to leave this Babylon: this desire to return to the homeland fuelled not by maudlin nostalgia and sweet remembrances but rather the craving to be a person, an ordinary person, an *individual*, damn it, warts and all, once again. This is individualism of a totally different species, individualism unattached to proprietorship, possessions and patents. Different yet banal in a human sort of way. Elementary and sacred, first among the things that it is racist culture's defining mission to confiscate and corrupt. Anti-racism is individualism. Profoundly so. Just not the kind sanctified in the ethics of capitalist society.

But there is more, much more, to what Fanon called the "absurd drama" scripted by racist culture. What the lore of race in the hands of white supremacists does to us is one story. What we who are subjected to that lore do with it – do to ourselves and to one another as a result of it – is something else.

IV

THE BLACK PROFESSOR'S BURDEN

> *It was always the black professor,
> the black doctor...
> I tell you, I was walled in.*
> – Frantz Fanon
>
> *What happens to a dream deferred?*
> – Langston Hughes

THE OTHER DREAM DEFERRED

What happens to a calling corralled, pressed into urgent service, that of the vindication of the rights and pride of a racial community – urgent service yet one arguably extraneous to the essence of that calling? What becomes of a craft when the prefix that names the specific albeit ancillary identity of the practitioner threatens to eclipse in significance the defining property of that craft? I am speaking of the agony no less than the ecstasy of the black professor's calling. In a diminishing regard for the particular and the universal alike, I am in this adopted homestead not importantly a professor, even an African professor, still less a professor of Ghanaian origin, I am a **black** professor. And that prefix trumps not only other possible prefixes, other available adjectival testimonies to my particularity and individuality. It threatens to overthrow the primacy of the concrete universal, professor, to which the prefix purports to minister. So that in a strange grammatical *coup d'état*, the adjective – here a generic label, eccentric, in truth, useless as a figure of individuation – usurps the authority of the substantive. The result is that it is no longer certain what is of paramount importance to my status in the academy: my being a professor or my being black. Am I even in the academy, to say nothing of the "real world," first and foremost black, and only in some secondary albeit useful sense a professor? That is the question.

It was thanks to the grip of the "white look" that the protagonist of Frantz Fanon's "racial drama" felt "fixed," "walled in," immured in a universe of perception that, even at its most benign, insists on seeing him not as *this* individual, this individual doctor, but as the *black* doctor. But the intramural look trained on the black professor by members of "the community" can be as tyrannizing as it is challenging, even exhilarating. It is the confining existential and moral geography of life lived according to the lore of race that Fanon memorably dramatized. But Fanon sketched not only what the oppressors do to the oppressed but what the oppressed do to one another and to themselves. For the transmutation of an individual, this individual practitioner of a craft, this individual professor, into *black* professor comes with peculiar duties and prohibitions, constraints and restrictions – a special case of the fraught blessings and burdens that come with certain scripts of identity that Kwame Anthony Appiah has with some justice cautioned us about.

PEDAGOGIC BOND AS RACIAL COVENANT

"Do Black Men Have a Moral Duty to Marry Black Women?" That is a question once posed by philosopher Charles Mills. This is my kindred question: Do black professors have special obligations toward black students? The answer – a benign instance of circular reasoning – is this: unquestionably yes. Yes, we do everywhere and for as long as there are *black* students.

To begin with, Who will begrudge the black student, especially the new black student, the thrill of a veritable epiphany, that of her first black professor, perhaps her first black teacher, period, in this empire of whiteness that rules over there in the adopted homestead? You can see on her face the smile of consoling recognition the first day that you walk into class. A covenant, unspoken yet unmistakable, is instantaneously enacted. Henceforth, I am going to be teacher, brother, role model and father confessor regarding race matters in these less-than-hallowed halls of the academy, but also regarding other regular human predicaments. I will be the trusted listener to myriad stories of slights, disrespect, unjust grading or assessment of work, but also stories of excellence construed as doing the race proud. To the "racial contract" that, according to Charles Mills, binds white men together and secures their mastery of the world, the pedagogic bond between black student and black professor responds with a racial covenant.

THE TEXT: READING AS RACIAL ALLEGORY

An epiphany and a covenant ordained by the racial agon. All the more momentous if the black professor, particularly in the social sciences and the humanities, teaches a subject that features writers and thinkers of African descent. For then, a double grace of proprietorship is secured, that of teacher and of the subject and texts taught. Above all, these texts become *black* texts. The university bookstore mimicking, undoubtedly with benign intent, the "geographical ordering" of the "racial polity" (Fanon, Mills), concurs with this taxonomy by placing these texts not in the philosophy or literature or history section as the case may be, but in the Black Studies space. All texts authored by black writers promiscuously put together and set apart in a zone exclusively assigned to them. There occurs thereby a double erasure, that of the finite particulars signalling the specific provenance of a work and that of its status as a local testimony to the essential tensions and possibilities of the human condition in history. At this point, adherents to a certain version of the politics of difference, multiculturalism and Afrocentrism, in rightful revolt against coercive and counterfeit universalisms, might cheer and shout: right on, right on. I hear you, sisters and brothers, I hear you. But there is, as they say, a price for everything.

An exemplary case. The foundational text of modern African literature written in English, Chinua Achebe's *Things Fall Apart*, is divided into three parts. The white man, blue-eyed devil or god-sent saviour, is entirely absent from the plot of the first part, the longest of the three parts. The white man enters later, much later. Yet the black professor is expected to read and teach this first part, with all its internal and integral metaphysical and moral drama – one that is at once particular and universal – in light of what happens when the white man later makes his fateful entrance. Makes his entrance and therewith inaugurates that process of annexation of native resources and stories to the invaders' design. With supreme irony, the black professor is expected to instruct the black student in the complicit subjugation of the native narrative to the imperial act. This has important consequences for the structure of reading the text: the very temporality of reading; the order of thematic significance assigned to the constituent parts; the process of evaluative judgment. The most crucial consequence is how the novel's principal character, Okonkwo, is to be judged. The black professor is expected to see Okonkwo as he appears in the first part of the narrative in his human, all-too-human reality, and despite the opprobrium that his more offensive actions repeatedly invites from his community, as racial hero destined to lead the fight against the white man which occurs at the novel's conclusion; the dénouement retroactively dictating the interpretation of the beginning. The novel's argument thus severely reduced to political history and a particular fragment of political history, albeit one invested with a world-historical import, the verdict on Okonkwo required of us – leaving matters at the political – is straightforward: Okonkwo not as an insufferable ogre, a violent misogynist and male supremacist, an abominable prefiguration of our post-independence despots, but a valiant anti-colonialist and noble warrior against white supremacy, literary ancestor or kin of Nkrumah, Malcolm, Mandela, Biko. The black professor is expected to read and teach the novel first and foremost as an allegory of racial conquest and resistance. A veritable and ironic violence, this, that of the history and politics of empire and race trumping all that precedes and transcends that history and politics, all that is indigenous to the world of the text, all that is special to "this separate earth"

(Soyinka), but also all that, with equal significance, is native to the *human* condition before the ordinance of race came calling. I am speaking of the countervailing lessons in the metaphysics and ethics of freedom and fate; the question of power in relation to the psycho-existential peculiarities of the individual and the moral status of men and women, the provenance of good and evil. Call these pre-colonial, pre-racial, transracial questions, questions unforgettably enacted in the crucial third and fourth chapters of the novel – precisely those scenes in which we encounter internal omens of ethical crisis and premonitions of Okonkwo's tragic fall. Reduced to racial antagonism, the common human agon and its local vicissitudes are excised. The black professor who, by the lights of this prior and unfolding internal drama, finds Okonkwo flawed, deeply and tragically flawed, who sees in the very possibility of that verdict evidence of the novel's richness as a work of art and moral argument, that black professor courts the suspicion of siding with the white interloper and scorning the African warrior.

The craft, the bond, the text: all three conscripted by reciprocal pressure into race work. Such is the black professor's calling. It comes in many shapes and forms, from the grievous to the innocuously risible. But there are times when it borders on the tragicomic, even as it challenges in the most profound manner the *raison d'être* of my vocation.

DISSERTATION AS RACE WAR

He came to me, he said, to seek protection from evil. What evil? The evil of "the white academy." I easily ignored the paranoid demonology that brought him to my door, to say nothing of the groundless faith that saw in me an agent of salvation from a nameless iniquity. But I readily accepted the task of guiding him as a black student. On his behalf, I performed duties supererogatory to the essential mandates of my calling. And after one seminar with, shall we say, indifferent results, I agreed to be the supervisor of his doctoral dissertation. I only wondered if acceptance of that duty precluded insisting that sentences should be grammatically and intelligibly written, in short, if that duty overruled standards of excellence. Standards! Aha, that's a damnably suspect, quintessentially colonialist locution. In retrospect, I asked myself: Did I, thanks to my concern for the blackness of a student, overlook serious shortcomings in his academic formation? Or did I fail to point out these weaknesses to him with sufficient clarity and unvarnished honesty? Did I, by this serious sin of omission, set him up for uncomprehending shock and genuine incredulity when I eventually let him know that the draft of the dissertation he gave me required massive surgery? So it was that my demand that he writes intelligibly, offer arguments for assertions, excise unnecessary and vacuous matter from an obese text, and correct innumerable spelling and grammatical errors, all this became tangible evidence of race betrayal: the case of the brother who uses his good fortune in the "white academy" not to help elevate his kith and kin but to shame them, the better to call attention to his matchless singularity. I was, I must confess, stunned. In nearly three decades at the university, I had no doubt committed many unspeakable sins. Betraying black students to please the white racist academy was not one of them. Indeed, I fancied myself as one in whom black students reposed considerable trust. Foolishly, I imagined that I had lighted upon a golden mean: a way of challenging black students, like all students, to excellence and at the same time showing special concern for those existential particulars that undeniably attach to their being black students. I flattered myself that I had earned a good reputation in that regard. But here I was: just another Uncle Tom masquerading as a brother of the left. The offended brother would have an occasion to expose the masquerade and undo the meretricious reputation. The oral examination of his dissertation would be that occasion.

Statutory rule has it that the defence of a doctoral thesis is a "public academic event," a description founded on an older understanding that makes the now fashionable name "public intellectual" something of a pleonasm. In practice, in my experience at my university and other Canadian universities, the "public" customarily consists of a few fellow graduate students and friends. In any case, the location is invariably a room at the university. Availing himself of a strict or rather elastic construction of the statute, our avenging brother demanded that the defence be held off campus at a place in the BLACK COMMUNITY. That demand having been rejected, the next best thing was not one of the rooms in which a defence is regularly held, all of them quite decent but, except for one forbiddingly ornate venue, in no way extraordinary. Heavens forbid. You see, for the examination of this magisterial thesis, nothing less than a lecture hall would do. You see, there were all these eminent brothers and sisters coming all the way from the United Kingdom and India and the Caribbean and the United States, all of them anxious to be present at the dénouement, the triumphant conclusion of an epic battle of Black Truth and its audacious protagonist against the awesome empire of white knowledge and its wretched black satraps.

On the appointed day, we, the examiners, educators evidently in need of being educated, arrived at the lecture hall on time. So did the chosen witnesses from THE COMMUNITY and the fortunate pilgrims from afar. We would have to wait patiently for Him to come at a time of His own choosing as befits one upon whom imminent victory in a long emblematic struggle had conferred a well-earned nobility. And did he make an entrance? He strode in with a measured gate and haughty bearing, resplendent in an African outfit, exactly like the magnificent chieftains, ancient and modern, with whom the motherland is copiously blessed. All that was missing from THE ARRIVAL were the royal drums, the *fontomfrom*, the elders' *oriki*, the praise singers, the men's acrobatics and the women's ululation. Clearly, we were about to witness not an exercise that regularly makes the bravest and the most brilliant of candidates secretly tremble with intimations of human vulnerability but rather a postmodern durbar. At this durbar, the black prince of academia would receive grateful recognition of his valour from acolytes, epigones, designated flatterers and, above all, young awestruck subjects in desperate need of uplifting lessons in education as racial *agon*.

Of the ensuing examination, what do you expect but that it would be the crowning act in the drama of racial vindication, a climactic settling of accounts with the white academy and the black professor as its pathetic vassal? How could it be otherwise? A candidate's opening statement is customarily a summation of the principal arguments of the work at hand, a review of its intellectual antecedents, its gestation and completion, perhaps hints of future lines of investigation, in fine, a prelude to a spirited conversation. Our black prince's version began with a rehearsal of the diabolical forces arraigned to smother a nascent prodigy of heretical thought from the very beginning. It told the story of a work so unsettling in its very subject matter, its findings and propositions so disconcerting to Eurocentric intellectual history and traditions, altogether such an impertinent anathema, that the original monument was summarily rejected. Rejected by the white academy and the cowered and cowering black supervisor. Regarding the details of these findings and propositions and what their momentous novelty consisted of, the audience was left in the dark. So cataclysmic were the truths they contained that they were evidently better left untold, ineffable truths. In any case, the document ultimately submitted and accepted, so the opening statement intoned, was but a truncated and paltry version of a majestic enterprise. Were it not for the prodding of loyal and supportive friends, friends from the "real world," friends untainted by the mire and miasma of the academy, even this picayune product before us would not have seen the light of day. It was to those people that the black warrior-scholar owed his achievements. To them alone was he accountable. In their "empowering" company, he found a genuine epistemic community, one possessing canons of validity of which the academy was blissfully ignorant. What is the self-sequestered tyranny of academic knowledge compared with the popular sovereignty of *the* community's Word?

It soon became clear that the mission of the black warrior prince's opening statement was to award to himself a preemptive exemption from the burden of being held accountable to the normal conventions of question and answer. Mission accomplished. To each question in the ensuing farce of an examination, the Black people's prince responded with a declamation, an appeal to the assembled brothers and sisters and pilgrims to testify to the utter vacuity of that question compared to visceral matters of life, race matters. Absolved by the grace of race, the black prince had no obligation to offer a decent answer to a single one of the questions posed by members of the examining committee. He fully availed himself of the people's preemptive absolution.

Here is the question: Why did we not fail his black ass? I had participated in countless doctoral oral examinations before this one. Although the black prince's written work, after significant revisions, was passable – we would not have convened the oral examination unless it was – the defence was abominable, an unmitigated disgrace. So why did we not fail his black ass? At the very least, why did we not send his black ass packing to the purgatory of self-mortification, contrition, and genuflection before human ideals of excellence, which we would otherwise invoke? The answer lies in qualifying his ass as black ass. That race-indexed designation of the lower regions of his anatomy encapsulated the agony of the black professor's calling. It signals the less-than-happy consequence of transmuting an ordinary, crucial human vocation into race work. Weary of being held hostage to obligations foreign to the regular scheme of human responsibilities, the "rediscovery of the ordinary" – the liberating prospect envisioned by Njabulo Ndebele at the formal ending of apartheid – is, to echo the Prince of Denmark, "a consummation devoutly to be wished."

CHIMERA OF PURE FORMS?

No doubt – to indulge for a moment in tell-tale philosophical jargon – I am flirting in these foregoing observations with a purist and (horror of horrors) an essentialist view of the academic enterprise. As opposed to what? As opposed to a history-conscious view (call it critical historicism) that would *not* see the drama of education as race work as something extrinsic to the real thing. What kind of otherworldly metaphysical thinking is it, frowns our postmodernist friend, that sees race (and its mandates), after eons of its material power in real life, as the accidental mistaken for the essential? What on earth are these normal obligations and regular schemes of human responsibilities you are talking about? What are those chimerical pure forms of social reality, those "fundamental contradictions" that make up the foundational terms of our moral and political argument and so drive our ethical commitments? Why think of the racial formation of our social *agon*, racialized kinds of moral and political life, as something of an impure species, even a distraction, a stubborn distraction, yes, but a distraction all the same, from the essence of "the ordinary," say, the essence of teaching as a vocation? Really, I should know better, shouldn't I? Neither immaterial accident nor something of intrinsic importance, "race" – and its mandates – belongs to the family of created things marked, as are all created things, by their *specific essence* (the phrase is that of the early Marx) and bringing a specific gravity to the drama of the human condition in history. There are no quintessential forms of social reality and social strife in history and in the world. What you see is indeed what you get. Deal with that.

OR UTOPIAN REALISM?

"Where Race Does Not Matter." So serenades Cecil Foster in praise of Canada as an exemplar of "the new spirit of modernity." True or false? False as a simple factual description. True as hortatory utterance, at once desire and injunction, an optative in benign disguise, the world-wise spirit's manner of keeping faith with things hoped for. Realism without dreams is supine. Dream without knowledge of this bitter earth is barren. Recalcitrant reality constrains me to living my calling here in the adopted homestead as race works, in part. Utopia informs my vision of it as a race-transcending enterprise. Race blindness, that serene evasion of reality and the dream it brings us is not an option. Nor is there ever such a thing as "professor" unmodified. There are, and there will always be, other prefixes, be they of defining or ancillary significance. All the same, I often wondered while I lived and worked in the adopted homestead: What must it be like to relinquish the compulsory collectivism of *Black* professor for the concrete universality and individuality of this professor, ultimately, the individuality of *this* person? Oh, happy day. Oh, a daunting prospect. Even as it recounts this other dream deferred, the story of the black professor's calling must be a prolepsis of that happy and daunting day.

CONTRAPUNTAL VIBRATIONS

What would it be like to live life away from the everyday metaphysics of race and the fraught peculiarities of existence-in-black? That indeed sums up my persistent ventriloquy in the days before the eternally deferred journey back, back to the homeland and the relative freedom from the dominion of race, a dominion you cannot escape even in the hallowed halls of the academy and its formal requirements and rites, practices and events: the recurring dream of a-racial existence, one blessed *and* burdened with the regular dramas of human affiliations, attachments, responsibilities. That was my chronic fantasy. On the second day of February 2006, I was honoured with a dinner organized by the Black Students Association and the Association of African Students of York University to mark my impending retirement. I was thrilled. Two other celebrations followed with colleagues from my Department and my College, celebrations with no particular protocols of racial belonging. I was equally and differently thrilled. And years later, in 2019, the Director of the Graduate Programme in Social and Political Thought, Gamal Abdel-Shehid, organized a conference in my honour on the theme "Partisan Universalism."[1] The participants were made up of a motley crew of former students and colleagues, current students in the Programme and eminent scholars from Canada and the United States. You would be hard-pressed to pin down the racial composition of the presenters and the attendees, to say nothing of the specific ethnocultural lineages of the topics of the presentations (now assembled into a book bearing that title). I was overjoyed and will forever regard that gathering and resultant publication as a high point of my intellectual life. So what to make of my mixed, even conflicting, reactions to these signal

---

[1] See: *Partisan Universalism: Essays in Honour of Ato Sekyi-Otu*, edited by Gamal Abdel-Shehid, Sofia Noori. Cantley, Daraja Press, 2021

events and the roulette of identifications and disavowals accompanying them? Racial kinship is recognized and re-signified, required and renounced, reclaimed and re-erased. What's going on? Contradiction? Paradox? Ambiguity? Perhaps I can summon to my aid Walter Benjamin's famous saying in the *Arcades Project*: "Ambiguity is the figurative appearance of the dialectic." Nice try, wryly retorts our satirist of the dialectic, detective of dodgy responses to the (undeniably) tangled truths of the world. And the rejoinder? Are these tangled truths not indeed bound to give rise to a skein of attitudes, beliefs and practices, sometimes necessary, sometimes questionable, often incongruous, and always in need of critical reappraisal and revision, lest they imprison us in hardened conventions and motionless certitudes?

V

HUMAN THINGS, BLACK KINDS?

SERENADING SERENA

Whenever Serena Williams plays, Mansa and I drop everything; we are glued to the television, all rapt attention. And if she wins, all joyful hell breaks loose. The first time was Saturday, September 10, 1999, when the seventeen-year old Serena won the women's singles tennis championship at the US Open, the second African American to do so since Althea Neale Gibson won at the US Nationals (the precursor tournament) in 1957. We were ecstatic, absolutely ecstatic. We jumped and screamed for joy. Not since Ben Johnson's ill-fated victory in the 100 meters at the Seoul Olympics on September 24, 1988, did the two of us erupt in such unrestrained jubilation because of the sublime triumph of a black athlete. Does this visceral reaction render suspect my disembodied discomfort with the culture of the-first-black-this-and-the-first-black-that, that measure of excellence underwritten by racism's normative expectations? Does serenading Serena the way I do make me guilty of self-referential inconsistency? Not in the least. I seek freedom from the dominion of race, yes. But that quest is informed by a visionary realism as alive to the obdurate truths of this world as it is open to its untried possibilities. Not even returning to the homeland, given the history of the present, will nullify the oppressive jurisdiction of race. And to this day, we continue to celebrate Serena's magnificence as a black athlete, even as we salute her transcendent greatness as *an* athlete, hell, as an exemplary human being. Such is the stubborn prose of the world and the intermittent poetry we dare to compose and impose upon its authority. The prose and the poetry. With the

HUMAN THINGS, BLACK KINDS?

extraordinary Serena, to witness the prose is at the same time to behold a glorious presage of the poetry in the very hardened script of the world. On Wednesday, the 10th of August 2022, Mansa and I were privileged to watch Serena play her last match in Toronto. She lost to her opponent Belinda Bencic of Switzerland. The real dénouement quickly followed: Serena's defeat at the hands of Australia's Ajla Tomljanovic in the third round of the 2022 US Open, the site of her inaugural triumph. But her grandeur was on full display on both occasions. So was her vulnerability. The human grandeur and vulnerability of a *Black* star: such is the irrevocable duality of the spirit in which we toast Serena. Impure joy? Celebration is compromised by lingering fealty to race, albeit in the service of reparative justice? Not exactly an ode to joy unmodified? Maybe. On the other hand, what should we make of rising star Coco Gauff's encomium to the effect that tennis was (and still is?) such a "white sport" until the fabulous sisters crashed the party and that it was Serena who made it possible for her not to feel different playing tennis? Perhaps what Serena has accomplished is far more significant than consigning designations such as "white sport," in Lenin's phrase, to the "museum of antiquity" – by itself a noteworthy achievement in the historicist book of things whose time has come or passed. Perhaps her greatest gift is to have led the way in rendering the very idea of *white sport* not just contingently untenable, contradicted by the realities of our time, not just an anachronism, but essentially unthinkable, meaningless. And not only tennis or even sports in general but all manner of (human) activities, practices, tastes and modes of conduct to which racial patents have been affixed, thereby rendering locutions such as "It's a black thing or a white thing" is fundamentally incoherent. No doubt, a welcome picture of things to come, whispers the pragmatist friend of moral and semantic revolutions. But isn't Alain Badiou just a little too impatient regarding what is to be done, what can be done? At the end of his luminous essay *Black: The Brilliance of a Non-Color*, he envisions and enjoins – as did his erstwhile mentor Jean-Paul Sartre in *Black Orpheus* – not indeed skipping the moment of realism and its mandates altogether, but undertaking, right here and now, to "go beyond" it. "Or, rather, go elsewhere." I am not unsympathetic to Badiou's desire. I am no less cognizant of the "prodigious labour of the negative" (Hegel), the daunting and miraculous work required to recast the world's recalcitrant script. I am afraid I have to tarry with the prose awhile even as, inspired by the world-wise visionary of Great Barrington Massachusetts, I dream of life "above the veil."

BLACK LOVE?

Poetry *interruptus*, constantly, cruelly, unavoidably. Constrained to tarry with the prose of the world. Conceded. But **Black** love? "Black ***Love***? A television show on the Oprah Winfrey Network actually bears that name: Black Love. Must be special, exempt from the regular ecstasies and agonies which mortal love in other earthly shapes and colours is heir to. The imputed difference, the difference in kind, I will be enlightened, is not the function of some natural essence but a matter of shared lived experience and affective practice, an object lesson – to talk philosophical jargon once more – in "racial nominalism" as distinct from reductionist essentialism. Still, isn't there something rather jarring about "black love"? What other particulars of our "spheres of existence" (C.L.R. James) are we going to classify, distinguish and name according to the ordinance of race? "Black love." Isn't that going a little too close towards the radical racialization of all "human things" (Fanon), human things in all their banal, promiscuous and marvelous incarnations? Or is the very idea of *human* things radically mistaken? Is it true that that idea is the conquerors' subterfuge? Can it ever be salvaged from enforced and skewed understandings? Just wondering.

AND BLACK FOOD?

The verdict, the answer to my naïve humanist question, is already in. In an article titled "Innovation and the incinerated tongue: Notes on hot chicken, race, and culinary crossover" (subtitled "How does black food go viral among white folks?"), historian

Cynthia R. Greenlee asks: "Is it possible to have Black culinary crossover without appropriation, in a country built on Black labor?" (*The Counter*, 11 May, 2021). How do you answer that question in a way that does not betray the affliction of historical amnesia, the amnesia which nourishes humanism and humanist innocence? Can it be that the most elementary of so-called "human" practices are, in fact, artifacts of race, always already perversely "racialized" as they say? Do they not then call for rituals of decontamination, expiation, and reparation to make them truly shareable human practices? Human practices so named without scare quotes, that is, without the cynic's ventriloquy murmuring suspicions of all vaunted universals? Or am I still hung up on the chimera of pure forms, hopelessly pursuing, in Césaire's iconic phrase, "the essence of all things," essence unsullied by history's corruption or, failing that, then restored to a pristine condition – where none ever existed?

VI

PROPERTY RITES

FORBIDDEN APPROPRIATION

I gather it is offensive, criminally offensive, for a white artist, Dana Schutz, to portray the mutilated body of 14-year old Emmet Till lying (as his mother insisted in real time) in an open casket, black youth falsely accused of sexually assaulting a white woman and gruesomely lynched in 1955. "It is not acceptable," goes the protest letter signed by Hannah Black and others, "for a white person to transmute Black suffering into profit and fun, though the practice has been normalized for a long time." (2017). It is not acceptable for a white artist to flirt with a dead black guy in effigy and get handsomely paid for it.

It is equally impermissible for white models to prance and strut on the runway wearing cornrow wigs (2020). The magnificent singer Adele, white and British, had no right to sport an African hairstyle to the 2020 Notting Hill Carnival in London. Or so her very appropriate and unforced subsequent confession stated. Well, while we are at it, Ghanaian lawyers and judges should be shamed for donning those blond wigs to court, not because they look downright ridiculous in them – although that alone is a good enough reason; black face in repulsive (medieval) white wigs – but because those wigs are the patented paraphernalia of another culture's "legal practitioners" (the Ghanaian media's preferred name for those ordinarily called lawyers elsewhere). And our lovely Ghanaian women, what am I saying, black women everywhere, should return the hair in all those intricate wigs they sport to their places of origin in a collective act of self-chastisement and reparation. A Special

International Court for Cultural Appropriation and Restitution should be set up to attend to these weighty matters.

A LUTA CONTINUA

It is all so suspiciously American, this rain of fatwas against inappropriate appropriation, all too recognizably American in its juvenile petulance and absolutism. We ought to resist the globalization of the arrant imbecility that is a product of racist culture in its peculiarly virulent American strain, American exceptionalism with a vengeance. But perhaps the fight is already lost. Here is the latest (2021) instalment of the Great Prohibition. It is verboten for a white person – "wrong profile" – to publish a Dutch or a Catalan translation of Amanda Gorman's much-praised Biden inauguration poem "The Hill We Climb." It can't be done. Hmm. A Luta Continua, in more ways than you think. Many hills to climb, evidently. "Many rivers to cross," indeed. But when he rendered the prophetic challenge in that unforgettable song of aching beauty, did Jimmy Cliff have in mind forbidding rivers of separation engineered into being by racial apartheid's erstwhile victims, thinking to find in willed chasms the pathway to sovereignty?

This is Karl Marx in 1844: "Private property has made us so stupid and one-sided that an object is only *ours* when we have it." Likewise, racist culture. Possessive individualism must fall. So must possessive particularism. They are twin ways of exclusionary hoarding: hoarding material things on the part of individuals, hoarding moral goods on the part of communities, and inventing fables of unaided effort and solitary striving and earned entitlement to justify the practice. There is a euphonious Akan word for the malady: *pɛsɛwoankoya*, wanting to have it all to yourself. Such a lovely word for such a ghastly habit.

REDUCTIO: WHO OWNS THE KENTE?

The plot, as always, thickens. So let's have some more fun, shall we? Let's repatriate the comedy of forbidden appropriation. Let's take the farce of possessive particularism regarding ownership of cultural treasures and fatwas against offensive appropriation to a theatre near you, back home to the motherland, specifically to Ghana. The *kente* has arguably become the iconic sartorial gift of the motherland to the African diaspora, particularly Black America: witness the spectacle of US Democratic members of Congress led by the Black Caucus sporting *kente* scarfs as they took the knee in the aftermath of the lynching of George Floyd in 2020. Although its putative Ghanaian nationality is not unknown, for the diaspora, the *kente* is an *African* artifact. The diaspora's relationship to that artifact is pan-African, even pan-African*ist*. But in its putative land of origin, Ghana – the Black Star – a crude recrudescent tribalism would rather shrink that gorgeous artifact's symbolic territory, make one ethnic group or the other, Anlos or Asantes, its original inventors and rightful proprietors, designate one town or the other, Agotime in Eweland or Bonwire in Asanteman, as its founding home; accuse one group or the other of patent-piracy. What right, then, have African Americans to Pan-Africanize this cultural treasure when Ghanaians are busy dragging it with other symbolic forms into the clotted bogs of vulgar tribalism and ethnic chauvinism?

ILLICIT APPROPRIATION, OTHER FELONIES

And here are queries regarding some other potentially actionable felonies chosen at random in order, as they say, to "problematize" – what an ugly word! – the claims of racial or ethnocultural ownership, this time as an intramural affair – that is to say, when the usual suspects, bloody white interlopers and predatory treasure-hunters are not involved.

There is this annual festival of the Anlos of southeastern Ghana called *Hogbetsotso*. It commemorates the organized escape of the Anlos from Notse (in what is now Togo) and the wicked tyrant, Torgbui Agorkoli, and their migration to what became their subsequent home in the Volta Region of Ghana during the fourteenth and fifteenth centuries. A climactic part of the festival is a rite of reconciliation and an open deliberative exchange between the chiefs and the people, enacting, as it were, remembrance of the motive – hatred of despotism – for their founding journey and thus the raison d'être of their political existence: public freedom. Contrary to exoticist mystifications dear to anthropologists, this is no otherworldly "religious" ritual but a secular tradition. Or rather, instead of a binary division, let us say that this is an exemplar of the sacred as a political act and of the political as a sacred practice. In these times of refashioning democratic cultures, would it be illicit for all Ghanaians, irrespective of their "tribe," to appropriate this story as a shared indigenous tradition of resistance to tyranny, a veritable "movement of Jah people" fleeing not white terror but a native ogre; reinvent it as the archetype of the insurgent constituent assembly of the people; have this taught in schools throughout the land? Or should we hold steadfastly onto ethnocultural originalism, keep the meaning of the festival in the jealous enclosure of one "tribe"; desist from conscripting it into the service of the nation's narrative institutions, the shared ways in which the political community as a whole elects, in Frantz Fanon's felicitous formulation, "to speak and to tell a story about itself"? Does it require a revolution in the country's official taxonomic practices to imagine renaming ethnic particulars as symbols of the national culture, to say nothing of prefigurative insignia of a Pan-Africa to come? Dream on. It is census time in Ghana, July 2021. It is not enough that I am to identify the town of my birth or place of domicile. Faithful to the colonialist tradition of classifying the natives, I am asked, six decades after "independence," to name my "tribe," codify my identity according to some scheme of denotation invented by the invaders and serviceable to the separatist interests and territorial ambitions of the chiefs. To what "tribe" does a Torontonian belong and be asked to name at census time?

But here is one more outlandish query in the same vein of taking poetic license with the "original intent" of ethnopolitical texts. Ken Saro-Wiwa memorably wrote: "Dance my people/For we have seen tomorrow/And there is an Ogoni star in the sky." Would it be outrageous to stretch this dream of one ethnos unbound, this invocation of a radiant Ogoniland not yet born, one set free from the depredations of Anglo-Dutch Shell, rapacious multinational capital and its local enablers, set free, more profoundly, from a captive way of being-in-history, would it be felonious to enlarge this ethnocentric dream into a vision of "this Africa to come," as Fanon the seer (again!) enjoined – perhaps even a vision of a fragment of *humanity* unbound?

And lastly: Was Wole Soyinka a thief or a prostitute or, worse still, a Yoruba imperialist when he bestowed upon that special Yoruba deity, Ogun, the Akan name for Pan-Africa, *Ogun Abibiman*? Are poets not permitted to enlarge the imaginary geography of their peeves and dreams beyond hearth and home? Are we ordinary mortals debarred from imitating the action of the poets, prevented from disrespecting property rights and rites with respect to empowering symbolic forms and moral goods, forbidden from making ours what we do not have and own in the service of human flourishing?

ETHICAL APPROPRIATION, HARD CASES

But are all iconic ethnocultural artifacts and practices shareable goods equally fit for ethical appropriation against the grain of identity politics in the malign form of possessive particularism, equally worthy candidates for the human commons? What of Kofi Annan accepting the Asante royal title of *Busumuru* conferred on him by the Asantehene Osei Tutu 11 in August 2005? Can it be said of the ceremonial sword awarded him that day that it is a stainless emblem of a shareable ideal, usable by dint of a generous understanding of inherited symbolic forms as a call to *Amandla Awethu*, Power to the People? Are there any insignia of the nation and its constituent fragments truly in the service of the people's power rather than political idolatry – the sanctification of the ruling order and the beatification of the rulers? That is a fair question. But is that sword not particularly burdened with a history that must give us pause? Captured in war, it became recast as an emblem of peace – the serviceable peace of the victors. Show me the cultural treasure, someone will no doubt enquire, with Walter Benjamin, which is free from such fraught antecedents and ethical ambiguity? Touché. Still, was it not rather jarring for Ghana's *national* hero, all of Africa's pride and joy – albeit one so accredited to us by the masters of the world – intercessor in our intranational and regional disputes, to sport paraphernalia of ethnic supremacy? Did the world's peacekeeper-in-chief have any business lending figurative legitimacy to trophies of conquest? By all means, let us make ours whatever serves the enterprise of human freedom and flourishing. But a trophy of conquest and internal imperialism? As Ghanaians like to say regarding such hard cases or things and acts of questionable virtue: "As for this one, hmm."

WHAT (CRITIQUE OF) IDENTITY POLITICS IS NOT

What of an organization for Latino migrant workers, disproportionately represented as they are in the meat-packing industry in the US, protesting their sordid conditions of work and their special vulnerability to Covid-19? Is that not also a species of identity politics? Not in the least. That, and others like it, is the work of solidarity untethered to particularism of the fundamentalist kind, to any exclusionary metaphysics of difference. It is a political act founded on class struggle "in the most materialist meaning of the word" as Frantz Fanon might say. No hardened product of collective narcissism, this is a possible presage of what Massimiliano Tomba calls "insurgent universality." I suspect that Asad Haider, a sympathetic critic of those interdictions that come with walled identities, will concur.

ETHICS AS IDENTITY POLITICS?

Women are much less vulnerable to the disease of individualism...we understand interdependence. –Jane Fonda (BBC World News, 28 November, 2020)

The disease of death, the white road, is also unconnected sight, the fractured vision that sees only the immediate present, that follows only present gain, and separates the present from the past, the present from the future, shutting each passing day in its own hustling greed...

Ato Sekyi-Otu

> *That the passion and the thinking and the action of any one of us should be cut off from our connected consciousness by mere physical things, walls of wood and walls of stone – that would indeed be the manic celebration of death's white empire.*
> –Ayi Kwei Armah (*Two Thousand Seasons*, 1973).

What should we make of these kindred curses against "individualism" pronounced by the American activist-actress and the African writer? Are they salutary examples of what philosopher Sandra Harding calls "the curious coincidence of feminine and African moralities"? Or rather (quite apart from the question of whether the substantive position they share is laudable), are they not a regrettable species of identity politics in ethics, moral thought predicated on identity politics? Are we to take what they mean to say literally and seriously, namely, that the cult of the isolate and autarchic self is, for the one, a male malady and, for the other, white people's thing, "the white possessive" as Aileen Moreton-Robinson calls it? And here is a follow-up question pertaining to the genealogy of morals: To what are these kindred expressions of aversion to "individualism" in the moral life attributable? On the one hand, to women's character, inborn or acquired, legacy of the gendered division of love's labour? On the other hand, to "Africanity" construed as racial essence, expression of a distinctive "physio-psychology of the Negro" and, by derivation, a defining characteristic of "Negro-African society" and worldview, as our famous philosopher-poet-statesman Léopold Sédar Senghor used to rhapsodize (in contrast to Frantz Fanon's demurral to the effect that "My black skin is not the depository of specific values.")? Or do these tropes of aversion to "individualism" name a way of being-in-the-world elected from among the extended family of shareable ways, variants of human things which are ultimately irreducible to gender or race or any ethnocultural peculiarities; ethics as premise and consequence of our shared human practices?

BLACK SKINS, DIFFERING WORLDS?

No doubt, the tortuous responses to the mandates of race and associated questions of identity expressed in the foregoing rambling, contrapuntal observations have something to do with the experience of being black in North America but born and bred a-racial elsewhere; more precisely, the fact of being born Ghanaian – with all the internal tensions with which that national identity is fraught – but becoming compulsorily and self-consciously black in the adopted homestead. The skin of black people famously comes in different shades. But so it is especially with "the souls of black folk." Such is the distinction between "the fact of blackness" and "the lived experience of the black." Different places of origin, different ways of living the agony and the ecstasy of existence-in-black. Consider the 2006 memoir of Lincoln Alexander, the first black Member of Parliament in the Canadian House of Commons, the first black federal Cabinet Minister in Canada, the first black Chair of the Workers Compensation Board, the twenty-fourth and first black Lieutenant Governor of Ontario, 1985-1991, quintessential first black supremo, we might say, in the racial polity. This is the title of the memoir: *Go to School, You're a Little Black Boy.* It is a mother's prodding words recollected in gratitude by an accomplished son as an emblematic counsel to be passed on to today's youth. Now, my mother and father never said that to me. I mean the part about being a little *black* boy; the part of the counsel that makes going to school a racial mandate and, by implication, the path to overcoming race-based impediments in life. My parents never said that to me growing up in Ghana. Come to think of it, I don't recall Mansa and I saying that to our children as we brought them up in Canada. Therein lies a crucial difference, a symptomatic difference. In Alexander's mother's talk and my parents' (and our own) unexceptionable silence regarding the constraints and obligations of being black in the pursuit of education is encapsulated a not insignificant difference in intimations of possibility. To say nothing of the whole eccentric exceptionalism of "the-first-black-this-and-the-first-black-that," lucky primus out of the band of the unheralded, putative figure of excellence corrupted by dependence on racist culture's predicates. Mansa and I did not begin the work of rearing our children here in Canada under the burden of that perverse culture of twisted expectations and in obedience to Mama Alexander's absolutely understandable race-conscious imperative as a goad. No doubt, matters became slightly more complicated with time. But that initial inadvertent silence of ours regarding race as encumbrance or as responsibility must have been of profound psycho-existential significance for our children. Racial profilers of the world – and I don't just mean racist police officers and tormentors of young-men-living-while-black; I mean all those who live by imprisoning scripts of "failing-black-students" and "the-black-family" and "black-on-black-crime" and other pernicious individuals-extinguishing allegories of race – take note: existence-in-black is not one story.

Not so fast, retorts the black native informer in possession of experiential knowledge we more recent immigrants did not have, at least in the beginning. You brothers and sisters from the motherland are delusional. The anti-black-racist eye is totalitarian, wilfully ignorant of the plurality and diversity of black lives, doesn't give a shit if you were born in Accra or Brooklyn. That is the point. What is more, adds our sober racist-culture-determinist ever alive to the habits that inevitably come with living life here as black life: in no time at all, those blessed children whose parents, like you, were born and bred in the motherland, to say nothing of the parents themselves, will ingest the toxic prescriptions and proscriptions that govern existence in the adopted homestead as existence-in-black. Sooner or later, they will have the scars to show, persistent injuries that will rudely awaken them from their a-racial slumber. But we need not dwell solely on the more negative consequences of living black lives here. Coming as you do from Ghana where, as you claim, you were not black in an existentially significant sense, it may indeed not have occurred to you to impart to your children from their earliest years here in Toronto some version or the other of Mama Alexander's injunction regarding the Black Child's Burden. Nevertheless, even the more positive consequences of existence-in-black, say, enabling forms of affiliation and commitment your children adopt, will carry the mark of racial identification, one thrust upon them but for which they will freely assume responsibility. Here is a heart-warming example, close to home, of such positive consequences of being black in Canada. In this season of Covid-19, one son enlisted self-consciously as a *Black* doctor in the work of combating vaccine-hesitancy among sections of the Black community in Toronto. Another son and his spouse are sponsoring a scholarship scheme for black and other students of colour entering the school their daughter attends. And straddling diasporic debts to their parents' homeland and race-conscious responsibilities in Canada, the same two sons are making financial contributions to a programme initiated by the Toronto Children's Hospital for educating paediatric nurses in Ghana. So, disabling burden or enabling constraint and goad, the sign of race follows, in kindred albeit distinguishable ways, the lives of the native-born African Canadian or native-born African American *and* the new African immigrant and her children. Black skins, differing worlds? Perhaps we are talking of differences in degree not in kind?

All the same, even little differences matter, sometimes matter greatly. All little differences.

THE GRAVITY OF SMALL DIFFERENCES

And none more telling than those we encounter when we view the world, in particular the United States of America, through the prism of this homestead, Canada. It is by no means a land without blemish, to put it delicately. Just ask the First Nations Peoples. Ask them about the confiscation of their lands. Ask them about the genocidal enlightenment of the "residential schools," the institutions to which their children were forcibly taken to exorcise the savage Indian lurking in their being, the mass graves into which the bodies of nameless creatures from those schools were ingloriously thrown, their souls condemned to haunt ancestral hearths and sacred shrines asking to be named and remembered, duly mourned and rightfully avenged. Did I say "their souls"? According to the good nuns, "Indians" have no souls. No, it is by no means a land without blemish, this Canada

ATO SEKYI-OTU

– hold the effusive hymns, please. All the same, it is a land not without the salvageable albeit fraught promise of decency. As the song asks: Compared to what?

VII

OBSERVATIONS ON USA[2]

PRE-CURSES

In the following fragments I set down some random observations on the United States of America. Americans prefer observers of their nation from other lands to be vicarious patriots, sojourners who rue the cruel fate which condemned them to be born in the accursed places from which they come and who bless the day a kind fortune brought them to their shores, there to bear witness to the marvels one exceptional people have wrought. That is the script written for those yearning and willing to take up the venerable tradition of foreign flatterers. It is the script awaiting my pen. I will not oblige. These scattered observations are going be harsh, very harsh. But they are no harsher, you will presently see, dear reader, than the strictures I visit upon the land of my birth. The difference, the crucial difference, is that the curses I bestow on my homeland emanate from burning fury comingled with profound grief, the sentiments of betrayed love, discredited expectations, mauled hope. My animadversions on USA do not derive from the same sentiments. Neither do they come from disenchantment with some beatific idyll. Growing up in Ghana, I was not untouched by xenophilia, the healthy and the morbid alike, a xenophilia, alas, heavily favouring things from one particular part of the human world, and inculcated with especial intensity into the hearts and minds of adolescents of a colonized society. But somehow in those years

---

[2] In remembrance of Frederick Douglass, witness to primal crime. In honour of Noam Chomsky, nemesis of Wilfred Owen's ogre - "The old lie: dulce et decorum est pro patria mori." In memory, with apologies, of Drucilla Cornell, American like no other, her questing spirit "porous to all the breaths of the earth."

of wondering and inchoate aspirations, for me America was never the cosmic magnet it was and still is for many young people around the world. Coming to America was never going to be the fulfilment of some all-consuming dream. Like many of my generation I came to the United States not because I was fleeing destitution or persecution, lured by the promise of material extravagance and unencumbered freedom, the motives American folklore attributes to anyone who undertakes the journey to the blessed country. I came for an utterly banal and unpoetic reason: to go to university, to be sure, to attend one of the great universities of the world – Harvard. With the self-assurance instilled in me and others like me schooled in one of those elite institutions of my native land, but also a self-assurance bred of blissful ignorance of the world's impediments, we deemed ourselves qualified and entitled to go to any place and to attend any university. Towards America, then, I arrived with neither worshipful admiration nor informed disquiet. That the country was born in sin, the radical evil of slavery, more precisely, the enslavement of Africans and the genocide of indigenous peoples, none of that registered on my mind with anything approaching retroactive revulsion. That race is the contrivance that organizes life in America in so many malevolent ways was thus no part of the body of knowledge I carried with me and with which I began my years in the United States. As for America's self-image as marvel of the free and democratic polity, I was at the time of my arrival, entirely agnostic, greeted that claim with neither enthusiastic endorsement nor educated incredulity. If the state of my mind regarding America was not completely a *tabula rasa,* a blank slate, neither was it encumbered with prejudgments so hardened as to court the shock of future refutation. In short, I was not set up, thanks to some great expectations, for disappointment. A great deal of things about America subsequently came to astonish me, but not because I did not expect to see them in some America I knew or thought I knew. They came to astonish me because they are, quite simply, astonishing. They are just not the kind of marvels that lyricists of the America Dream – native panegyrists and foreign flatterers alike – consider praiseworthy. The following observations, while they do not come close to exhausting all that I have seen and learned of the United States, are products of the years I spent there, and pictures I formed from the much longer period of studying, living and working next door in Canada, observing USA, so to speak, from a respectable distance.

HYPERBOLE NATION

A very short list of samples:

> "The greatest country in the world." American axiom, before and after Trump, Covid-19, and the emperor's disrobing.

> "The best political team on television": CNN's modest description of its election pundits.

> "Ronald Reagan single-handedly ended the Cold War and brought freedom to Eastern Europe": American historical truth.

> "The *world* series": Designation for a local American sporting event.

Hyperbole is as American as the gun.

BIPARTISANSHIP USA

From the Balkan expedition to the invasion of Iraq and Afghanistan to the intervention in Syria, to the systematic aggression-as-sanctions against Cuba, Iran and Venezuela, Republicans and Democrats regularly vie with one another to hike budgetary allocations for the military. Let someone propose an infinitesimal fraction of those amounts for the care of the sick, the poor and the homeless. We are certain to hear a cacophonous rage against taxing and spending and useless social experimentation and the debilitating culture of dependency. Not when it comes to the costs of such military expeditions. Here all the famous fiscal restraints are jettisoned. Nobody asks the ritualistic question: "How is this going to be paid for?" The most recent and especially callous instance of this selective allergy to spending and deficits and other cardinal sins is the swift appropriation of humongous sums for defence while a bill to aid the furloughed and the evicted and the suffering as a result of Covid-19 stalled. That paragon of selective parsimony, the humourless bane of the destitute, Senator Mitch McConnell, will declare any such proposal "dead on arrival." Something rotten stinks here. And it is the unbearable stench of a nation utterly indifferent to the harrowing woes of its own citizens, unmoved by its inner infamy. If that is not evil, what is?

THAT BIG BEAM IN YOUR EYE

If only America would cleanse its own native landscape; atone for the violence and the cruelty that accompanied its birth and its growth; stop killing its own (Black) citizens, heal the festering wounds of its despoiled and dispossessed peoples, be forced to remember its use of Agent Orange in Vietnam and Cambodia, be made to pay reparations for the destruction of Iraq, to name only the most recent of its marauding deeds, then perhaps its self-appointed mission of taming the savage fields of the entire world would begin to be half believable. It can then hector the Putins and Assads of the world with some credibility, enlist the consent of the "international community" to punish this or that regime guilty of atrocious violations of human rights.

In December 2021, Joe Biden, faithful to the tradition of rushing to pull the mote out of another person's eye while electing not to see the beam in your own, hosted a virtual "Summit for Democracy," with a band of pretenders of his choosing as the fortunate participants. The open secret and message behind the summit and the gleeful participation of obsequious vassals like the seventeen African leaders? Why: Beware of the Chinese *et dona ferentes*, even when, especially when, they bring gifts. Their "model" of prodigious growth and accelerated reduction of poverty under the aegis of the authoritarian state is not worthy of emulation. Our democracy can quell the aches of the belly and set you free at the same time. All this cant, while the right to vote in the USA was under sustained assault by a band of state legislators sworn to restoring the glorious days when the voice of slaves was deemed unreliable in court and their votes were non-existent, irrelevant for certifying America's credentials as a democracy – and at the very moment when a congressional bill intended to safeguard the endangered right faced opposition (and eventual rejection) from the Reaction. The reason Biden could hold that "global" summit at this very moment without blushing must be that he too regards the political participation of descendants of slaves, whose right to vote is under siege, to be inessential to America's self-definition and status as a democracy, nay, as "the greatest democracy in the world." But the charade would continue with a follow-up summit in December 2022 at which Biden declared a bidding war with China for the servile love of mendicant Africans by pledging billions of dollars in "aid." Murmurs warning of China's evil intentions, the unsavoury nature of its investments in Africa, the repugnant character of its "model" of development, could be heard throughout this august gathering. It is difficult to tell how many of our leaders greeted these entreaties and admonitions with the incredulity they deserved, or discerned the colossal beam in America's eye while it demonized China and excoriated its terrible human rights abuses.

"THE AMERICAN PEOPLE"

"Are the American people ready for a black president?" That was the question often posed at the inception of the Obama adventure. Dear questioner, I was always tempted to say, by "the American people" you mean white American people, don't you? You are not speaking of the whole of the American citizenry, certainly not of the black part of the blessed whole, are you? This is a case of the fraction impersonating the whole, isn't it? Or, to put it a little more fancifully, this is a species of the specious synecdoche.

Ato Sekyi-Otu

THE LIBERTY OF SAVAGES

The second amendment to the U.S constitution grants "the right of the people to keep and bear Arms." This is because "A well-regulated Militia" is said to be "necessary to the security of a free State." Let us put aside for a moment the perennial disputes in second amendment jurisprudence and go along with the manufactured consent according to which the article guarantees an individual right to bear arms: the interpretation now rendered evidently unassailable by the 2008 Heller decision crafted under the auspices of Justice Antonio Scalia's performative originalism (nice postmodernist jargon for the invention, retroactive certification and enforcement of that which never originally existed). But even if Americans acquiesce to this quintessentially Nietzschean act – the forcible triumph of an interpretation – does that make individual ownership of a gun the necessary, not to say sufficient, condition of liberty, as the NRA claims? Does that make "the firearm the fundamental symbol of our freedom," as Charlton Heston used to rhapsodize? That would make freedom a required instrument of survival in the primeval forest rather than a miraculous product of what Nigerian philosopher Emmanuel Eze called "achieving our humanity." That is neither the liberty of the ancients nor the liberty of the moderns, in the language of Benjamin Constant's iconic distinction. Defying classification according to recognizable divisions of human history, the NRA's version of freedom must be *sui generis*. The liberty of savages? That cannot conceivably be the foundation of what Newt Gingrich (boastfully) and C.L.R. James (generously) called "American civilization." Or is it? The founding rivalry between Hobbes and Locke for possession of the American soul is encapsulated in this debate concerning the relation between freedom, firearms, and the second amendment. Not that I consider Locke a saint and Hobbes utterly in error.

POSTSCRIPT

Sadly, the liberty of savages is in danger of being embraced by others around the "civilized world." In some quarters in France and even Canada, opposition to mandatory vaccination against Covid-19 and other related restrictions – a matter of public health – is voiced in the jungle cry of animal freedom. Right-wing truckers blocking principal Canada-US border crossings call their movement FREEDOM CONVOY. Echoes of that roar can be heard all over the "free world."

MASKS OF FREEDOM

Queried during the vice-presidential candidates debate on 7 October, 2020 about Trump's failure to require his followers and his officials to wear masks as protection against Covid-19, Mike Pence waved the libertarian flag on behalf of his boss. Trump, he averred, trusts the American people to make their own personal choices. A woman's right to choose whether or not to carry a pregnancy to term is evidently excluded from the sacred articles of the libertarian faith. State intrusion is perfectly fine in this instance. Firearms – even when sported in public places – and health care are private matters. A woman's womb is not. This is presumably the message that the United States of America, with the great state of Texas as torchbearer, should proudly take to the global public square in this season of rivalry between liberal democracies and autocratic regimes. What shall we call the substance of this message? Casuistic individualism? Selective libertarianism? Just plain arrant sophistry? The choice is yours. You have imprescriptible semantic rights.

INFANTILE INDIVIDUALISM, JUVENILE PATRIOTISM

In a television interview on 15 May, 2020, Tom Nichols described the view of freedom displayed by armed men protesting against Covid-19 lockdowns in Michigan as a "very childlike, I-can-do-whatever-I-want" view of freedom, nothing less than "confusing freedom with nihilism." Asked how that nihilistic egocentrism is consonant with the protestors' fervent patriotism, a sentiment evidently marked by acceptance of shared transpersonal obligations, Nichols sensed a contradiction. How wrong. That patriotism is but the collective version and constant companion of nihilistic egotism, twin infantile disorders. One licences "I can do whatever I want"; the other licenses "We can do whatever we want," or as Elon Musk recently declared, "we can coup whoever we want." That patriotism unilaterally exempts the US from adherence to international agreements and authorizes wanton, unprovoked aggression around the world, just as infantile individualism brooks no restraints on the will in the interest of the common good.

RESTRICTIONS: MOTIVE AND CONSEQUENCE

The wave of legislative measures restricting voting in some American states predominantly target black people, intended to stop them from influencing the outcome of elections. Uncomplicated motive, this, for the iniquitous exercise of white supremacy. And uncomplicated result. The relation between motive and consequence gets more tricky in the case of new laws restricting abortions or virtually making them impossible. They also predominantly disadvantage African Americans. The cruel irony of the latter restriction, however, is that it is not as if the prohibitionists are keen on seeing the black population of America multiplied. Nor is it the case that they are religiously devoted to public support for destitute mothers and their children, some of them brought into the world as a result of those restrictions. You see, the foetus and the *idea* of motherhood are sacred, even if real sentient mother and child are condemned to material conditions of deprivation. The right to life ends with the birth of the child. That way, the interests of the faithful demanding obedience to the word of god and of racial bigots sworn to making black lives unliveable are both fulfilled. Votaries of the right to life and those indifferent to the material conditions of black lives are thus united, are in fact one and the same people. God, after all, works in mysterious ways. Taking care of apparent incoherence, resolving the most antagonistic of contradictions, is one of them.

AMERICAN JUSTICE, CANADIAN PRISM

23 April 2018. A raving women-hater by the name of Alek Minassian rams a van into pedestrians in Toronto, killing ten people and injuring many others. A police officer, one Ken Lam, manages to arrest the maniac without firing a shot. The world, in particular Americans, are utterly in awe. Under the aegis of American justice, the outcome would have been somewhat different. Such is the prodigious significance of minor differences. But Canada, let's not sing fulsome hosannas unmodified. A satanic deed that put unspeakable dread into all who witnessed it was somehow spared the designation ready-made for it in today's taxonomy of evil: "terrorism." Why? Because this deed had merely to do with INCEL (a crazed tribe of sex-famished, "involuntarily celibate" misogynists) and nothing to do with ISIL or Muslims or Arabs. And Canada, let's not gloat with unrestrained pride. Had Minassian been black, he would quite likely have been unceremoniously dispatched to Hades, the worthy recipient of the famous, entirely understandable and undoubtedly exculpatory operation of the "split-second-decision." Yes, even in this fair and civil land. Pity, but our ode to Canada will have to sound this jarring note. Still, small differences, as I say, are not inconsequential. Particularly after the clarification that is Trump. After this recent unveiling of the culture that birthed him, the relative civility of Canada – ridiculed as boring by the fevered and frenzied populace to the south – is not unwelcome.

HENRY KISSINGER AND THE INSUFFERABLE EXALTATION OF THE WICKED

In the aftermath of the 2002 Salt Lake City Winter Olympics bribery scandal, Henry Kissinger was seriously touted as a member of the body charged with the task of cleaning up the International Olympics Committee. Now, that's an unimpeachable symbol of purity for you. The butcher of Indochina, architect of murderous coups against democratically elected governments in Latin America, "statesman for hire" according to an adoring portrait in Canada's right-wing *National Post* some years ago. What is the difference between Dr Kissinger and Dr Mengele, specialists in the science of selecting who shall live and who must die, avatars of the onerous craft of realism in the conduct of human affairs? Don't ask me. Awaken the victims from their stupefied sleep. After pouring a libation of atonement to the ancestors for such an impious act, sit on a mat with those victims and ask them to measure and compare the relative gravities of the stupendous horrors they endured on earth. Herbert Marcuse, our sorely missed doomsayer and irrepressible utopian all in one, would have described this exercise in macabre mathematics as a "calculus of suffering." Its findings would no doubt be quite enlightening. Not that those findings are likely to win the assent of a Niall Ferguson, zealous griot of the white man's feats, deftly trading worthless nostalgia for fallen Rule Britannia for rewarding adulation of ferocious Pax Americana.

MILTON'S SATAN OR NIETZSCHE'S KANT

Not too long ago, American pundits were calling the new breed of neoconservatives "idealists." Really. Those "brains" behind the baneful missions of *meurtriers sans frontriers*! Yes, "idealists": well-intentioned albeit overzealous warmongers to be distinguished, one gathers, from the "realists," that rival band of war counsellors possessed of a keener attention to intended targets and a judicious calculation regarding scale and scope, exercised less by the goal of slaughter and subjugation than by the economy and efficacy of its execution. When the saints of realism go marching in, they will count among their number the self-same Henry Kissinger. By your deeds shall you be judged. By their deeds we should expect that extended family of mandarins of war, "idealists" and "realists" alike, to gleefully join Nietzsche in sneering at the naïve proponent of "perpetual peace." They have for their tutelary spirit not the Immanuel Kant cruelly pilloried by Nietzsche, but Milton's Satan as he rallied his coalition of the willing – aka "the international community" – "To wage by force or guile eternal war" in their gallant mission as enforcers of a wicked world order. I will take Nietzsche's Kant anytime, real warts (pernicious anti-black racism among them), caricatures, and all.

NEW ORLEANS, OLD USA

Tragedy in classical Greek drama is the occasion of *anagnorisis*, the trauma of recognition. Its kin, crisis, is according to the Akan people of Ghana, the occasion of the proverb, the inventive work of thought and language concerning the human condition. In the torrential and pestilential waters of Katrina the world witnessed the open yet disavowed secret of the United States, its foundational and abiding apartheid: two nations under one partial and wicked god. The question I asked myself at the time was whether the revelatory shock of that catastrophe would reduce the American mind to speechless stupefaction or rouse it, for once, to the labour of the proverb. The jury, as they say, is still out. We are still waiting.

FROM KATRINA TO THE PANDEMIC

Will the knowledge that Covid-19 disproportionately devasted African Americans because of pre-existing conditions of deprivation and woefully inadequate health care inspire efforts to redress inequities? Or will the re-unveiling of this open secret rather fortify the right-wing claim that racism and racial injustice have nothing to do with it, that it is all a matter of individual responsibility, and that money spent on health care and other public goods only benefits "those people"? Will the response be an echo of Rick Santorum's unprompted and unguarded outburst during his bid for 2012 Republican presidential nomination to the effect that "I don't want to give black people other people's money" (the deep reason behind all the horror of reckless spending, deficits and talk of fiscal responsibility)? Will the reaction to the unequal distribution of affliction and death caused by the virus then be "Let them fry," uttered, of course, in coded but easily decipherable language? Just listen to the response to Biden's proposals for economic relief (such as it was). Don't tell me the opposition was entirely innocent, devoid of racial animus, a matter of colourless principle, no muted echo of Santorum's crude but undisguised outburst. Unfortunately for putative devotees of pure economic reason and fiscal conservatism innocent of racism, the disingenuous Machiavellian Senator Graham gave the game away. He called the part of the Biden plan offering debt relief to black farmers "reparations." How is that for tearing off the veil of innocence, innocence of racist motives for deep convictions regarding public policy? How is that for a guileless blow to the myth of disinterested commitment to principle?

MALCOLM'S TRUTH

George Walker Bush was judged criminally uncaring for his (non)response to Katrina in 2005. When he got around to reacting to it, he famously described the horrible scenes of deprivation and suffering as something belonging to another world, the "Third World." But after the spectacle of sustained buffoonery and gratuitous cruelty that is Donald Trump, George Bush, swaggering architect of Iraq's dismemberment, must in retrospect appear to some – the beloved Michelle Obama among them – as Mother Teresa's acolyte. The bar, shall we say, has been severely degraded. Or perhaps we should rather say that thanks to Trump, Malcolm's truth now stands nakedly irrefutable: the chickens have indeed come home to roost. Trump marks the comprehensive repatriation and verification of American thuggery. Perhaps we should be grateful for this clarification.

OBSERVATIONS ON THE USA
THE AMERICAN EVASION OF INFERENCE

Here is a commentator on Donald Trump's refusal to condemn white supremacy during the infamous presidential debate of 29 October, 2020: "Donald Trump says racist things; he does racist things. I am not saying he is a racist." What's worse, Trump's refusal to condemn white supremacists or this craven evasion of an inescapable inference? But that evasion of disconcerting inference is part and parcel of the American Ideology in practice. "The American evasion of philosophy" is Cornel West's paean to American pragmatism. Strange the pragmatist culture that so stubbornly evades calling its habitual practices and representative agents by their name. Perhaps the problem is the evasion of "philosophy" not just in the practice of American philosophers – their vaunted freedom, according to West and Richard Rorty, from the tyranny of "foundationalism" – but in the public culture as a whole: evasion of philosophy understood as the trained inability and unwillingness to draw rationally warranted albeit unpalatable inferences from a chain of facts staring you in the face. How else do you explain the phenomenon I am going to describe in the observation which follows, the habitual way America's leaders speak when they come face to face with abominable deeds committed by one of their own?

"THAT'S NOT WHO WE ARE": METAPHYSICS OF/AND THE NATION

Charles De Gaulle famously begins his monumental *War Memoirs* with the profession of tenacious adherence to "a certain idea of France," a mythopoeic image of an eternal France beyond its temporal deformations, periods of mediocrity that struck him as "an absurd anomaly, to be imputed to the faults of Frenchmen, not to the genius of the land." Here is the American version, in American prose: "That's not who we are." This is the regular exclamation we hear in the USA after every hate crime, every mass shooting, every atrocious deed and abominable word directed at some hapless member or members of communities of "the other," more recently, after every cruel act and repugnant utterance by Donald Trump. And of course, no event in recent memory provided a more apposite occasion for reciting that serviceable catechism than Trump's last act: instigating the 6 January 2021 siege of Capitol Hill. The fact that the siege featured, among the invading patriots' heraldic emblems, the very familiar, indeed the quintessential American historical artefact, the noose, did not in the least undermine the tradition of selective self-identification and disavowal. Forget living memory of Emmett Louis Till's gruesome fate. Forget Fannie Lou Hamer's blasphemy: "the land of the tree and the home of the grave." According to the nation's mythopoeic chroniclers, 6 January and the display of that archetypal symbol which graced it were no sequel to an old story. "Those acts do not represent who we are." Thus intoned Joe Biden. The President-elect said this in the teeth of what Donald Rumsfeld would have called "known knowns" as he went about meticulously classifying logistical facts pertaining to the unfolding invasion of Iraq, finessing the order of knowledge, and in the process marshalling the English language (American version) into the enterprise of aggression. "That's not who we are," then, signals the moment when American self-understanding, conveniently giving short shrift to Rumsfeld's "known knowns," goes philosophical, more precisely, goes scholastic – distinguishes essence from accident. Here then is a very brief history of forgettable times and ephemeral things, forgettable and ephemeral because they are extraneous to the nation's essence, to American Being: Genocide of indigenous peoples as founding act to be duly consecrated on Thanksgiving Day. A memorable follow-up: Indian Removal Act and the Trail of Tears, 1830-1850, the deed that, with Andrew Jackson's gentle prodding, forced the people of the Cree nation to leave their ancestral lands in Georgia and Alabama in order to make them free for habitation by specimens of the chosen people called upon to build "God's own country." Plantation slavery and the invention of the tradition of forced separation of families, happy prologue to the epic history of "family values." Lynching, exemplar of American justice. Agent Orange in Indochina and Abu Ghraib in Iraq, Black Sites and Extraordinary Renditions

OBSERVATIONS ON THE USA

after 9/11. The CIA's Gina Haspel, highly praised administrator of those Black Sites, splendid personification of the possibility that satanic brutality in its exceptional(ist) American form is gender-neutral. The caging and forced separation of children of "illegal migrants" from their parents in 2018-2019, the ideal of family values redux, a continuity that makes you wonder, just a little, about the lament of a kind Catholic Sister to the effect that "family separation violates our values." How, you want to ask, can a *catholic* nun, votary of the whole – the whole as ghastly fact and prophetic word, the ghastly fact that, precisely, cries out for the word as redemptory act – how can she say a thing like that, worship at the waters of American oblivion? And so here for further reminders is a compressed rollcall of ghastly facts culled not from the bad old days but today's breaking news, more precisely, from the vintage lethal years of 2014 and 2020: Gregory Vaughn Hill Jr., shot to death on 14 January 2014 by the police for getting drunk while black and playing loud music in his own (?) garage in St. Lucie County, Florida. Eric Garner choked to death on 17 July 2014 by David Pantaleo, one of NYPD's finest, while Garner screamed the new song of lamentation in the canon of African American literary history: "I can't breathe." Michael Brown, killed on 9 August, 2014 by the police in Ferguson, Missouri for walking-in-the-middle-of-the-street-while-black. Twelve-year old Tamir Rice shot to death on 24 November 2014 by the police in Cleveland, Ohio for carrying a replica toy gun. Ahmaud Arbery, mowed down on 23 February 2020 by a close-knit team of father and son (with a little help from a friendly neighbour) for jogging-while-black. Breonna Taylor, slaughtered while-black-and-sleeping-in-her-own-bed on 13 March 2020. "Her *own* bed"? Not without justice, the formidable Frank Wilderson 111, Afropessimist-all-the-way-down, asks if such a thing as "your *own* bed" or "your *own* space," standard idioms and signposts of inviolable proprietorship, can be coherently predicated of black lives in America in the first place. And the *pièce de résistance* of recent acts of casual savagery to be duly filed under the category of things alien to American Being: George Floyd, asphyxiated on 25 May, 2020 with cavalier composure by Minneapolis police officer Derek Chauvin while

Floyd repeated in writhing pain the very same line, so recently crafted, from that freshly published edition of the sorrow songs – "I can't breathe." Rayshard Brooks shot to death by Atlanta's finest even as the streets of the world screamed with rage and grief over the lynching of George Floyd. No need to risk evidentiary overdose and bring up the freshest of today's breaking news: the November 2021 acquittal of Kyle Rittenhouse of the charge of murdering two unarmed men protesting yet another (unpunished) police killing of an unarmed black man, Jacob Blake, in August 2020. Anomalies all, these mortifying acts, discrete deeds with no shared pedigree, if we are to believe those purveyors of scholastic American folklore practicing selective self-identification, one wilfully averse to pattern recognition.

So it is that of the age of Trump, liberals such as Anne-Marie Slaughter lament the grotesque aberration that age must be seen to be: "I just don't recognize my country anymore," she tells (mainly-white-establishment-stars-only-on-my-show) Fareed Zakaria. They must be harbouring tearful nostalgia, these liberals, for those civil days of the recent past when moral giants such as the inimitable Donald Rumsfeld proudly exhibited American exceptionalism by raining on the people of Iraq arsenals spewing "shock and awe." That pornographic sadism must have been uncharacteristic, alien to "who we are." True votaries of "the conservative sensibility" – with the learned George Will doubling as principal hymnist and Jeremiah – concur with this narrative of monstrous misdirection. Twin voices of the American Aeneid, liberals and authentic conservatives regularly contrapose to the sorry epoch of Trump an America before the Fall, the prelapsarian time of the virtuous republic bequeathed by the ancestors, the slave-owning founders. Such is their amnesiac originalism and the transcendental patriotism it licenses. Thinking to deliver a knock-out punch against "essentialist arguments" allegedly proffered by left-wing critics of American aggression – those weird empiricists all-too quick to draw (unwarranted) inferences from repeated evidence of serial crimes – Michael Walzer mockingly asks: "Does the long history of intervention in Central America reveal the essential character of the United States?" Yes Michael, it does, unless, of course, you are an initiate of some occult science of human conduct, the science that teaches that the phenomenon before your eyes is but an exception not an expression of the real national self, never mind that phenomenon's eternal recurrence and gruesome ubiquity. The evil that America does evidently belongs to another order of being and time. Quintessential essentialism, this, albeit of the exculpatory kind, exculpatory essentialism, if ever there was one. Against this reassuring scholasticism, the true and truthful patriot would offer this riposte: It is one thing to say with young David Hogg, survivor of the February 2018 mass shooting at Marjory Stoneman Douglas High School in Parkland, Florida, survivor turned gun-control activist: "This is not the country we should be, and it's not the country we have to be." It is one thing to enjoin a people not to accept today's iniquity as their destiny. It is one thing to exhort them to be better than they are. It is another matter entirely to recite the catechism of disavowal in propositional form – "This is not who we are."

But perhaps it is by such serviceable metaphysics that people expiate their sins, grant themselves absolution, avoid insomniac nights and get to live another day. Did Nietzsche remotely have this in mind when he wrote: "We have abolished the real world: what world is left? The apparent world perhaps? ... But no! *with the real world we have also abolished the apparent world*!" To flirt fleetingly with a usable Nietzsche: Was his critique of metaphysics ethically motivated? Was it, in fact, ethics, unpalatable exacting ethics of responsibility? Where is the debunker of dodgy metaphysics when we badly need one?

WITNESSES WITHOUT (DODGY) METAPHYSICS

There is absolutely no way that descendants of those who walked the Trail of Tears or those whose ancestors' bodies were turned into specimens of a "strange fruit" will call the Incident of the Noose on Capitol Hill and Torture at Abu Ghraib aberrations. Or do so with a straight face, that is to say, a face not shrouded in a white mask. Call that identity politics or epistemology or ethics if you want. For once I will welcome the opprobrium. Hail to those chosen by bitter knowledge to bear witness to life and history without mendacious metaphysics, those who, thanks to that very truthful testimony, hold on to the tenacious hope that a new day in human affairs promising another way of being-in-the-world is possible. Malcolm should be living at this hour.

HOW NOT TO INSULT THE OTHER AMERICAS

And you liberal, amnesiac critics (if that is not a contradiction) of the American state's more egregious domestic misdeeds, stop your habitual calumny against the peoples of the other Americas. Stop adding insult to injury by saying that these are misdeeds that only occur in "some banana republic." To the point and more specifically, cease and desist from attaching that pejorative label to the most recent proceedings in the laughing-stock of a polity you call "the greatest democracy in the world" – the pathetic post-elections antics of an entirely homegrown tyrant abetted by obsequious legislators and frenzied followers. Stop it. The societies you so blithely contemn as "banana republics" are human societies birthed from fraught antecedents and possibilities, possibilities derailed and disordered by the greed and violence your nation planted. For goodness sake, stop outsourcing templates of evil. Reminders of the long history of American justice, at home and abroad, will do just fine.

TRAVESTIES OF PROUST

But here, in a characteristic refusal of such reminders, is Thomas Friedman invoking the essence of the American character: "Americans are slow to go to war," he tells Fareed Zakaria in the course of that mockery of an inclusive conversation of humanity – "The Global Public Square" – he hosts. Let me come to the aid of the renowned journalist and provide him with this incontrovertible probative evidence culled not from the long twelve score years and more of the USA's existence, but from the very recent past: irrefutable evidence of America's pacific essence and the world's gratitude for its recurring manifestations. I have lived in or next door to that exceptional country on and off since the Year-of-Our-Lord-of-Suffering-Humanity-1962. There has not been a single year, not one, out of those many decades that the USA has not been at war, unfailingly in the honoured role of initiator of war, aka the aggressor, repeatedly. A rather incongruous fact, if Thomas Friedman is to be believed, a fact disfiguring, one supposes, the real national character and the pristine time when it shone radiant from sea to shining sea at home and all over the known world. *A la reserche du temps [et du pays] perdu*: Such is the vulgar Proustian fantasy entertained by American liberals such as Friedman. And so here again is Friedman mourning the precipitous Fall from that angelic nature, lamenting what has become of America and the world's view of the country in the four lamentable years of aberration under Trump: "For the first time people are afraid of us." That first night of "shock and awe" when those beautiful bombs came raining down on innocent Iraqi mothers and their homes must have been an uncharacteristic albeit sublime exhibition of Pax Americana that struck no fear whatsoever in the bones of those mothers. Indeed, those mothers, hailing the bombs as harbingers of their liberation, were getting giddily ready, as Dick Cheney and Paul Wolfowitz prophesized at the time, to dance in the streets and shower American troops with flowers. Two decades on, that wonton aggression and the hubris which sanctified it, far from being cause for retroactive atonement, is invoked as an exemplary act of America's beneficent world-historic mission in light of which the 6 January 2021 assault on Capitol Hill by fellow American citizens seemed nothing less than sacrilege. Horrified by that parricidal act, Representative Seth Moulton of the House Armed Services Committee bemoans the inversion of America's metaphysical calling thus: "We went to bring democracy to Iraq." And now a barbarian horde of our very own citizenry, untutored in civics, the national epic and the history of our redemptory work, bring mayhem to democracy's very own native temple. *O tempora*. Fatal misapprehension born of stubborn delusion.

Ato Sekyi-Otu

HOW AMERICAN EXCEPTIONALISM IS MADE

John Kasich, former Governor of Ohio and "moderate" Republican, supported Joe Biden in the presidential election of 2020. His modest fee for ditching Trump and helping Biden to victory? Biden should let it be known to the "far left" wing of the Democratic Party – a phantasmagorical, entirely non-existent entity – that you can't be an American and be a "socialist" at the same time. Members of that wing must be forced to be free from their eccentric convictions, if they have any claim to share in America's essence. It seems that "American Exceptionalism," that unique devotion to freedom unknown to other sentient beings, is itself not a matter of free choice. It must be enforced as must the substance of that commitment, the permissible articles of faith consistent with it, as well as the list of ideas adjudged incongruous. Chief among the cardinal sins that "far left" adherents are accused of committing and which true Americans like Biden must disavow and disallow is, naturally, the deadly sin of advocating "Health-Care-For-All." American exceptionalism, one gathers, means unquestioning fidelity to the principle of Health-Care-Only-For-Some.

ALTERNATIVE DEFINITIONS OF AMERICAN EXCEPTIONALISM

"The capacity to kill so many people so quickly is uniquely American." Those are the words of Harvard Kennedy School Professor Juliette Kayyem after yet another mass shooting, the one that happened at an Indianapolis Federal Express facility in April 2021. Since this concerns American exceptionalism in the matter of killing, permit me to add a rather more sanguine example, sanguine in an idiosyncratic way: Only in America is the rightful conviction of someone for killing – I am speaking of the April 2021 conviction of Derek Chauvin for murdering George Floyd in May 2020 – be a cause for jubilation as a momentous event, augury of the Second Coming. A visitor from Mars may be forgiven for not understanding what makes this an anomaly, a highly commendable anomaly: the murdered person was a black man, the killer a white police officer. Likewise the rightful conviction in November 2021 of the trio of white vigilantes who hunted and mowed down jogging-while-black Ahmaud Arbery in 2020, and the joyful thanksgiving that greeted the conviction. The befuddled visitor from Mars may be forgiven for asking what all the fuss was about, for not appreciating the strange albeit welcome exception, the exception that is an eloquent indictment of the general rule.

THE SORRY FIGURE OF THE AMERICAN LIBERAL

To be a "liberal" in America, that is to say, to stand two feet to the left of Atilla the Hun, is heresy. If you are to avoid total ostracism, you need to perform flamboyant acts of renunciation and compensatory orthodoxy tantamount to ritual cleansing. You have to be an unwavering "friend of Israel." You cannot voice support for the Palestinian cause. Indeed, you are allowed to be "progressive" (in the utterly defanged sense permissible in the USA) in all matters except Palestine, "PEP" in Marc Lamont Hill's crisp acronym. You cannot be or be seen to be soft on Russia. You are obliged to have called Putin – way before he invaded Ukraine – a killer, but don't you dare pin the same moniker on Saudi dauphin Mohamed bin Salman for the arranged murder of Saudi-American journalist Jamal Kashoggi on 18 October, 2018 in the Saudi chancellery in Turkey. You have to adhere to that shifting standard because of the alternative ethics mandated by "our national interests." Doctrinally, the American liberal must insist on a radical contradistinction of his creed from socialism, I mean, communism – same thing in the American political lexicon. If you are a Rev. Raphael Warnock, Georgia Democratic candidate running for a US Senate seat in 2020, and you are asked in a CNN interview if you were present at a speech given by Fidel Castro at a church you belonged to twenty-five years ago, you must squirm and offer a dodgy answer. You are not only required to prove your non-attendance even though you were in fact present, but, more pertinently, you must offer a retroactive disavowal of Castro. Didn't the candidate know, then and now, that Castro was a "murderous thug"? Why this hesitation to reduce the event of the Cuban Revolution and the phenomenon of Fidel to this crisp moniker? To be permitted to be one without guilt or fear, the American "liberal" must hold and be seen to hold such truths to be self-evident. In matters of foreign policy you must be an exhibitionist in your chauvinism. In the pursuit of "our adversaries," the American liberal, like every true warrior but especially the American liberal, must, as Prince Hal memorably exhorted, "disguise fair nature with ill-favoured rage." That is to say, the American liberal must be merciless, inoculated against anxiety over the death of children resulting from America's actions. If asked, as Madeleine Albright was asked by Leslie Stahl in a May 1996 interview, if the death of half-a-million Iraqi children as a consequence of sanctions imposed by the US on the country under Saddam Hussein was worth the price – "that's more children than died in Hiroshima," Stahl explained – the American "liberal" must respond as Albright did: "We think the price was worth it." Out of such unseemly admixture of craven inerrancy and gratuitous sadism is the figure of the American liberal cobbled.

INTERPRETATION OF MIGRANTS' DREAMS

September 2022. Heartless Republican Governors Ron DeSantis of Florida and Greg Abbot of Texas transport migrants to New York City, Washington DC, Chicago and Martha's Vineyard. Their mission? To punish hypocritical Blue States for Democratic President Biden's sins of omission: failing to secure the country's borders and putting the burden of receiving and maintaining undocumented migrants exclusively on their states. Here is a sample of enlightened reactions to this Unamerican ("this is not who we are") cruelty. New York City Mayor Eric Adams tells CNN anchor Jake Tapper that the migrants should be allowed to come and pursue the American dream "the same way our ancestors did." Mayor Adams is an African American. Mayor Adams must be in possession of an alternative history of the United States, one which, by transfiguring or totally erasing the story of how African Americans became African Americans, enables that edifying analogy. It appears Mayor Adams shares that fable of the Middle Passage as theodicy with that certified hymnist of the American Experience, Dr Ben Carson, for whom the journey from the slave dungeons to Virginia was but an instantiation of the archetypal immigrants' odyssey. But Mayor Adams is only retelling half the American Romance, the part evoking the cherished destination of the migrants and the generic prize that is their due. Listen to Jake Tapper summing up the other part, the story of what necessitated the journey in the first place, telling it for the enlightenment of obtuse Republican Governors and their ilk: "These people [the migrants] are fleeing Marxism." They are fleeing, that is to say, not just material conditions of destitution, in the case of Venezuelans, destitution aggravated if not caused by cruel boycotts and sanctions imposed by the US. And they are fleeing not just "socialist dictatorship" or "communism," the generic label attached to every social and political system that tampers ever so slightly with the rule of capital, say, by instituting Public Health Care for its people. No, they are fleeing a doctrine. Having perused the *Communist Manifesto* and, above all, *Das Capital* and found their contents pernicious, these learned and intrepid men and women undertook to revolt with their feet and their bags against the teachings these texts embodied and were being enforced by the state, and as a result decided to flee. Flee Marxism. This a revolt against *Capital* somewhat different from, albeit no less consequential than, what Antonio Gramsci had in mind when he penned "The Revolution Against *Capital*." All this and more evidently actuated the migrants' flight and is what deeply touched Jake Tapper's liberal sensibility. Tapper's only plea? Would that the Governors of Florida and Texas were equally touched, given – he assumes – not just their shared revulsion towards the communist system but, more profoundly, their educated antipathy towards the entire theoretic edifice that is Marxism in all its exacting and repulsive intricacy. Such is the discerning liberal's interpretation of the migrants' dreams and the ethical obligations they urge the famously knowledgeable American citizenry and especially their erudite leadership to accept as a result.

Ato Sekyi-Otu

AMERICAN THEODICY

A strange threesome of constitutional autocracy, predatory plutocracy and impetuous ochlocracy: that, in truth, is what the American polity is made of. Invoking the glossy form masking the ghastly innards, the regular retort you get from apologists each time you bring up the latest of America's domestic evils and foreign crimes is this: "but it is a democracy." Only in America are these alleged evils and crimes even aired and debated. Only in the USA will the highest court of the land have the independence and the courage to declare the actions of its government in violation of international law and the constitution alike (I am referring to the Supreme Court's ruling in 2006 on the status of so-called "enemy combatants" at Guantanamo Bay). Only in America are social divisions such as those made manifest by Katrina even recognized as unjust in the first place. Only in America, only in America... Hmm. Thus does the revelation of evil serve as a confirmation of goodness. At their finest hour Michelle and Barack sang the enchanting hymn: "Only in America is our story possible." Well yes, only in America, long-reigning monarch of THE FREE WORLD, is the very idea that in the year of our world 2009, any citizen can *in principle* become a nation's chieftain astonishing. Only in America is a banal possibility transfigured into a glorious exception. True, in the unforgettable words of Jean-Jacques Rousseau's dismal report on humanity's condition – "born free but everywhere [they] are in chains" – everywhere there are arrangements designed to enchain individuals, classes and particular communities in imprisoning enclosures fatal to the free development of the human prospect. But can it be that the American design of these arrangements, with their material and mythic coordinates, is to this day *sui generis*, one of a kind, truly a "peculiar institution" stubbornly and perpetually reconfigured such that the rise of a black man to the highest office of the land is indeed a miracle to behold? In which case Barack's and Michelle's extravagant jubilation, "only in America," is spot on. But it says less about America's praiseworthy singularity among the family of nations than about

its lamentable uniqueness, the exceptional form of the limitations inherent in it
s social order particularly for citizens who happen to be black.

LAMENT FOR THE NATION

Here is one American patriot's lament for the nation regarding recent schisms: "What happened to when we were united against one common enemy?" This is political commentator Michael Smerconish's idea of the good, a nice Manichaean model of the nation and the world, object of mournful nostalgia. This is our American patriot's *cri de couer*. But not to worry, Smerconish. The idyll *E pluribus unum* will endure. Help is coming. A saviour for the endangered unum is at hand: China. That new demonic upstart of a country will unify not only all decent nations of the "international community" in this epoch's defining *theomachia*, the sacred contest between liberal democracies and authoritarian regimes (remember to always refer to those nefarious states as "regimes"); more pertinently, the "threat" of China will unify America itself, salvage it from disastrous divisions. What is the invention of the enemy for?

WRONG DIAGNOSIS

And here is Alan Bloom's earlier lament: "The closing of the American mind." When did *that* happen? Just yesterday? A recent event? An altogether abrupt and shocking turn in the life of a national psyche hitherto known for being self-questioning, capacious, "porous to all the breaths of the earth," as Césaire said in praise of a way of being and thinking that is faithful to the special promise of a human community but does not fence it off in a walled enclosure? In addition to getting the time when the disaster set in wrong – how long has this been going on? – Bloom and precipitous-decline-and-fall fabulists like him also misidentify who and what is responsible for the catastrophe, and even more fundamentally, what that catastrophe consists in. He and fellow threnodists blame it all on the work of cultural infidels and perverse intellectual intrusions from outside in recent times. Anything but the American *geist*, its congenital and untreated pathology, and its terminal metastasis.

MISTAKEN ETIOLOGY

What a nation! So deeply imprisoned in the cave of narcissism and for that very reason so utterly incapable of self-scrutiny. Even the leaders who appear at moments of supreme crisis miss the opportunity to undertake a deep accounting of the nation's ailments. Consider a pivotal part of the opening words of Franklin Delano Roosevelt's fabled First Inaugural Address on Saturday, the fourth of March, 1933: "In such a spirit on my part and on yours we face our difficulties. *They concern, thank God, only material things.*" How mistaken, how woefully mistaken. The most generous thing we can say about that exordium is that the ensuing condemnation of the ruinous culture of greed allegedly responsible for the Great Depression is a case study in what philosophers call the performative contradiction: the reductive materialism of the diagnosis contained in the famous line – "They concern ... *only* material things" – is at odds with the causal explanation which follows, the irate indictment of the moral turpitudes responsible for the economic disorder. FDR is not the first nor will he be the last American chieftain to confound cause and consequence.

USA BEFORE AND AFTER TRUMP

Do we need further evidence that Donald Trump – to say nothing of contemporary ancestors like Gingrich, Cheney, Rumsfeld and Wolfowitz, worthy premonitions of Trump without the arrant buffoonery, deadly serious precursors of the cruel clown – do we need further evidence that Trump is not the only thing the world has to fear from America? Listen to Elon Musk celebrating the divine right of king of the universe to act with arbitrary freedom as recently demonstrated in the coup against Evo Morales, the coup to make Bolivia safe for lithium: "We will coup whoever we want. Deal with it!". That hubris predated Trump; it will quite likely survive his incumbency.

BOLIVIA'S REVENGE

It is one year after the coup executed at the command of the earthly god to Elon Musk's delight. On the 18th of October 2020, the people of Bolivia, in a supreme act of impudence, gave a landslide victory to the ousted leader's party, MAS, in an election that was indisputably, as they say, free and fair. A glorious administration of the middle finger to the emperor, this. And a preemptive shaming of American "democracy" and the laughable farce it would become three weeks later, starring Donald Trump as leading man. This did not stop votaries of "American exceptionalism" from saying, once more, that that kind of farce belongs to "banana republics." So, to invoke the inimitable Aretha – "Who's zooming whom?" – we have to ask: who is peeling whom, in more than one sense of the word; that is, peeling the veil off the self-deluding face of the emperor?

THE WORLD APRÈS TRUMP

We know there will be Trumpism after Trump, just as there was Trumpism before his advent, honoured lineages and enabling presages. So unexceptional, so non-idiosyncratic, so not-unamerican, is the phenomenon. And it's not just that seventy four million people voted for him. I am talking of the quintessence, not mere figures. Trumpism as synecdoche, the defining American way of being, the collective psyche with its petulance, infantile narcissism and insufferable hubris, and not just that of its dominant class exclusively – all that will still be with us. That's the awful news. The good news is that the long-lingering allure will have worn off. The peoples of the earth will henceforth confront an entity stripped of its last deceiving masks. And after the recent exquisite exhibition of Democracy-in-America featuring a master class in the management of transition from one administration to another, the world, we hope and pray, will be mercifully rid not only of their ubiquitous election observers, but also of all those tiresome instructors in the arts of transitional justice. With unimpeachable justice, the world can now say to them, in the polite language of the Akan people of Ghana: "*Dzi wo fie asɛm,* take care of business in your own homestead." Reverence for the ancestors forbids me from rendering this counsel of prudence born of self-scrutiny in a more colourful idiom. You know what I am saying?

And no, no xenophobic nativism is being proposed here. Peoples of the world less self-adoring, less imperious and impertinent, peoples and persons known to be regular members of the community of finite and fallible humanity, *karibuni, akwaaba,* welcome. Even – especially – for work in the service of unforced political education and collaborative enlightenment. Prophets bearing arms, averse to foreign interference in *their* nation's affairs but freely wielding missionary cudgels as tutorial instruments in *our* business – that's another matter entirely. Those types need not apply. Not in this glimmering future that beckons after the long-overdue but inevitable death of god.

RIGHT NAMES MATTER

Yes, death of god. That is no hyperbole, if you think of the demiurgic power this one nation has wielded or imagined itself to have wielded in the long night of its short reign over human affairs. At its finest hour it could, at will, summon governments into being and turn others – and their countries – to dust. It reserved the full force of its fury for those "regimes" which committed the grievous error – the impertinent and infectious error – of attempting to bring some relief to their peoples' wretched conditions of existence and in the process dared to tamper with an unjust order of things ministering to American power and the obscene opulence of homegrown plutocrats. "Death of god" is no hyperbole if you consider what is at stake. The sycophantic establishment-toady Fareed Zakaria's anodyne name for the ending of this monocratic dispensation is "The Post-American World." That does not come close to capturing the coming Nietzschean moment in the recent history of the world, the palpable demise of the most frightful incarnation of mortal gods humanity has ever known, the bracing prospect, as a result, of an unshackled future for other sentient beings dwelling outside the enchanted animal kingdom that is the USA. The question is whether we, yesterday's worshipful creatures, dare recognize the event and begin to live a life worthy of its meaning. Or dread, as Nietzsche feared, the daunting consequences of our deicide and seek the protection of surrogate divinities. It all begins with naming the event right in the first place.

AFGHANISTAN: AUSPICIOUS DOMINO?

As it happens we don't have to wait long to witness propitious omens of that event. August 2021. The comprehensive, inglorious rout of US power and its satraps in Afghanistan after two decades of wrecked lives and wasted resources, an infinitesimal fraction of which the American ruling class would not deign to expend on the destitute of their own country, to say nothing of the wretched of the earth. But don't get me wrong. To echo the bard with extreme impiety: I toast the rout not because I detest Taliban less but because I loathe empire more. Above all, because I cherish with a passion the right of all persons and peoples to design their own plan of life. So don't call me anti-American. That is truncated naming, an impoverished definition by negation. I stand *for* something. Call me by my full name: partisan of human self-determination. Whatever or whoever stands in the way of that possibility must fall. Yes indeed.

WHAT A WONDERFUL WORLD

Here I am delivering – in remembrance of Frederick Douglass ("What to the Slave is the Fourth of July?"), in honour of Noam Chomsky, icon of resistance to empire and lies, and in respectful memory of Drucilla Cornell, exemplar of a spirit "porous," as the poet enjoined, "to all the breaths of the earth" – here I am heaping curses upon America's ancestral and abiding sins; celebrating omens of its coming eclipse. I do so not out of hatred for its people, this vast and variegated part of the human community, but in the name of a paramount principle. And here I go murmuring misgivings even about this adopted homestead, Canada, Oh Canada, hinting at its imperfections, its congenital and lingering blemishes, homestead built by human, all-too-human hands. Again, just ask those who were here from time immemorial and whose ancestors were invited to make their abodes free for habitation by specimens of the chosen race. Still it is, as I say, a land in which the glimmer of decency threatens to break out any day now. For six decades it has been the tree that, planted as it was on stolen soil by sinful hands, buffeted by the vortex and vices of the encircling world, housed my strivings and hopes, sometimes with sturdy succour, often with wavering and inconstant resolve, but always with this furtive tease of the possibility of human goodness. So why even bring up those blemishes? What insufferable ingratitude. Thus scream the outraged voices of true bloods. By what ethereal standards do you judge things made by earthlings? So murmur the polite voices of realists. The chastisers have a point. Truth is, I will return to my homeland and there witness rifts in the social body that are second to none in their inhumanity. Racism? Its enabling logic is alive and well here in the odious shape of ethnic chauvinism, withering contempt for Northerners by Southerners, animosity between Asantes and Ewes; it breathes with foul odour in the belief that a person is not really a person, not really an individual, but is what he is, possesses these vices and those virtues, *because* he is Fanti or Ga or Ewe or Conja. Remember the racist syllogism deployed with murderous consequences by George Zimmerman? Tribalism is homeland racism. I can hear the objection: "It's not the same." Tell that to those on the receiving end of benign disrespect, non-racial disrespect, just harmless intramural dissing. Tell that to Ghana's Northerners of whom ethnic supremacists from the other regions say that they are constitutionally lazy and that they vote for a certain political party because of their low intelligence as a group and because of affirmative action policies enacted in their favour by an indulgent government. Sounds familiar? Obscenely familiar? I can hear the protest ringing in my ears, intoning the last maxim of every people's moral protectionists: *"Obi mfa ne nsa atabin nkyerɛ n'egya kwurow mu.* One does not point to the fatherland's location with the left hand." You don't say sinister things about the homeland. So whispers an Akan admonition. But how can we know racial apartheid to be a radical evil and call it by its name, if, heeding the taboo of supine patriots everywhere, we dispossess ourselves of a universal standard by means of which we can judge and curse what Miriama Bâ – her searching gaze fixed not on the ills and iniquities of the larger world outside but on our very own native infamies – what she called the "internal ordering of our society with its absurd divisions"?

But surely, however real and absurd these internal divisions, life in the homeland is different from life over there in the adopted homestead of Canada, to say nothing of the colossus to the south and the overpowering miasma oozing from its fevered body? Homeland has to be different from these two places where, notwithstanding undeniable nuances and marks of distinction, the lore of race decrees that human existence, with all its intrinsic prospects and perils, is first and foremost existence-in-black, first and foremost Black life, with consequences – pernicious and glorious alike – that uniquely derive from that condition, consequences lived from the streets to the hallowed halls of the university? Free from the totalitarian dictatorship of race, life in the homeland *is* different. True. But it is, alas, a human place, human-all-too-human.

Prayer to the muse: Of journeys of return not aroused by paradisal pictures and maudlin nostalgia, sing.

VIII

HOMELAND IS NOT YET HOME

The place of my birth is an irritant.
–Patrick Sylvain, *Haiti: A disavowal*

BESSIE'S QUESTION, ERNST'S DREAM

"*Fie ara ne fie*, there is no home like the native homestead" is bullshit, of course. Unless you mean to tell the ironic truth of the saying that there is indeed no place like home, no place, that is to say, which looks like the lodestar called home or comes close to fulfilling the promise of being a just space of human flourishing, and that homeland is *not* that place. But surely, homeland, such as it is, and adopted homestead and neighbourhood cannot possibly share resemblances in the forms of human divisions and degradations? Or can they? Was Bessie Head on to something when she voiced these disconcerting words in *Maru*: "How universal was the language of oppression?" And not just the language? Can it be that I will find or rather rediscover here in the homeland conventions of subordination and exclusion – from the soft separatism of social distinctions as an unavoidable necessity of the relationship between employer and employee to neo-feudal boundaries between masters and servants as a natural feature of the social bond? That I will find here replicas of the rules and rituals of hierarchy that are racist culture's normal procedures? Here where race indeed does not matter as the principal axis of social power and idiom of existence, Ghana having dodged the fate of settler colonialism? Here where we flaunt our faith in the equal worth and dignity of all persons and say with casual certitude: "*obiara yε nyame ne ba*; everyone is god's child"? Just how far is homeland from home, the imagined destination, according to Ernst Bloch's bracing vision, of humanity's sempiternal longing? How far is homeland from home? Today, as some of our African American sisters and brothers, weary of the lethal consequences of the Zimmerman syndrome, contemplate returning to the motherland – and after George Floyd this is no longer a beatific romantic dream but a pressing existential necessity – that question is no idle philosophical query, a rumination concerning our universal "transcendental homelessness." Or is it?

"TAKE BUT DEGREE AWAY": HOMELAND VARIATIONS

To my query regarding why the driver should be kept waiting outside in the scorching sun all afternoon until summoned to drive me to this place or that, or why he shouldn't be served a meal at the same time as my buddies at a gathering of high-school classmates, I was told: "That's the American way. Matilda felt the same way as you do and asked the same questions when she first came back. But she eventually learned the facts of life here. You will soon learn to forsake your American way" – presumably, a half-decent, if not exactly a radically egalitarian, way of relating to the driver, the help and the like, a way supposedly characteristic of the social bond in the USA.

A strange counsel, I thought. I had never thought of myself as a votary of "the American way," to say nothing of the fact that Canada is the country in which I lived and of which, together with Ghana, I am a citizen – a country whose distinctiveness, for all its imperfections, I rather appreciated and still appreciate. Nor did I ever think of the American form of the social bond – with racial and class subjugation as its foundational and enduring bedrock – as a laudable template, one that, in the estimation of my interlocutor, is fine for life in "America" but unworkable, except in the imagination of well-meaning and naïve returnees, in the real world that is Ghana. Here on this other side of utopia, I was instructed, you flirt with erasing boundaries, with fancy "liberal" experiments in everyday life at your own risk. Let them know their place. Tweak the accepted design of separation ever so slightly, invite these people from "the boys' quarters" into your world and what do you know? We know the archetypal answer: "Take but degree away…" and cosmic disorder erupts. But was I prepared for local copies of that lore in the common phobias and taboos of the Ghanaian elite? Allow a little breach in those walls of separation and presently, so goes the admonition, you will be hearing of their families' penury, the children's unpaid school fees, funerals of their loved ones to attend, monetary contributions to make. Next they will be sitting at your table, breaking bread with you, dancing to your music, discussing weighty matters of society and politics, inviting you to share with them all the aches and pains which, as the man said, "this mortal flesh is heir to." Very soon, immortal gods, you will be asked to-be-human-with-them! They've got to know their place. Does that mean that you don't value them? Not at all. But you've got to keep them in their place. By all means have a Kantian heart or mind or soul – choose your preferred organ of saccharine sanctimony – but be a feudal overlord in the practice of life.

In the beginning I was revolted by these sentiments, by the mortal dread of equality they harboured and the habits they sanctioned. How could it be otherwise? How could I possibly stomach these interdictions and the very language in which they are voiced, evincing as they do a recognizable kinship with the rules of existence in racial orders? Can it be that rules of life presumed to be *sui generis*, belonging to particular places and the more atrocious social orders of the world, are not so at all, not so special? Can they nevertheless serve as moral templates, useful for recognizing or at least suspecting abominable affinities between practices in different times and places? So it is with living memory of existence-in-black in the adopted homestead and its consequences for judging the nature of things in the homeland. And so it is that in the beginning I felt nothing but revulsion with homeland reminders of unsavoury things away. The beginning was short, the revulsion not entirely unmixed for long. Soon, shockingly soon, you begin to copy those conventions of separation and exclusion taken for granted in the homeland. You begin to craft excuses – I mean offer reasons – say, for lodging yourself in that privileged place in the car, the right corner of the back seat, which the geography of social power with culture's arranged blessing has decreed to be naturally and exclusively yours. Your knees and legs hurt crouched in the front passenger's seat. More seriously, were you to occupy that seat, the consequences of the driver's proximity, say, intermittent conversation with you, could be fatal, given the life-menacing habits of drivers in this rules-averse society. Imperceptibly, thanks to the serviceable silence of your conscience, you come to partake in all those serial acts of self-absolution ritually practiced by kind, gentle and sensitive souls upon whom has been thrust privilege they cannot refuse. We should be grateful for kind, gentle and sensitive souls.

OF ABDUL AND MASTER

"Abduuuul." The name is barked as though it were a summons to answer for some heinous crime, the barker's face contorted with inexplicable fury, his very nose instantly rearranged into a figure of imperial disdain for all those cursed with the sorry fate of being merely human. "Saah," the summoned one responds and runs with a sprinter's speed, hands behind him with trained servility. No need to tremble, because there is no wrong in question. This is the normal mode of encounter between Abdul and Master. This is the regular practice of "dutiful submission" characteristic not of "*black* subjectivity," as Saidiya Hartman says of the conduct of the enslaved in antebellum America in *Scenes of Subjection*, but the trained habit of a member of the free and equal citizenry of postcolonial Ghana. These are the rituals of "performing before the Master" enacted, to repeat, not by a *black slave* but by an enfranchised albeit subordinate being in an all-black nation, one that, precisely because it is all-black, does not regularly think of itself as black. And this is when Abdul has done nothing particularly grievous to incur his Master's displeasure. You don't want to see *this* Master truly angered by a real error, a specific lapse or serious sin of omission committed by Abdul. This is regular stuff, part of the normal rituals of subordination in this our *post*colonial society. To be sure, it is nothing as violent and gory as the peculiar "pageantries" of subjection, as Frank

Wilderson delicately calls them, enacted by slaves for their masters' pleasure; but it is every bit as mandatory.

Abdul's Master's native tongue is Fanti. Abdul understands and speaks Fanti. Indeed, Abdul is perfectly fluent in Fanti in addition to other Ghanaian languages. You would think that the natural thing is for Master to speak with – I mean to speak to – Abdul in Fanti. You would be mistaken. Fanon should be living at this hour. Fanon should be living at this hour to help us make sense of a colossal pile of excremental detritus in everyday life: help us decipher not the drama of the black man and language in racial orders but the rituals of language performed by the Ghanaian master and his servant (I mean his "boy") right here in this our post(???)colonial homeland. Fanon says of "the problem of language" in the colonial-racial context that here is an instance of a human commonality that the most discerning of philosophers knew not of: such is its eccentricity as a form of communicative action, even as a species of the practices of power. But Abdul's relationship to his master and language is something else again, a whole other "problem of language." The master in Fanon's account of the "racial drama" speaks "pidgin" to all black people irrespective of their real level of competence in standard French or English or Portuguese. He does so in order to enforce the "dividing line," to interdict the possibility of a world in common. Abdul's master, in a strange twist to conventions of hierarchy, pursues the same goal – that of interdicting the possibility of a shared moral community – by studiously avoiding speaking a native language with him, speaking the people's tongue. That is why the insults and reprimands and orders that follow the barking of Abdul's name are delivered in English only, standard authoritative English. That way, the sentinels that guard the "dividing line" in this our free, independent and democratic land will remain on duty. The twist is that the Ghanaian master enforces his dominance over his Ghanaian subordinates by means of the colonial master's tool. But that borrowed weapon of dominance is of a piece with the "boys' quarters" and sovereignty over the right corner of the car's back seat. Fanon should be living at this hour so that he may revisit with us the rites of power under the sign of race and witness their weird replications in the internal ordering of our society: this tangled dance of archetype, copy and eccentric affinities enacted in conventions of hierarchy in our very own homeland. *Yɛn ara asase nyi*, this land is our land, we proclaimed on Independence Day and still proclaim. Evidently, we do not dwell on this land of ours with equal moral status. The ritual comedy of language enacted by Abdul and his master is eloquent proof.

LANGUAGE, LIFE AND DEATH

But perhaps I overplay the degree to which this tragicomedy of language in the homeland has to do with class-hierarchy, the enforcement of its rules and its hilarious absurdities. For today the will to forget the native tongue, the determination to make your children speak English and only English at school *and* at home – perfectly atrocious English, mind you – is no longer the affectation of a specific class but a collective malady that cuts across class and social status in its incidence and severity. Or perhaps I should say that, thanks to a delusional logic, hierarchy is at once affirmed and erased by this decision by members of all classes not to speak an indigenous language with their children. What will history say of this era's parents, elders and teachers, putative custodians of our cultural resources, who gleefully promote indigenous-language-amnesia and suppose that "I tink therefore I yam" is standard English and the surest certificate of arrival at the portals of cosmopolitan modernity? In this society of imitation, fads and fashions quickly become unstoppable forces, with dire consequences. The mania for speaking English at school and at home fostered by parents and educators who themselves clearly need elementary lessons in English is a prescription for cultural suicide.

More than cultural suicide, this is a serious matter of physical health, a matter of life and death. Among the rare hopeful things I have encountered in this land of inverted priorities was a discussion of the risks of stroke I heard on the radio one morning in 2013. I listened in awe to an explanation of the causes of stroke delivered almost entirely in Akan (one of Ghana's languages) by a doctor with matchless pedagogic skills and equal mastery of the language. The idea that competence in indigenous languages as formative foundation is of enormous benefit in the acquisition of other languages and bodies of knowledge is now pretty much unarguable, except in places such as this one where wilful darkness is regularly confused with enlightenment. That it is a marker of cultural distinctiveness as an end in itself is an acknowledged principle. That it is also a vital necessity, a matter of physical health, perhaps even a matter of life and death, was made resoundingly clear in that incomparable discussion on the radio. Will that doctor's work – the most essential of "essential services" in this season of the pandemic – be continued by the next generation of doctors? That is the question. The indigenous language amnesia fashionable in the homeland today is imbecilic in intent and disastrous in its consequences. It is a macabre death wish.

CRIMINAL PRUDERY

Speaking of language, consider this gem: "He inserted his manhood into her private part." That is the way a journalist in Ghana – where else? – describes what a pastor did to a woman who came to him seeking help for her infertility, That is the journalist's uncensored report of the Man of God's healing deed meticulously performed because, as he said, he needed to exorcize the demonic forces causing her condition. What is more atrocious: the rape perpetrated by the pastor or the violent assault on language committed by the journalist in a shameful failure to call evil by its unadorned name? Criminal prudery. It competes in its wide currency with this other obscenity: "He had carnal knowledge of her." This is not a biblical citation uttered in some medieval English parish. It is ordinary twenty-first-century Ghanaian speech, the everyday locution of the inhabitants of a moribund society, more specifically, the language of journalists reporting a rape, for goodness sake!

ABDICATION OF THE GUARDIANS

Nothing better epitomizes the death wish, the psychopathology of a people who have forgotten to remember the future, than this society's depressing culture of funerals, with its unending days, weeks, and months of mourning. Mourning for the recently departed as well as the long gone, for the praiseworthy no less than the utterly execrable: endless days and weeks and months and anniversaries of manufactured grief vying with extravagant feasting. The vital resources and sacral practices of a culture transmogrified into a veritable festival of necrophilia.

It was on one such occasion that, with minds and tongues set loose by copious booze for unscripted thoughts on everything but especially on the nation's condition, I heard a classmate deliver an angry lament for the nation and a fulsome panegyric to the idyllic days of colonialism. And a panegyric to J.B. Danquah, Kwame Nkrumah's neo-feudalist adversary, as unheeded prophet of what will happen when you demand and are given freedom you are not prepared for. And this fellow pronounced his elegy to colonial tutelage and lament for its rude interception by nefarious demagogues in the presence and to the incredulous ears of no less a person than Ama Ata Aidoo. Later, musing about that unamusing encounter, I told Ama Ata of an infinitely more awful one some time back: a full-throated rant of contempt for Africa, visceral self-hatred, a hideous hymn to white supremacy and unabashed adulation of whiteness from hair to foot. It was, I said to Ama Ata, utterly dispiriting, coming as it did from a chief (albeit of some inconsequential principality), putative custodian of African essences, guardian of what is left of our inheritance and our promise. Progressive chiefs? Now, if that is a generous oxymoron and not a flagrant contradiction – how can we forget their starring role in the capture and sale of our people for export? – this chief is no specimen. He is a goner, prime exhibit of vacated responsibility on the part of our would-be guardians; hopelessly failed "Captain" – if you will permit an irreverent echo of the Charles Wesley hymn – of Africa's "host, and guide of all who seek" not indeed "the land above" but Ebibiman's earthly sustenance and flourishing.

"NO SAVIORS"

Where is the healer to suck with
thick lips the obstinate secret at the
heart of the open wound?
 —Césaire, *Notebook of a Return to the Native Land*

The knowledge there was no one left to guide us, as also
the knowledge we would surely perish if we attempted
going back, produced in all a profound consternation.
 —Ayi Kwei Armah, *Two Thousand Seasons*

The flight of the gods; the treason of the chieftains; the fright of the people: such is the African condition. Where is the healer? Who will shepherd work towards remembrance of things not yet done with our inheritance? The answer? Just us, you and I, the acephalous community of the quest for "this Africa to come." As always, "No Saviours." Our wounds are much too deep and widespread, no part of the social body kept immune from the general decay and ruination, to warrant faith in the redemptory work of a particular organ of society, still less in the magical hand of a solitary healer. It is difficult to count on those at the apex of the social order to take up the enterprise of regeneration as a result of some radical conversion of the collective mind. As the saying goes, they are the problem not the solution, certainly not the collective mind of rightwing folks among our elites.

MIND OF THE RIGHT

Presently, under the rubric of "STRANGE THINGS OF THE WORLD" I shall invite you, dear reader, to join me in peering, with rage and revulsion in our guts, into the fevered souls of rightwing black folk in America and other societies in the world where history has contrived to assemble different races under the aegis of white supremacy. And I will be asking you to join me as I stare with astonishment and sorrow at the words and deeds of rightwing Jews, in the process sharing with you the sources of my astonishment and sorrow. But what of rightwing kinsfolk here in this homeland? Unlike our rightwing African American brothers and sisters, they are not direct products – grotesque products – of the racial order, hell bent on hustling their way out of its adamantine partitions. Nor are they, like rightwing Jews, creatures of that tragic mutation that makes some forget to remember that they were once slaves in the land of Egypt, or rather remember that history all too well and are persuaded that there is no third alternative to servitude or dominance. The kinsfolk of the rightwing in the homeland are, of course, also progenies of history. But out of history's constraints they have fashioned a culture of self-inflation, calculated social amnesia and what Fanon labelled "wilful narcissism" that places on their shoulders irrevocable responsibility – as a class and as individuals – for their actions and inactions, their conduct and judgment. More than others elsewhere, we can say of them that they are free agents in a world of their own making, albeit under conditions not entirely chosen by them. Such is the irrevocable burden of accountability that provokes in me unmixed fury with their utterances, their deeds and their sins of omission. Here, dear reader, is a sample to savour.

NPP'S CREED AND ITS VANGUARD

A bizarre marriage of Burkean ancestralism and Thatcherite solipsism: such is the ideological personality of Ghana's rightwing New Patriotic Party. In their pure forms these two persuasions clash. The one flaunts pedigree, genuflects to antecedents, inheritance, habit, as constraining sources of social circumstance, judgment and moral action. The other says: I came into this world with nothing; I am what I am and I have what I have by virtue of my unaided industry. Owing nothing to precursors and society for my fortunes, I am entitled to dispose of them the way I bloody well please. In their Ghanaian incarnations, however, the twain meet in the soul of the NPP. Egoism cohabits with a certain communitarianism. But it is the bounded community of ethnos and class, of kith and kin defined by tribe and status, not the civic community of equal citizens. It is that bounded community which is here the primary object of what Edmund Burke called "public affections." Collective egotism and, worse still, that homeland version of racism known as tribalism, are the odious consequences of this ethnic communitarianism. The Akyem and Asante rivalry and warring loyalties within the NPP is one expression of this ethnocentric form of allegiance to community. In that sense it is entirely compatible with the everyone-for-himself-get-the-state-out-of-the-way species of individualism officially espoused by that party. Collective egotism of the ethnos *and* egoism of the individual self; ethno-nepotism *and* social Darwinist Thatcherism; chauvinistic ethnic loyalism tinged with royalist ritualism and adherence to neoliberal market fundamentalism: these apparent antipodes are here joined in kinship. The outcome is a kleptocracy that practices at once a pseudo-traditionalism and a perverted modernism, a caste of impatient hustlers with custom-revering and aristocratic pretensions.

Upon Margaret Thatcher's death in 2013, Nana Addo Dankwa Akufo-Addo, born-to-rule- and-destined-to-be-President, and Gabby Asare Otchere-Darko, the party's vainglorious would-be think-tanker-in-chief-cum-principal-superintendent-of-procurements, paid fulsome homage to her as a tutelary spirit. And why shouldn't they have, these two scions of the holy family? From birth, they have been privy, have they not, to the groans of the belly and aches of the spirit familiar to those upon whom Thatcher visited her nefarious policies? Otchere-Darko for one was particularly taken by Thatcher's "resoluteness," her refusal to subordinate sturdy conviction to the tepid politics of compromise, a quality, he thought, worthy of emulation by Ghana's and Africa's effete political leaders. He forgot that were dogged resoluteness in pursuit of a programme a cardinal virtue, Adolf Hitler would be a peerless laureate. Some British wit had averred that a fitting tribute to Thatcher and her legacy would have been to privatize her funeral rather than bestow upon her in death a regal version of support from the public purse that she gleefully denied others in life. Impressed with his own powers of discernment, Otchere-Darko concluded that this posthumous transfiguration of the "there-is-no-society-only-individuals" ideologue into beneficiary of an extravagant state-sponsored funeral showed that the notorious "Iron Lady was after all Irony Lady." Our Danquah-Busia wit forgot that irony begins where dogma fails. He forgot that market fundamentalism of the sort espoused by Thatcher is, like every dogma, the enemy and not the friend of irony. Mistaking for a vindication what was arguably a shaming lesson, an oblique censure by the living presaging the ancestors' chastisement – shame on you wicked architect of life-extinguishing privatization of public goods for enjoying publicly-funded honours – Otchere-Darko forgot, lastly, that it is one thing to be an unwitting butt of irony's *ananse* wiles; it is quite another to be its praiseworthy exemplar.

But it turns out that our Thacherite zealot's adherence to the primacy of conviction and the principle of coherence is not exactly inerrant. That same year 2013, Otchere-Darko was miffed by criticism from NPP gadfly Wereko-Brobbey to the effect that it was illogical for their parliamentarians to boycott the vetting of nominees for ministerial offices in the rival and, at the time, ruling party's government while fully availing themselves of the privileges and salaries of MPs. Otchere-Darko's answer to this rebuke of inconsistency amounted to a thuggish parody of Nina Turner's question: what's (love of) logic got to do with it? His party's intent in undertaking the boycott, he offered with shameless candour, was not to do logic, proffer rational argument informed by principled conviction, but to mess up the governing party's game. Since Socrates, the name for advancing a stance in the service of particular interests and immediate advantage rather than truth, justifiable claims and shareable ends, is sophistry. And so it came to pass that acolyte of the woman who bragged that "this lady is not for bending" and got credulous souls in the neocolonial satrapy to believe her words and praise her deeds will stoop and stop at nothing, will vengefully bend political and moral reasoning in ways that would have made Nicolò Machiavelli and, farther still in ancestry, the sophists, visibly blush.

BROTHERS UNDER THE SKIN

Upon winning the presidential election in 2016, Donald Trump got a congratulatory letter from Akufo-Addo in which the Ghanaian celebrated the Republican Party as "Sister Party" to his NPP. Perhaps like the famous exceptional blacks of racist folklore, the Ghanaian leader was seeking preemptive exemption for his party and his class from the president elect's imminent verdict on Africans and "their shitholes." Perhaps we should be grateful for small mercies, here full disclosure of lineages of insensate imbecility, extended family resemblances in character traits among figures of the Reaction in today's world.

"PROPERTY-OWNING DEMOCRACY"

Naturally, the Party of "Property Owning Democracy" – the hoary idea the NPP's feudalist ancestor J.B. Danquah copied from early twentieth century British "progressive" Tories – fervently supports and promotes the "private" sector." Why place the word private in scare quotes? Because the private sector is no self-generated entity, a miracle of autogenesis; the private sector is a creation of public power. Here and everywhere, from the beginning to this day. How do the owners of these private enterprises secure the means of accumulation and production? I will not detain you, dear reader, with a disquisition on a more foundational fact: private property is a public artefact. No state, no law, no property. That is the open secret which, of the philosophical godfathers of liberalism and the cognate socioeconomic system of capitalism, Thomas Hobbes was honest enough, brutally honest enough, to avow. Unlike the sleazy John Locke who claimed – mendaciously, we now know – not to have known Hobbes and Hobbes' preemptive refutation of his obfuscating teaching according to which the right to property precedes the forcible blessings of state power. That is why votaries of property and the so-called private sector like NPP ideologues should read Hobbes; it might force them to come clean. But will they? The dispossessed and the destitute of the land most certainly have a partisan and shareable interest in reading Hobbes in vernacular translation. They should do so the better to answer triumphalist fables of individual investment and arduous exertion and just rewards unaided by the state as the source of wealth. And the better to confront what avaricious "traditional" authorities like the kleptocratic chiefs do with the people's lands and other resources, misusing for their personal enrichment power delegated to them as custodians of the commons. "Property-owning democracy" my foot, if I may invoke the more polite expression Ghanaians employ – consider the alternative – to indicate the measure of their contempt for deceit and cant. The constitutive function of property is the dispossession of the demos, robbing the people of the commons. Proudhon got it right. Property is theft. Here in the untamed jungles of capital's dominion and the dictatorship of a predatory bourgeoisie in the heat of primitive accumulation, the sun shines with especial clarity and ferocity on that primordial and persistent fact, NPP ideologues notwithstanding. Take a look at any appropriations procedure, procurement rituals and the open secret of how contracts for the construction of public goods are assigned – before the subsequent consecration of the products, creatures of the public purse, as gifts of the private sector. In contradistinction to property, the defining mission of democracy is placing power over a community's material and civil goods in the hands of the people. The essence of property is exclusion, of democracy sharing. "Property-owning democracy" is not an oxymoron, it is a logical howler.

THE METAPROCEDURAL REPUBLIC

> *Democracy is form and substance.*
> –Karl Marx, *Contribution to the Critique of Hegel's "Philosophy of Right"*

In the 1980s, American political philosopher Michael Sandel crafted the phrase "the procedural republic" to describe a public philosophy and political culture in which substantive commitments and controversies regarding the common good yield pride of place to formal principles for adjudicating disputes concerning justice. He was speaking of the American republic and a dominant version of its public philosophy as articulated by John Rawls in *A Theory of Justice*. Today, Ghanaian political discourse has gone one step further. It is mired in the infinite regress of disputation regarding procedures and rules about procedures and rules for procedures and rules... It is in this rarefied world of self-referential citations, incantations and otherworldly scholasticism, replete with all the borrowed paraphernalia and quaint vocabulary, that political adversaries and public intellectuals of the Ghanaian elite dwell. It is to this sublime farce that public business is almost completely reduced. No, I am not disparaging ritual, theatre and form in political practice and argument. Still less am I depreciating assiduous attention to due process. No one who has observed shameless manipulations of procedure in the US Congress or infractions of due process by right-wing legislators and jurisdictions in that country – especially in matters regarding women's reproductive rights and voting rights – would make light of the importance of procedural rules *tout court*. But when all you hear all the time in the Ghanaian public sphere is the endless refrain of objections to alleged violations of rules and procedures of legal and constitutional matters, then you have to ask: What ever happened to objections to human misery? What ever happened to substantive questions of social justice? What about enlarged understandings of rights, including the right to liveable life, or even of political representation and democratic accountability? Where is the consuming concern for what Ama Ata Aidoo's Anowa calls "the common pain and the general wrong" in its many stinging hurts? At what point does legalism become vacuous or rather tyrannical formalism, one that usurps, by virtue of a fetish worship of words, the imperative work of attending to public things? Public *things* in all their materiality, ubiquitous, odious, painful, exigent materiality: water, light, air, sanitation, toilets, filth, poverty, inequality, domestic violence. The lordly indifference of "our learned friends" to these earthly things is infinitely more nauseating than the acrid matter from which they wilfully avert their busy eyes and noses in order to concentrate on "praying the court." Let me be clear. It is the time-devouring, mind-numbing, prodigal inversion of form and substance, it is this idolatry of form as the very substance of political argument, which I deplore. It is this obsessional self-referential fixation upon procedure that I call meta-proceduralism. Meta-proceduralism is the persistent and pernicious evasion of substance.

Nor am I casting aspersions on constitutionalism, that larger concern with the force and mission of provisions and stipulations of the constitution – the constitutionalism that underwrites proceduralism and its ultimate sublimation into meta-proceduralism. But I am struck by what appears to be a certain selectiveness that characterizes invocations of constitutional provisions and stipulations by our political and legal elites. I am struck by the relative paucity of references to, say, Chapter Six of the 1992 constitution, "The Directive Principles of State Policy (Article 36 (1 and 2)." It is here that the framers, perhaps compensating for the predominantly liberalism-inspired power-restraining, state-phobic thrust of the document as a whole, stipulate what is to be done in pursuit of substantive democracy and integral justice. It is the articles of this Chapter which, in contrast with the "negative liberty" thrust of the totality, enjoin upon the state "positive liberty" responsibilities (to echo a conventional but contested distinction in political philosophy made famous by Isaiah Berlin). To this chapter and other provisions inspired by what may be called socially-progressive constitutionalism our learned votaries of procedure have responded with audible silence. They will not deign to broach what American political philosopher Drucilla Cornell calls "transformative constitutionalism." They will not be caught doing what Puerto del Sol, Spain's activist movement, does, namely, taking seriously "the social provisions of the Constitution." Don't bet on hearing them support the dual intertwined demands of recent popular movements in Chile: change of the constitution *and* an end to scandalous social inequalities. Dual and intertwined, because the existing constitution, "the [Pinochet] constitution," in the words of one demonstrator, "is our original sin" by virtue of enshrining private property rights in the interests of the oligarchy and ignoring socioeconomic rights in the service of the people. True, there is no happy ending to report here. In September 2022, a referendum on a new radical constitution enshrining the people's rights was soundly defeated after a campaign of vilification by sentinels of the old order. Such are the vicissitudes of the path towards a fundamental transformation of the social order. But in Chile the argument has been broached; the work of transformative constitutionalism is on the horizon. Not in comatose Ghana under the rule of a reactionary elite captive to the fetishism of form and procedural rules, wilfully averse to vital questions of social substance. The rare exceptions to this notable disuse of constitutional instruments and arguments for progressive ends in Ghanaian political discourse in recent years, to my knowledge, are the following: the Progressive People's Party's insistence on executing the mission and injunctions of Chapter Six pivotal to its programme, central, for example, to its consideration of nominees for ministerial offices by the Appointments Committee of Parliament in 2013; Kwami Agbodza's persistent and explicit invocation of Article 25 to indict the policies of successive governments and the Central Bank of Ghana; journalist Kwesi Pratt's audacious progressive-legalist defence in 2013 of future Minister of Gender, Nana Oye Lithur, in the face of attacks on her for speaking out against violence against homosexuals, in the name of the law and the equal protection of all citizens; a similar defence of the same appointee on the same grounds by the Domestic Violence Coalition in January 17, 2013; Yao Graham's spirited protest against lawless police violence and his call for amending the Public Order Act, which in his view enables that violence; and, most recently, the opposition by eighteen academics and civil society groups, invoking provisions of the 1992 Constitution, to the the "Draft Bill for the Promotion of Proper Human Sexual Rights and Ghanaian Family Values" currently (July 2021) under consideration in Ghana's parliament, a bill that criminalizes homosexuality and even advocacy of the rights of gays and lesbians. These rare examples of heretical legalism apart, the proceduralist tradition in Ghana has been decidedly cowardly and largely inconsequential. "Their legalism and ours," I am tempted to say (echoing Leon Trotsky's 1938 *Their Morals and Ours*) in vindication of a proceduralist legalism and constitutionalism committed to the defence of the powerless and in pursuit of substantive egalitarian democracy, as opposed to a proceduralism placed at the service of the ruling order. That was the kernel of validity – and the missed opportunity – in the rhetoric of "true democracy" in the early Rawlings years, a political vocabulary that seems now utterly quaint and forgotten. But that vocabulary is by no means discredited, notwithstanding the contempt for due process and civil liberties that came to mark Rawlings' long rule, to say nothing of the subsequent capitulation to neoliberal dictatorship and, with it, the comprehensive abandonment of the popular-democratic programme of substantive social justice. Such a programme might have found sustenance in a left proceduralism underwritten by transformative constitutionalism, thereby fulfilling Marx's 1843 understanding of the democratic enterprise as the meeting of form and substance.

PRAY TO GOD OR PRAY THE COURT

In its serene evasion of concrete matters of social misery and injustice, the (meta)proceduralist tradition shares a family resemblance, and indeed roots, with the surfeit of god-talk which has come to usurp the place of critical social vision in these parts. Invocations of god's grace buttressed by a cornucopia of biblical quotations compete with proceduralist formalism and its plethora of textual recitations as panaceas for social and existential despair, cure for the disorder of the polity and the disarray of the soul. But are these the only reparative resources available to us? Know what the bible says, leave it up to god, *fama nyame*; or get the rule and the procedure right and go to court; pray to god or pray the court? Are there no alternatives to the twin obsessional distractions provided by narcotic faith and formalist proceduralism?

Of course, faith can be an insurgent commitment rather than an agent of social amnesia and a numbing opiate. As for proceduralism and its parent, constitutionalism, Ghanaians need only look at the work of the South African Constitutional Court to observe that this near-total subordination of substance to form, of critical social vision to procedural ritual, is one telling and unenviable feature of our vaunted Ghanaian exceptionalism, just like our all-consuming religiosity. While our courts and "learned friends" droll on and on and on about infractions of this rule and that rule, the South African Constitutional Court has been known to attend – horror of horrors – to such profane questions as the appropriation of land by extractive industries, evictions of destitute squatters from privately owned lands, objections to such evictions on the grounds that they infringe provisions of the 1994 Constitution. Proceduralism and the fine subtleties of constitutional jurisprudence are not foreign to public discourse in South Africa, but they are here marshalled in the service of addressing the people's material conditions of existence, in the service of law *and* life, as American legal theorist Catherine McKinnon might say, not for onanistic indulgence in the thrills of legalist drivel. Dismembered from life's needs and their regeneration, the rites of law do not deserve our fulsome allegiance any more than the claims and conventions of faith.

SINS OF THE "NATIONAL CATHEDRAL"

Public things ought to be public things.
–Frantz Fanon, *The Wretched of the Earth*

In the labyrinth of misery,
Despair has erected a cathedral
Where the prayers of the poor
Smolder on the ground.
–Patrick Sylvaine, "And So…"

Ever since Kwame Nkrumah came and wrecked their genteel party with uppity impertinence, the founders and successors of the Danquah-Busia tradition in Ghana have been telling us this: They are the club of men and women of substance, endowed with superior intellect and wisdom, and, thanks to those qualities, the natural rulers of this country. Listening to today's representatives of the tradition, a visitor from Mars may be forgiven for sneering and thinking that either this claim was always bogus or that the present generation are a rather sorry breed of the caste. I will set aside their reaction to last year's demonstrations against the unbearable rise in the cost of living: the mixture of contempt and manufactured fear of terrorism with which they greeted the phenomenon of the youth of comatose Ghana, at long last, doing what young people around the globe, from Chile to Lebanon to South Africa to Nigeria to Panama to Sri Lanka have been doing in very recent years and days: saying no to social misery and scandalous inequalities, daylight robbery of our national treasure, police violence administered at the behest of the government. I will pass over the extraordinary poverty of spirit that led the NPP's vainglorious think-tanker-in-chief, Gabby Otchere-Darko, to dismiss the substance of the demonstrators' cause, reduce it to a numbers game, and dwell on how many people showed up: such is the moral obtuseness of sated stomachs and stunted minds. For now I'll invite you to just listen to the arguments – and that is a very generous characterization – regarding the so-called "national" cathedral, the sickening brew of insufferable arrogance and crass illogicality these spokespersons display on morning talk shows. Perhaps we cannot hope to correct the arrogance, so stubbornly ingrained in their members' DNA. That overweening arrogance breeds wilful ignorance and indolence, the unwillingness and inability to submit a programme or proposal to the labour of rational justification and the risk of refutation. But we must not let their perverse reasoning and the illogicality of their utterances go unanswered.

The "national" cathedral project bristles with multiple wrongs. I call them "sins" in a half-facetious compliance with the idiom of its promoters. I will highlight three of them. The first has to do with principle; the second considers what is a priority in the scheme of national necessities; and the third concerns procedure. I will dwell in these brief comments largely on the question of principle, because I suspect that from that original sin – the transgression of principle – the other wrongs almost inexorably flow.

PRINCIPLE

On 23 November 2019, defending the planned building of a "national" cathedral and its exorbitant cost in this time of desperate need, Finance Minister Ken Ofori-Atta declared in the most fatuous reasoning and garbled language to match:

> From 1957 to where God has brought us and the blessings He has given us and now a small land we are giving to God should rather be given to real estate agents? I get afraid. Because we are a Christian country, even if we don't do it, the stones themselves will get up and do it. It is a beautiful thing and it is a memorial to God. This huge country God has given us, we are taking a small 3 acres for God and we are crying. The things of God make me afraid. God will build his thing but we have to do our part. It is certainly about 100m dollars.

My immediate reaction to that utterance was the following: Eject this character from the ministry and send him to some monastery. That, however, would be to dishonour the good priests and impugn their intelligence. Quite seriously, Ofori-Atta would subsequently ask that every Ghanaian contribute 100 cedis monthly to the project. He would make this demand in his mid-year budget review statement of July 2021. In a budget statement! Now, according to the American civil rights leader Rashad Robinson: "Budgets are moral documents." I don't think he meant to include soliciting funds towards expenditures on an edifice serving one faith community in the *political* morality of budgets and the tasks it enjoins, or what the 1992 Constitution calls "The Directive Principles of State Policy." Nowhere in the 1992 Constitution is it written that Ghana is a Christian country. And it is a good thing too. For that would have enshrined in the constitution – the constitution of a civic republic – not only the supremacy of one religion but also the tyranny of the majority, something distasteful to avowed adherents of *liberal* democracy. Nor is it written that the citizenry should commit millions of cedis to an enterprise that the mighty divinity will command into being anyway, with or without our pitiful, merely human, contribution. I will pass over that incoherent theosophy. We should be infinitely more alarmed by the more fundamental matter of principle, namely, the proposition that the state in a modern constitutional republic has any business in the religious life of the citizens any more than in what they do in their bedrooms. We should take strong exception to the very idea of "the religious activities of the state" in which Akufo-Addo places the construction of the cathedral. "What touches all must be approved by all," goes an old adage. Unless and until our country becomes a theocracy – a fate too horrible to contemplate – an edifice honouring one religion and the religious life of one fraction of our people is not among the public things that touches all of us and so demands our collective approval. It is even less legitimate to ask all of us, whether we are Christian or non-Christian, religious or non-religious, to bear the costs of realizing a personal commitment Akufo-Addo made to his god. The point appears to escape a particularly witless and belligerent spokesperson of the governing party who sees no difference whatsoever between Akufo-Addo's promise to his divinity and his pledge to implement the Free Senior Secondary School programme if he came to power, since they are both, according this discerning spokesperson, personal pledges. But it is, as they say, elementary. One is an oath enacted in the silence of your conscience or prayer – inaudible, unverifiable, an entirely private affair beyond the *political* requirements of accountability. We cannot even tell whether it is the shared commitment of a votive community born of their considered judgement or the product of a solitary individual's fevered hallucination. The other, be it praiseworthy or ill-conceived, is an electoral promise, a civic act made to the citizenry in the full glare of the public realm – verifiable, knowable, subject to the scrutiny of public reason, and one for which the successful candidate can rightly be held accountable. I should have thought that these avatars of democracy know that an enterprise is not "national" just because you call it so by fiat. Strange is the democratic culture in which declarative edict usurps the work of deliberative judgment. But such, it would seem, is the understanding of democracy and democratic consent entertained by our party of the best and the brightest. I have heard it said by more than one NPP spokesperson: "As for the national cathedral it *will* be built no matter what". Prophecy or commandment? Voices of reasoned dissent and disagreement are of no consequence. Certainly, dissenting voices marshalling secular arguments need not apply. Even the brilliant and tireless Samuel Okudzeto Ablakwa of the opposition National Democratic Congress, choosing to fight with the adversaries' weapons, found it necessary to bring a humongous bible to a morning talk show and cite scriptural passages in support of his objection to the cathedral. Are there no earthly human grounds for opposing this project? Here is an old philosophical question: Is the "national" cathedral a bad idea because god, if he exists, would disapprove of it, or would he disapprove of it because it is a terrible idea? We can, you and I as equal citizens of a democratic polity, marshal the resources of public reason to debate the second option. The first option is available only to those among us privy to divine wisdom. Even if the latter group make up seventy percent of the populace, as Ofori-Atta and Akufo-Addo keep harping on, their verdict is essentially neither verifiable nor falsifiable. But it is profoundly anti-democratic, if by democracy we mean not rule by caprice but the government of public reason where those who govern implement ends to which we consent. With perverse consistency, Ofori-Atta would respond to criticism of his performance as finance minister and calls for his resignation with the declaration that only Jesus can judge. That stance is not only anti-democratic; it is profoundly anti-political, a view of human affairs according to which you and I, sentient human beings and voting citizens, have no agency. On that path lies the totalitarian dictatorship of faith. But the ironic upshot of Akufo-Addo's stance is that this is a private obsession transformed by his absolute-monarchist hubris – *l'état c'est moi* – into a public matter. We are therefore entitled to subject it to scrutiny and lay bare the wrongs it embodies.

PRIORITY

On Monday 11 July 2022, I watched with aching sorrow in my guts a report on *Metro TV* showing children in a "school" located in a "defunct cemetery". A *defunct* cemetry! The symbolism alone, dear reader, should make you weep. In the place where the life of the mind is to be nurtured, that is to say, seedlings of our future planted, the young live in intimate communion with decay, detritus and death. Only a society that has forgotten to remember the future, that pays no heed to the injunction *kae dabi*, will condemn our children's faculties to certain atrophy at the very time and place of gestation. Only an insensate chieftain presiding over such a moribund society will declare in his Solomonic wisdom that the building of a "national" cathedral is the "priority of priorities," commit himself to erecting a majestic edifice in praise of the heavens while our people have no decent toilets in which to relieve themselves of their earthly burdens. When I heard Akufo-Addo's solemn invocation of "priority of priorities," I thought of John McEnroe's iconic exclamation: "You cannot be serious." But that cruel inversion of priorities is of a piece with the penchant for luxurious jets and roaming around the skies of the universe for entirely inconsequential "international" undertakings while students of our famed secondary schools face shortage of food supplies, their elementary earthly needs uncared for. Deputy Finance Minister John Kumah's assertion of an analogy between building the cathedral and building of schools would be half credible if in fact building schools with decent facilities were the norm. Giving pride of place to providing a "sacred space" for the care of the soul in the midst of a crisis of affordable accommodation to house sentient human bodies; "bread of heaven" and soup devoid of meat; the ultramodern shrine and the prehistoric shithole: such are the dual emblems that have conspired to define our chieftains' idea of priorities and the choices they have elected to foist upon us. They don't find it necessary to justify these rational choices to us mere mortal citizens. But they may have to do so as they go to meet their Makers, the masters of the world's so-called "national" economies coming to our shores from afar and bringing with them instructions our rulers cannot refuse. Our rulers may have to explain to the lords of the earth their idea of equal opportunity: on the one hand, demolishing the homes of potentates and securing rented residences for them with public funds in order to make room for the cathedral; on the other hand, blissfully ignoring the desperate cry of ordinary citizens for basic housing.

PROCEDURE

They go on and on about the rule of law and their unequalled fidelity to its dictates and attention to the minutiae of rule-based transactions pertaining to implementation of public policies. You can't tell that from the way in which they have gone about the business of the cathedral. From the beginning the project was not even submitted to parliament for debate and approval. That contempt for democratic deliberation evidently flowed from the foundational lie that the whole thing would be built with funds contributed by private individuals and faith communities, principally Christian churches, and those opulent pastors preoccupied with saving the souls of their flock while their bodies writhe with pain and anxiety and insomniac nights. Having dispensed with democratic procedure in the very decision to build the shrine, the selection of architects, contractors and builders, and the disposition of requisite monies followed the same autocratic path. The very land on which the cathedral is to sit comes from the confiscation of properties, in some cases without prompt compensation, the case of Waterstone Property being one of them. This, from the party of "property-owning democracy" evidently turned into the party of property-seizing autocracy, perhaps an unintended disclosure that "private" property is, for better or for worse, a public artefact, a state-sponsored right. The business of the cathedral – and it is business for all the sanctimonious shroud of piety – has been marked by the familiar fake freedom of the "free market" and the phony rituals of arranged competition, in truth a system resting on the toxic triad of caste prerogative, dynastic ethno-nepotism and party cronyism. Non-competitive procurement, single-source dispensation of contracts, flagrant infractions of requirements of transparency, inconsistencies in the estimates and reports of costs, inscrutable details regarding how much the state is providing and how much comes from private resources: such are the rules-thrashing proceedings which have characterized the whole sordid business. I used to think that our political culture or rather the political discourse of our elites is much too obsessed with questions of procedure and disputes concerning procedural rules to to the detriment of substantive matters of public goods and social justice. So much is this the case, I thought, that I was led to describe the political culture preferred by our elites as a meta-procedural republic, a political practice fixated upon procedures about procedures regarding procedures. Now I would qualify that characterization and say that while the concern of our elites with substantive matters of public goods is indeed desultory, their vaunted attachment to procedures and rule-based transactions is rather selective, entirely dispensable when it suites their interests.

In sum, the "national" cathedral is riddled with flagrant infractions of procedure, utterly indefensible in the scheme of pressing national necessities, and dead wrong in principle. The entire project is beyond redemption.

I began this brief with two epigraphs, the first of which is taken from the work of Frantz Fanon. I can think of no better closing argument than his prophetic admonition delivered in the first days of our post(?)colonial life:

> *The national government, before preoccupying itself with international prestige, ought first to give back their dignity to all citizens, fill the brains and feast their eyes with human things, and create a prospect that is human because conscious and sovereign persons dwell therein.*

Ato Sekyi-Otu

RAISON D'ÉTAT ACCORDING TO THE PARTY OF REASON

March 2018. It is revealed that Ghana has entered into an agreement that will allow US soldiers to roam free with their gear in a sequestered area of this land. To expressions of outrage by members of the opposition parties, the minister of defence, a certain Dominic Nitiwul, responds that such an agreement was nothing new in Africa-US relations. Senegal, alas, was the first to become a "beneficiary" of such an arrangement in the noble race to be the elect among America's African satrapies. Call that house-slave-envy. As for Ghana, latecomer beneficiary of New Rome's imperial beneficence, his NPP government, the Honourable Minister averred, was not the first to enter into such an agreement. Governments of the Opposition National Democratic Congress did it in 1998 and 2005. Unsure whether NDC did the right thing or did the right thing but in the wrong way, he tells Ghanaians that the NDC Minister for Foreign Affairs "sold us" by signing a precursor agreement in 2005, and sold us in secrecy. His government's action had the entirely marvellous merit of taking place in the public realm, of submitting the deed to parliament for debate and ratification, thereby displaying in exemplary fashion the democratic mode of selling national sovereignty, the splendid paradox of open transparent voluntary and consensual bondage. It does not occur to Nitiwul the nitwit that the issue is not the relative stupidity and duplicity of our leaders but the inalienability of our sovereignty. It is true that I had no illusions and expectations of prudent governance as I contemplated coming back, but I did not return to the homeland to witness such inane debates over variants of the slave mode of exchange. This is personal.

NAANA: A POLITICAL AND PERSONAL CELEBRATION

The following remarks are intended to address some of the questions raised by the selection of Professor Naana Opoku-

Agyemang as the NDC's vice-presidential candidate for the 2020 national elections. They are not meant to indicate my party affiliation. I am not a member or follower of the National Democratic Congress or indeed of any of Ghana's political parties. But I am not neutral, politically or personally.

Politically speaking, I am partisan. I belong to the independent left. In defiance of today's arranged neoliberal consensus, I am left and proud, dreamer of an infinitely more just society than the one we currently inhabit. Moreover, I am a member of that weird human subspecies, the male feminists, those who believe that women and men are endowed with the same capabilities, are entitled to the same rights, freedoms and duties, and are equally fit to be guardians of the material and moral resources of our society. Prompted by that conviction I salute the historic selection of a woman and, in particular, Professor Naana Opoku-Agyemang, as a major political party's candidate for the office of vice-president. This is not just a matter of symbolic significance. This is an event of enormous substantive importance, one that is long overdue. That should do as an answer to the bizarre question someone posed after the announcement: "Is Ghana ready for a woman vice-president?" I vividly recall an analogous question often asked at the inception of the Obama adventure: "Are the American people ready for a black President?" I was always tempted to say the following to the questioner: By "the American people" you mean white American people, don't you? You are not speaking of the whole of the American citizenry, certainly not of the black part of the blessed whole, are you? This is a case of the fraction impersonating the whole, isn't it? In a similar vein I say: By "Is Ghana ready for a woman vice-president?" you mean Ghanaian men, don't you? Are Ghanaian women likely to ask that question? I could be wrong but I will swear by the ancestors of Kurankyekurom, Akyemfo that only a guy and a slowly recovering male-supremacist would even ask that question? And what, may I ask, have we men wrought all these years – marvellous regime after marvellous regime – anyway?

Nor am I neutral on a personal level either. Or rather, I should say that my personal view of Naana, her competence and preparedness for the office is not unconnected with my political understanding. Full disclosure: although I am a recent returnee to Ghana, I have known Naana Opoku-Agyemang for over four decades beginning in the 1980s. Teaching in the Graduate Programme of Social and Political Thought at York University, I was a member of Naana Opoku Agyemang's PhD dissertation committee and present at the brilliant defence of her work in 1989. I do not hope to convince the misogynistic Neanderthals who have been bleating out all manner of drivel and appalling comments impugning her competence, but let me assure the genuinely curious of this: Naana Opoku-Agyemang possesses a formidable intellect, one demonstrably capable of enlarging the fruits of her speciality into other institutional and societal domains. That is what a great intellect does, not to dwell immured in the enclosure of one discipline but, if called upon to do so, to see and attend to connections among varied problems of our social world. That is what is especially required of the aspirant to political office, more specifically, presidential and vice-presidential office – the ability to gather the disparate facts and special needs pertaining to all societal domains into a coherent and compelling vision of national purpose. Where is it written that the vice-president who assists in crafting and executing that vision, or for that matter the president, should be an economist or this and that specialist? Curiously, one person who voiced this stipulation is a University of Ghana political scientist, someone presumably familiar with the requirements of political office as a vocation. My answer to our learned friend is this: might as well require, in view of the current plague and pressing needs, that they ought to be virologists or immunologists. The offices of the minister of finance and health would be entirely superfluous.

Yes, we need engineers and technicians. So, the philistines and tunnel-vision fetishists of science and technology declare: a pox on literary studies and the like. Say goodbye to a generation of scholars who will cultivate and preserve knowledge of the arts. These humanities-abolitionists are not content to cast aspersions on Naana the accomplished scholar, educationist and administrator. Let the sins of the mother be visited upon her children. And so, one commentator on the Ghanaweb scoffs at the fact that two of Naana's three children have doctorates in literature and one in economics. Even the hallowed discipline, economics, it seems, is woefully inadequate! This is stupid. That view is the most eloquent proof that some acquaintance with the modes of reasoning fostered by the humanities is not a bad thing. What we desperately need now are leaders capable of thoughtful practice, visionary and inventive work, leaders able to conscript competent specialists and practitioners to help execute the discrete parts of a designed whole. I would say that Naana Opoku-Agyemang is supremely qualified to be such a leader; she is such a leader. And it is not insignificant that she is a woman, an audacious and accomplished woman. We should all be dancing in the streets – if it were not for this pernicious plague.

POSTSCRIPT: THE PITFALLS OF PRAISING THE LIVING

But is it true, Naana, that, barely a year after I penned this celebration sparked in part by livid scorn for hateful voices of the country holding your name and women's name in contempt, you were sighted in Naija attending the lavish funeral of that consummate fraudster of a "man of God," T.B. Joshua? If true, is there a lesson to be learned here? Didn't the ancestors, privy to the tragic inconstancy of our mortal will, caution us to beware of bestowing extravagant praise upon the living? Didn't they admonish us, at the very least, to place all creatures human like you and me on moral probation? Indeed the ancestors did so caution and admonish us. All the same, I will not disown the conviction and the affection that spurred the encomium. Aren't all attachments and commitments of today inescapably vulnerable to the wry wisdom of a later day?

TRICKLEDOWN PREDATION

Let the private sector do it, never mind the fact that the "private sector" gets its padded contracts from public funds through arranged appropriation procedures or outright untendered procurements. Cut taxes, remove all those regulations, and business will flourish, provide jobs for our youth and eliminate poverty, or at least bridge the gap between rich and poor. This is the neoliberal creed preached with especial ferocity in these satrapies. The reality? In the supply chain of power, privilege and predation, a slightly better-off guy sets up shop as a petty money lender to those infinitely more impecunious. He quickly becomes a loan-shark, terrorizing the indebted with exorbitant interest rates. This is the true nature of trickle-down economics and ethics – what Marx sardonically called "the ethics of political economy" – in their local forms and consequences, the informal sector's version of that material culture and moral order. And we know that in these parts of the world economy, the "informal sector" is the major actor, its governing ethics well-nigh normative, the unwritten public philosophy that shapes everyday conduct. There will be no trickling down of beneficent goods from on high to the inhabitants below, but there will be a flourishing trade in the malevolent arts of usury and bribery.

ENLIGHTENMENT'S AVATARS

EXHIBIT 1

A sheep was slaughtered at the forecourt of the Nasariyya Mosque at Aboabo Number Two in Kumasi after hours of fervent prayers by Muslims to thank Allah for the lives of Nana Addo Dankwa Akufo-Addo and other petitioners challenging the outcome of the [2012] presidential election at the Supreme Court... Organized by Free Education Prayer Group FENG, a pressure group with links to the NPP, the religious affair, which started around 8 am, was attended by people from all walks of life... Nana Antwi, the NPP parliamentary candidate for Asawase and other influential officials in the region graced the occasion...Ardent NPP members at Asawase and other parts of Kumasi also attended the event.
(From the *Daily Guide,* June 15, 2013)

Behold the party of torchbearers of the African Enlightenment. Behold the rites and rituals of modern constitutional democracy enacted with inimitable pageantry by our learned friends and their village kinsfolk.

EXHIBIT 2

Listen to Samuel Atta Akyea, Member of Parliament for Abuakwa South, scion of the same region and the same political party, NPP, from which significant figures of the nation's self-anointed *crème de la crème* hail, enjoining cooperation by parliamentarians from rival political parties for the good of the country. Listen to his fine version of the hallowed trope of the unitary body politic enlisted to foster that cooperation: "Ghana is like a husband servicing many wives." It is is the sixth day of February 2021, that is to say, the beginning of the third decade of the twenty-first century, high tide of late modernity featuring Neanderthal barbarism. But perhaps we should be grateful to the honourable legislator for unwittingly practising ideology-critique, inadvertently unmasking power-serving pieties for what they are. We should thank him for reminding us that from Roman antiquity and Menenius Agrippa cajoling the insurgent plebs against secession in the name of the inextricable interdependence of the parts of the body politic, to this call for collaboration among rival factions of postcolonial Ghana's political class, the trope of the unitary body politic is a hoax. It is a hoax whether it comes wrapped in the irenic poetry of the political community as an indivisible organism or is bleated in the farting prose of male supremacy. That hoary trope has little to do with shared care for the common good or just enjoyment of its blessings. It has everything to do with cementing the established order by securing solidarity among rival factions of the ruling class, the better to ensure the subjugation of the people and exact their acquiescence; it is figurative language in the service of primitive power. That is my unapologetically vulgar Marxist analysis of a venerable idiom of political rhetoric. Our Ghanaian potentate's version of the tired old trope doesn't even have the decency of being a "*noble* lie" as Plato's *Republic* famously and shamelessly named an archetypal version of the fable. It reeks of harem-hopping license, masculinist dominion and violence, guileless, crude, unalloyed. No doubt, the honourable lawmaker will call it part and parcel of "our culture" and "our traditions," frowned upon only by arrogant alien ideologues and their native acolytes.

EXHIBIT 3

18 January, 2022. Ghana's football team, THE BLACK STARS were ingloriously sent home from the Africa Cup of Nations (AFCOM) tournament, defeated by Comoros, among the lower ranked teams in the group to which the two nations belonged. True, the once mighty BLACK STARS have not won the nations' cup since the year 1984. But these are descendants of the team that shone with unforgettable albeit doomed lustre at the 2010 World Cup in South Africa. The last time such an early exit at the group stage occurred was 2006. Today is truly a day of matchless ignominy. It's only sports, only football, we know. But it is a symptomatic event, and so an opportunity, you would think, for self-scrutiny regarding the general disarray of the social body and the collective spirit of which this defeat is a possible consequence. An occasion, then, for reflection on the part of our people and our leaders concerning this moment in our *national* history, perhaps in relation to the African condition as a whole. To say nothing of contextual matters such as the pandemic and the worsened conditions of life the majority of our people face. But no, this is the propitious time, while the nation sighs a collective sigh of dismay, that two traditional regional potentates, Asantehene Osei Tutu 11 and Dormaahene Oseadeeyo Agyemang Badu 11, have chosen to wage symbolic tribal war, conduct an acrimonious wrangle regarding relations of authority, supremacy and autonomy between Asanteman and Dormaa. As evidentiary material for his case in this world-historical disputation, the Dormaa potentate – a high court judge in private life no less – has let it be known that to this day his people have in their proud victorious hands the head of an Asante chieftain severed in the seventeenth century. Such are the matters of momentous consequence that deserve to be excavated in the

service of the pressing socioeconomic needs, political arguments and public policies of today. Especially in this hour of badly needed national reckoning occasioned by the disastrous performance of the Black Stars. What would Yambo Ouloguem, that wicked satirist of our old potentates' picayune might and laughable puffery, what would Yambo have to say about today's copycats?

EXHIBIT 4

August 2022. A certain Akwasi Addae thought he might avail himself of Ghana's vaunted status as sterling haven of freedom of speech in darkest Africa. And so what does the credulous fool do? He launches an attack on a radio talk show on the chiefs of Asanteman for failing to stop the destructive practice of illegal mining in the region. He even hints at the operation of royal dirty hands in the whole business. Worse still, he promises to rally the youth of the ancient "kingdom" to protest against the official dereliction of duty. The response of the principalities and powers is swift and scary. The lords of the Kumasi Traditional Council perform a time-honoured ritual in Manhyia Palace – a ram is slaughtered, the gods are summoned – banishing the miscreant from Manhyia. There follows an order to the radio station to close shop forthwith. And irate youth, evidently more concerned with guarding the honour of their chieftains than the future of their lands, mount a violent assault on the office of the impious Akwasi Addae, the latter just managing to escape gruesome lynching. Naturally, upon these proceedings of naked power and primitive accumulation, entirely modern in their motives and effects albeit conveniently hybrid in their enabling instruments, fabulists of the ruling order laid the sacred livery of inviolable tradition. And so it is not the thieving chiefs and self-serving manipulators of customary laws and offices but rather Akwasi Addae, would-be protagonist of the commons and tribune of the people, who stands guilty of traducing tradition. Any time you hear the invocation of tradition, sneer, or do worse. Train your eyes and nostrils on the sins of omission or commission which that invocation is sworn to hide. As for the national government, the police and the courts, they have reacted to this display of prehistoric atavism and violent contempt for the rule of law with deafening silence. Evidently, it is not their mission to protect the rights and liberties, indeed the life, of all citizens irrespective of the region in which they happen to reside or the putative "kingdoms" that purport to usurp the sovereignty of the nation.

"PREHISTORY IN A TAIL-COAT"

Brand me a zealot of reason, if you wish. Call me a fervent partisan not of *the* Enlightenment, accursed name for the hubris and delusions of the modern Western *geist*, but, yes, enlightenment (small case, please). Here is why. If you heard a friend – a man of science, no less – relate with a straight face, that is to say, with complicit credulity, a gravely ill acquaintance's claim that had this friend visited her in the hospital but a few minutes earlier, he would have seen the face of Jesus by her bedside; if you heard the President of the nation – a civic republic, mind you – say that he is all for the erection of a national cathedral because it is the fulfillment of a pledge he made to god (not to mere voting citizens) that he would do so if he won the last election – erect a majestic cathedral in praise of the heavens while our people have no decent toilets in which to relieve themselves of their worldly burdens, and thereby honour with the public purse a personal covenant with the divinity in place of a social contract with the people; if you listened to this our very own Solomon implore us at the outbreak of Covid-19 to fast for one day to beseech god's favour; if you listened to an archbishop who found it necessary to explain that "God is not responsible" for the pandemic; if you listened to another scientist schoolmate declare that God's protective love, evidently playing divine favouritism (contra *Galatians* 3:28 and *Romans* 2:10), is the only explanation for the fact that this Neolithic Africa of ours has (thus far) escaped the holocaust Covid-19 was expected to wreak upon us; if you heard another (self-anointed) archbishop whose everyday life is mired knee-deep in mammon proclaim that the answer to the fall of Ghana's currency, the cedi, is prayer; if you heard a young man report a medical doctor's serious

HOMELAND IS NOT YET HOME

diagnosis of his bleeding nose that the cause was not physical but "spiritual," a demonic curse; if you encountered these specimens of arrant criminal actionable imbecility emanating from the half-educated no less than the intelligentsia – *la trahison des clercs* of a form Julien Benda knew not of – you will nod in agreement with the words of Epicurus adored by the young Marx: "Not the man who denies the gods worshipped by the multitude, but he who affirms of the gods what the multitude believes of them is truly impious." And you will assent to Yambo Ouloguem's stinging calumny uttered in 1968: "Prehistory in a tail-coat: there stands the African." Ouologuem must have meant to say: "There stands your typical member of the African elite." For to pin the crime of willful retardation on "the African" is as wrongheaded as blaming all Africans, as opposed to our villainous chieftains and merchants, for the capture and sale of our people and the unspeakable horror of THE DOOR OF NO RETURN. Listen again to Ouloguem's irate mockery of dandy darkness. Listen again, and then you will shout, you will have to shout: What do we need? Light. Real light. When do we need it? Now. More light. Better light, light radiating from every face of the sun and every corner of the earth, peering into all the hidden abodes of our existence, dissipating in so doing the oppressive fog. More and better light, whether it is borrowed from other lands or generated anew from our own disused energies and faculties of body and mind, it does not matter. We desperately need to excrete from our mind demonological causation together with indolent faith in the blessings of a despotic divinity. For goodness sake, we need to subject all our beliefs and conventions to the searchlights made available by forms of thought and practice that are, when all is said and done, humanity's commons. For our own good.

TWO CONCEPTS OF HOPE

9 February 2021, the week the construction of the multi-million-dollar Ghana National Cathedral was resumed after a hiatus, the United Arab Emirates' *Hope* mission performed a successful orbit entry maneuver on Mars. Perfect timing. Same day, same week, same year. Somewhat different priorities and different

understandings of hope guiding public policy in the two countries.

"PERPETUAL SOLICITUDE" AND ABSOLUTE FAITH

The air in this land is filled with a strange brew of religiosity: strange because misanthropic and cheery, melancholic and ecstatic, otherworldly and crassly this-worldly and materialistic, serving god and mammon with equal fervour at one and the same time. Of course, Ghana is hardly unique in this. Some years ago, the Catholic Bishop of Nairobi, commenting on the growing hold of evangelical Christianity on ordinary men and women in Kenya, called the phenomenon an opiate. What? The good bishop echoing Marx's description of religion? Actually, Marx's account of religion in the famous 1844 text, *Critique of Hegel's Philosophy of Right: Introduction*, was far more intricate than the caricature has it. Read together, that is to say, the notorious "opium" passage in conjunction with the sentences that precede it, the text describes religion as anything but mystification and concealment; rather it is revelation and disclosure, truthful testimony regarding the human condition, even a latently insurgent response to that condition: "*Religious* suffering is at the same time an *expression* of real suffering and a *protest* against real suffering. Religion is the sigh of the oppressed creature, the sentiment of a heartless world, and the soul of soulless conditions." Only after these hardly negative sentences do the notorious words appear: "[Religion] is the opium of the people." Religion, Marx is saying, "tells it like it is." The customary construal of the passage as offering a view of religion as nothing but mystification and sedation is dead wrong.

Two centuries before Marx, the English philosopher Thomas Hobbes offered, in the *Leviathan*, an equally sympathetic account of religion, one that has a familiar resonance in the homeland. Hobbes paints a stark picture of human beings tormented by "anxiety for the future time," fearfully "inquisitive into the causes of the events they see, some more, some less; but all men so much, as to be curious in the search of the causes of their own good and evil fortune." Particularly apposite is Hobbes's portrait of a life lived in "perpetual solicitude of the time to come," of a human being who "hath his heart all day long, gnawed on by the fear of death, poverty, or other calamity; and has no repose, nor pause of his anxiety, but in sleep." To such a harried soul the figure of god – "a first, and an eternal cause of all things" – offers an answer to the brutal enigmas of the world and the inscrutable vicissitudes of fortune. Today, we can hear Hobbes's voice in the fearful question of Femi Kuti's song, "*What will tomorrow bring?*" But in our societies, the god of the First Cause who answers the daunting queries of these lyrics need not eject from the turbulent landscape of the soul other spirits, deities, principalities and powers. On the contrary, the latter act as complementary warrants of meaning in what Jean and John Comaroff call "occult economies" – the mixed metaphysical economies – of the postcolonial world. We have here what Alexender Saxton, in *Religion and the Human Prospect*, calls "pagan pluralism," one which Christianity in its delusional idea of spiritual progress thinks to overcome but which, in a "reverse movement," according to Saxton, recurrently returns to the landscape of belief in the incarnation of witches and "local saints and roadside shrines [and] amulets and prayer wheels." It is a phenomenon that Christian fundamentalists bemoan as a recalcitrant but not an ineliminable survival of superstition! Yet "pagan pluralism" is the perfect answer to the multiple needs of body and soul. There is no point lamenting, with a Summerfield Baldwin writing in the 1920s about the fate of the Church in the later Middle Ages, that it traded mystery and "an appeal to the religious hunger of the human heart" for ghastly earthly things like power and wealth. Here in this world of the damned of the earth and the fortunate salvaged few, that dualism of body and soul, the sacred and the profane, does not apply.

Hobbes's explanation of "the seed of religion" is, of course, of a piece with his account of the necessity of the state. The state is that "mortal god" whose mission is to put an end to the incertitude and terror of the "natural condition of mankind" and guarantee security of person. Today, in the "emergent market" societies of the world under neoliberal occupation, it is taboo to want to extend the protective function of the state beyond the most minimal obligation of providing peace. The "mortal god" has fled, abdicating even the picayune rescue operations it provided or promised to deliver in the immediate post-independence years. A new orthodoxy regards these functions, such as they were, as intolerable impediments to personal responsibility and productivity, in a word, as socialism and the road to serfdom. The sole purpose of the state these days is to *enforce* the permissive conditions for the unrestrained accumulation of wealth by a new class of hustlers. Neoliberal newspeak calls this enforcement "reforms" and "providing a hospitable environment for business." With the "mortal god" absconded, with the buffer of a sustaining community gone, a desperate and destitute people have but one true and unfailing god to count on. Absolute faith in that god is the sole and incontestable answer to the condition of "perpetual solicitude." Hymns from the traditional Christian liturgy such as "Blessed Assurance," and "Lead Kindly Light" have always had a material impulse, have always answered to a *physiological* need, as Nietzsche might say, in places such as this. Only now, the staid cadences of the traditional hymns have been reanimated with an enraptured exuberance born of compelling necessity. You have not witnessed the agony and the ecstasy of body and soul, inescapable in this time and place, until you behold a reggae-resonant orgiastic, hips-stirring, civility-be-damned rendition of the hymn *It is well with my soul* at evangelical gatherings of the impoverished and the struggling no less than at the Calvary Methodist Church in Accra, one of the sanctuaries of the votive bourgeoisie: veritable theatres of faith made flesh.

And it is *faith* that is accorded primacy in this land of "perpetual solicitude." This constitutes a significant reordering of the teaching contained in a famous passage in Paul's first epistle to the Corinthians. It is a passage of such powerful beauty and unmistakable meaning that I cannot resist citing a fragment of it:

> If I speak in the tongues of mortals and angels, but do not have love, I am a noisy gong or a clanging cymbal. And if I have prophetic powers, and understand all mysteries and all knowledge, and if I

have all faith, so as to remove mountains, but do not have love, I am nothing. If I give away all my possessions, and if I hand over my body so that I may boast, but do not have love, I gain nothing ... And now abide faith, hope, love, these three, but the greatest of these is love.

Of the triad of supreme goods invoked in 1 *Corinthians* 13, the Christianity of our bleak Hobbesian world gives pride of place to faith. Here faith rules, not hope, still less love, which the passage declares to be "the greatest of these three." Why is this so? As I read it, the biblical passage makes love the elementary school of the moral sentiment and moral responsibility. Of the three things named, love is at once the primitive and paramount virtue. Strictly speaking, love is the only one which is a *moral* good. That which is supreme is love, the exacting labour of responsibility towards others – finite knowable beings – rather than faith, the showy, vacuous and ultimately non-moral devotion to a transpersonal being and an unwilled truth.

On this reading, the primacy accorded to faith in what I am calling the Christianity of our Hobbesian world is doubly significant. Firstly, faith offers preemptive and general amnesty for all the necessary evils committed in the frenzied business of existence. Faith expiates all the daily dirty deals and duplicitous deeds required of a hustling humanity mired in what Derek Walcott calls "the industry of survival," to say nothing of the industry of accumulation. Faith pardons, even sanctions, the loveless habits of acquisitiveness and possessive egotism let loose in this society in these times. Faith in God is the necessary double of what Frantz Fanon excoriated as *"le démerdage,* each one shits for himself, the godless form of salvation": God's grace as expiation for godless conduct. John Locke, Hobbes's future interlocutor, got it all wrong regarding the moral consequences of belief and unbelief. In his *Letter on Toleration* Locke had this to say as grounds for excluding atheists from the blessings of toleration: "Promises, covenants, and oaths, which are the bonds of human society, can have no hold or sanctity for an atheist. For the taking away of God, even in thought, dissolves all." Were

Locke to be living at this hour and in this place, he would have to recognize that it is precisely faith that permits its adherents to traduce "promises, covenants, and oaths" – traduce them with the blessed assurance of remission. Faith is the constant companion of the sly and shifty instrumentalist morality that governs human transactions in this society. Faith absolves and absolute faith absolves absolutely.

At the same time it helps to hold as a cardinal article of this faith the conviction that we are all sinners, tithe-devouring pastors and credulous flock alike, born sinners; that nothing we do or omit to do will ever erase this our congenital sinfulness. *Si pecasse negamus falimur et nulla in nobis est veritas.* "If we say we have no sins we deceive ourselves and the truth is not in us." That way, we can cheat, lie, take bribes, hate relatives, betray private and public trust, all in the imperturbable belief that we are merely human, all-too-human, born sinful and to sin condemned. Only grace, utterly undeserved and freely given, will save us. Better, then, the serene sinecure of faith than "love's labour." Better the gospel and the blessed assurance of divine grace than the demanding work of loving care of finite beings by finite beings for finite beings.

Doing the less than exalted and exacting work it does in this place, it is difficult to see, by the most generous stretch of the imagination, how faith here fosters "criticism of the earth," harbours intimations of resistance to the world the masters have made, acts in the service of human emancipation. We don't do seditious prayers around here. More fundamentally, we don't do prayer as sedition. We don't practise religion as an act of disobedience. According to Saidiya Hartman's historical narrative, our enslaved sisters and brothers of America worshipped as a transgressive act, one undertaken in defiance of the masters' prohibition in a "forbidden space," by virtue of the political act of transforming this fugitive space into a sacred grove, invoking an authority superior to the enslavers' law, and envisioning their inevitable liberation. From the plantation to the pandemic: Today in the time of coronavirus, leaders of the African American Church, faithful to their ancestral calling and earthly mission, are in the forefront of the fight to dissipate vaccine scepticism rampant in their communities. The sacred and the profane conjoined as always in a common cause. Here in the homeland, our "men of God" are otherwise engaged, busy attending to things not of this world. Or rather, in an obscene parody, quite busy attending to things very much of this earth – extorting tithes, amassing wealth, fucking chosen specimens of the flock. When it is not in the service of securing absolution for the myriad crimes of everyday life, worship is here an education in enraptured obedience and docile quietism.

THE SACRAL AND THE CARCERAL

It is appropriate, is it not, that the Ghana Church of Pentecost is erecting splendid facilities for the Government of Ghana to relieve overcrowding in the nation's prisons? And it is fitting that the government is spearheading the erection of a national cathedral. Marvellous example of the collaboration of Church and State towards shared ends. On the one hand, the Church's sanctification of captivity and institutions of repression. On the other hand, bestowal of civil authority upon the holy and the management of the soul. Nice reciprocal delegation of tasks by sacral and secular disciplinary bodies, mutual outsourcing of responsibilities in the interest of economy and efficiency. Where is our Foucault to show us why we should withhold effusive gratitude for this new addition to the economics of austerity?

CONCERNING FAITH: A SOLILOQUY

Yet none of this my "exercise in suspicion" – the incipient atheism of every explanation of religion – resolves the question of the human need for answers to the enigmas of the world. I hear you, Richard Dawkins. I hear your counsel of reason. But seditious preacher Cornel West is surely right. The "tragicomic sense of life," he says, is utterly overpowering, "propels us toward suicide or madness unless we are buffered by ritual, cushioned by community, or sustained by art." That tragicomic sense, always present in these parts, has undergone an exponential growth in more recent times, thanks to the wounds to body and spirit inflicted by the neoliberal siege, the bleak blessings of the lawless market and the general disorder of postcolonial life. What Pierre Bourdieu calls the "permanent condition of insecurity" which afflicts the working class in advanced capitalist societies is the defining feature of all human existence in our postcolonial world. And what Ali Kadri says regarding Egypt is so true of life in this society: "In the totality of existence…the word crisis has little or no meaning for it is an everyday occurrence." Confronted with this ever-menacing abyss, can human beings live by a belief with neither a creator-god nor a finished dogma at its centre? The kind of belief which, according to Ayi Kwei's visionary recollection, our ancestors explained to the invaders' priests the first time they brought to our shores their laughable "fables of gods and devils and a supreme being above everything":

> We told [the white missionary] we knew soft minds needed such illusions, but that when any mind grew among us to adulthood it grew beyond these fables and came to understand that there is indeed a great force in the world, a force spiritual and able to shape the physical universe, but that force is not something cut off, not something separate from ourselves. It is an energy in us, strongest in our working, breathing, thinking together as one people; weakest when we are scattered, confused, broken into individual, unconnected fragments.

This is not liberation theology. This is liberation from theology. And to what end? In order that, left on our own together, we will eschew the depraved solipsism of "each one shits for himself," the precept of human conduct which that revolutionary humanist of all people, Frantz Fanon, called "godless" – "*la forme athée du salut*, the godless path of salvation." Liberating news, the ancestors' wager as reimagined by Armah and Fanon's challenge to us to remain faithful to it. But it is no gospel. It has no blessed assurance to offer. And that is the problem. It is much too daunting and exacting. How on earth are our people to endure the relentless onslaught of existential terror that is their daily lot? Can they possibly grope their way, as the hymn says, "amidst the encircling gloom" with no "kindly light" to lead them, no authoritative Word – one of majestic simplicity – which announces the way? What use is Armah's surrogate for the apophatic divinity, his "made-in-here" anthropomorphic Ra who dares not flaunt his might because he has none to flaunt, none at all beside what we engender in concert?

> Ra's no self-created god
> Ra is our self-creation
> Ra is us
> embracing space
> traversing time.

How can this power of our own creation, ministering to our very own needs and chosen ends, how can this purportedly prodigious but, in truth, picayune power ever rival the benevolent grace of a despotic divinity? We are talking of a divinity who, in addition to healing the "vexation of the soul" Peter Tosh sang so poignantly of, just happens to bring ample gifts of material prosperity? Not a chance. So who the hell, literally, am I to call that faith fatuous – that faith in faith – which brings solace to our people? What gives me the right to scorn it in the haughty name of reason, earthly reason? What unfeeling hubris.

And yet, and yet... Why Christianity and the Christian god of all things, this god invented by others to minister to *their* needs? What needs? You ask. They built a wall around the self, made it sovereign owner of itself and its possessions, freed it – or so they thought – from all dependence on other beings. Lo and behold, they discovered very quickly that we are finite, vulnerable, dependent beings; that, as the Akan saying goes, "a single tree left to brave the storm all alone is doomed to collapse." So upon the ruins of a monumental but unsupportable ego they erected, by virtue of a putative conversion that in truth amounts to the most unrepentant narcissism, an all-powerful, all-knowing, all-owning god. A god that pretends to self-sufficiency, independence, sovereignty. A god every bit as imperial and monomaniacal as the solipsistic entity that brought disaster upon itself. A god whose impossible mission is to repair the wreckage caused by this very ruinous solipsism. Monotheism, abject obeisance to this one god, is the price paid for the terrifying emancipation of the subject. So why, oh why, do we grovel before this god, we who have at our disposal native resources for eschewing that desperate totalitarian solution to the anguish of the sequestered self? What self-loathing folly drives us to embrace, virtually as an anthem of racial redemption, John Newton's *Amazing Grace*, the very song of a bandit-sailor responsible for delivering captured African women and men to demonic destinations; the very same pirate who scripted *How Sweet The Name of Jesus Sounds* in between savouring the malefic mission, as C.L.R James acidly notes in *Black Jacobins*, of loading the cargo? How did we consent to transforming his depravity, his starring role in the heinous trade in human beings – this extraordinarily "vile" deed committed, in the self-chastising words of his own hymn, by an abominable "wretch" – how did we manage to turn this uniquely inhuman crime into an emblem of human *being*, symbol of *our* collective, inescapably sinful humanity? How did we come to acquiesce to this monstrous substitution, this misanthropic metonymy, the breathtaking gall by which a singularly atrocious life and nefarious activity are made to stand in for the essence of human conduct, the regular permanencies of human nature? It boggles the mind to think that we would consent to being tricked and deceived and fucked, not once, but twice! What am I saying, fucked many times over, repeatedly, recurrently, again and again and again! Serial comprehensive consensual violation, spiritual complement to our material complicity in our subjugation, continuation of the supportive part played in the original crime by our villainous chieftains and merchants.

And don't get me wrong. I hold no special brief for Islam either, the other half of the faith duopoly, that other companion of enslavement, that other sadomasochistic whip of the interlopers. I see little to choose between the lived histories of the two creeds. So no, I will not consent to the Talibanization of the African world. Not that I regard Taliban as the logical fulfilment of Islam, any more than I regard killers of doctors who support women's reproductive rights faithful disciples of Christ.

But where in this our African world is the ferocious daring that declares with Heinrich Heine, inveighing against the condition of the Silesian weavers in 1844:

> A curse on the god we prayed to, kneeling with cold in our bones, with hunger reeling; We waited and hoped, in vain persevered. He scorned us and duped us, mocked and jeered – We are weaving, we are weaving!

Where is our Kashav Mishram with the fortitude to refuse every lying solace for the unspeakable condition of the Dalits, every theodicy invented to befuddle suffering humanity:

> On my birthday, I cursed God.
> I cursed, I cursed him again,
> Whipping him with words, I said
> "Bastard!
> "Would you chop a whole cart of wood
> for a single piece of bread?"
> One day I cursed that mother-fucking God.

Intrepid words. Insurrectionary blasphemy crying for imitation in these parts, in this society of conspicuous injustice and stifled discontent, simmering resentment and trained docility. And yet this question of the human, all-too-human need for meaning, in its existential universals and sociohistorical particulars, cannot be evaded. Wanted, desperately wanted: conventions of the sacred that speak in our name, "a sacred devoid of any God," as Alain Badiou puts it; worldly rituals, solemn songs that honour our earthly holiness, numinous names for human enterprises and exertions and expectations. Is it not this exultant humanism – one summoned by love, chastened by awe and enlivened by hope – that at the end of *A Question of Power* Elizabeth invokes in aid of the willed ending of her torments in these luminous words?

> That's what she felt about people's souls and their powers; that they were like sky birds, aeroplanes, jets, boeings, fairies and butterflies; that there'd be a kind of liberation of these powers, and a new dawn and a new world. She felt this because the basic error seemed to be the relegation of all things holy to some unseen Being in the sky. Since man was not holy to man, he could be tortured for his complexion, he could be misused, degraded and killed. If there were any revelation whatsoever in her own suffering it seemed to be quite the reverse of Mohammed's dramatic statement. He had said there is only one God and his name is Allah. And Mohammed is his prophet. She said: There is only one God and his name is Man. And Elizabeth is his prophet.

Is that not what Bob Marley proclaimed when he sang "In the kingdom of Jah *man* shall reign...The mighty God is a living man."? Purged of their masculinist attributions, replanted as shared seedlings of human possibility, are Bessie's and Bob's visions so different from the one evoked by Marx in these magnificent words: "Criticism [of religion] has plucked the imaginary flowers from the chain, not in order that the human being shall continue to bear that chain without fantasy or consolation, but so that s/he shall cast off the chain and pluck the living flower"? "Pluck the living flower." How to wrest such proverbs of possibility from the most desolate regions of body and soul? Apart from Ernst Bloch's "red hero," so named in *The Principle of Hope*, who is capable of surmounting "lethal nothingness" and "can get by on the way to death almost without traditional consolation," where shall we regular mortals find the chthonic resources with which to face the abyss and keep educated hope alive? How to entertain the very idea of redemption without ordained directions, without what the same John Locke in the same *Letter on Toleration* – this time mocking "zealots" – sardonically called "that way which, according to the sacred geography, leads straight to Jerusalem"? Where is the path towards home devoid of a "sacred geography"? "Imagine there is no heaven." Thus sang John Lennon – but listen to Ray Charles' stirring rendition – in words infinitely more audacious than anything the English philosopher could muster. Is this bitter earth bearable if we heed John's song? That is the question. For in this quintessential place of "perpetual solicitude," continual crisis and overpowering fear which is the homeland, there is no scarcity of ready-made potions for attending to the aches of the belly and the tumults of the spirit.

OUR HOLY FACTORS

And there is no shortage of bile brewed from faith's more noxious juices, mixed with toxic ingredients or interpretations of "our culture," ready to be spewed upon the nonconforming and the "deviant." In the forefront of the holy war against the ordination of gay bishops and homosexuals in general are priests from Africa. Yes, from Africa. From these shores were once abducted into captivity millions of our people, doomed to be branded less than human, children of Lucifer devoid of souls, nature's abhorrent monstrosities. In the eyes of our holy men and their ardent followers, gays and lesbians are also less than human creatures, deserving, perhaps, of the ethereal love of god but not the earthly company of human beings. I was about to call this new act of damnation of our own by our own an irony. I almost forgot that our villainous chieftains and merchants in the role of native "factors" were waist-deep in the wicked work of capturing and selling our kith and kin. History repeats itself in the unseemly shape of the vanguard role played by today's holy factors in the persecution of homosexuals. Today's preachers of hate are the direct descendants of those chieftains and merchants whom Olaudah Equiano in 1789 called "these sable destroyers of human rights." Their condemnation of homosexuality as an "unnatural" abomination ought to remind us of the fate meted out to one descendant of those captives: In 1912, Jack Johnson, world heavyweight boxing champion, was convicted of violating the Mann Act, which forbade transporting women across state borders for "immoral purposes." Johnson's real crime? His relationship with a white woman, Lucille Cameron, was adjudged a "crime against nature." Our "men of God" are in perfect company. It is the unholy company of enforcers of established orders of all times and places who in hysterical dread say of every challenge to the reigning powers and mores what a deputy to the French Legislative Assembly said of the demand for the right of women to bear weapons in 1792: "the order of nature would be inverted." The question posed in Bessie Head's *Maru* has lost none of its pertinence: "How universal [is] the language of oppression?"

Brothers and sisters, especially you brothers, sentinels of "the order of nature," sovereign legislators of native ways and taboos, self-anointed guardians of our cultural treasures quick to issue fatwas against all things "Un-African," all of you devotees of natural law and enemies of human rights, this is my plea: Each time we are tempted to join in the damnation of *any* portion of humanity, let us remember what Ayi Kwei, our relentless archaeologist of crime and complicity, will never let us forget: *our* "fearful holocaust." Let it be our template of terror, terror in all its prodigal variety. You cannot house in one and the same breath, on pain of self-asphyxiation, hatred of racism *and* love of the subjugation of women *and* complicity in the persecution of those who, heeding their nature's promptings, elect to love differently. You just can't. Call it naïve but such is the inferential ethics of the fight against white supremacy and racism. Why? Because that fight awakens us, ought to awaken us, to other iniquities and in so doing commits us to other struggles, to an extended family of demands and ends. In a word, that fight answers to a larger cause: our striving after what Frantz Fanon called "human things," human things in all their shareable and distinct forms. No wonder Ayi Kwei once bestowed on that unsparing opponent of "*all forms* of exploitation," that enemy of every species of dehumanization, the *nsabran* or praise-name "Fanon the awakener." Fitting *oriki* for that exemplar of ethical labour without exemptions and without exceptions, precocious ancestor of *médicins sans frontiers*. As though they were intended for the ears of today's "men of God" – those avid avatars of citation in the name of inerrancy and in the service of the persecution of fellow sentient beings – Fanon's words deserve to be cited in full: "All forms of exploitation are alike. They all seek their necessity in some decree of a biblical nature. All forms of exploitation are identical, for they are all directed at the same 'object': the human being." This is first principle. I insist that its overarching transcendental validity, that is to say, its consistency with the logic of Fanon's egalitarian humanism, stands in spite of his homophobia, his disparaging comments on homosexuals in a notorious passage in *Black Skin, White Masks*, a passage all too often taken to represent an inexpungable core of his teaching. That passage is incongruous not indeed with an embalmed entity called "Fanonism" but with the pulsating thrust of Fanon's thinking, the path towards which his thinking takes us, takes us, like all enabling pathfinders, sometimes *malgré lui même*. We can hardly say the same thing about our "men of God" in the homeland, extend to them such hermeneutic generosity.

FIRST PRINCIPLE

A note for our priestly caste and their acolytes and persecuting lawmakers: You don't have to be a homosexual or approve of homosexuality to recognize gays' and lesbians' right to their sexuality. Likewise, you don't have to approve of abortion to recognize a woman's reproductive freedom, including her right to choose to carry or not to carry a foetus to term. It is important to insist on that distinction. Adherents of totalitarian morality regularly conflate the two stances. So do our legislators. Currently (July 2021) under consideration in Ghana's parliament is a "Draft Bill for the Promotion of Proper Human Sexual Rights and Ghanaian Family Values." As in other "democracies" of Africa in the grip of moral panic, the bill criminalizes homosexuality, criminalizes even advocacy of the rights of gays and lesbians. With impeccable logic the Speaker of Parliament intones: "We will not legislate to infringe on the Human Rights of people, but we will legislate to ensure that culture and traditions are not violated." Our "culture and traditions" include the idea that the proper measure of man is to father multiple children with multiple womem, leave the majority of these children uncared for, condemn the boys to a life of crime and the girls to prostitution. Do you, Mr. Speaker, count such pathogenic paternity among things that must not be violated? If not, then your definition of inviolate traditions is not universalizable and so is no definition but sheer sophistry. That means that what our "culture and traditons" are, what makes them praiseworthy, and how we promote them, is essentially constestable and not exempt from the province of Human Rights. Sadly or rather predictably, the Honourable Speaker is not alone. A prominent Catholic Archbishop concurs. He accuses supporters of gay rights of being under the spell of postmodernist subjectivism and relativism, but then offers as an argument against gay rights the claim that they are imcompatible with Christianity and Ghanaian culture. Is that the best argument you can offer, Holy Father, this quintessential resort to relativism, to the claims of a particular religious and cultural tradition, more precisely and worse still, to a particular interpretation of that tradition, this bow to the forcible triumph of one interpretation? Is any thing more guilty of idolatry? Is that the best you can do, Catholic prelate of all people, putative votary of the whole? Tell us Holy Father: the Christian values and Ghanaian traditions in the name of which you support the draconian bill before Parliament, are they good and praiseworthy simply because they are Christian and allegedly all our own? This is moral tyranny dressed up as cultural piety. This is talibanism without the Taliban. The theocratic Islamic Republic of Iran has a morality police – "Guidance Patrols" is their polite name – charged with ensuring respect for Islamic law. The Archbishop and the Speaker and all those honourable members of parliament have a marvelous template to emulate in the spirit of ecumenism.

FRAUDULENT FAITH AND FATAL FOLLY

One day in early May 2013, Prophet T.B. Joshua, the General Overseer of the Synagogue Church of All Nations, stages a mammoth day long service in Accra. It is a Tuesday, mind you, that is to say a regular working day in human affairs for people in societies intent on planting, cultivating and harvesting the means for their earthly sustenance – but evidently not in the Republic of

Ghana where every day is a holy day, unvarying time of waiting prayerfully for the divinity to take care of the needs of body and soul. The event causes a major traffic havoc that generates widespread displeasure. But that was only a minor prelude to a far more serious disaster later that month. A throng of desperate people assembled at that fateful church go on a riotous stampede for a free bottle of "anointed water" that promises an instantaneous ending to penury and pain of every variety. Four people die in the mêlée. Several more are injured. In the aftermath, a young woman is hauled before a credulous audience and media to confess that she was an instrument of the devil's design. Her appointed mission? To cause lethal disarray at this gathering of the pious and thereby discredit the vaunted salvific powers of the concoction. A young *woman*. Who else? Why not add to an injury caused by fraudulent faith and fatal folly a reprehensible insult launched straight from the time-honoured arsenal of male supremacist, misogynist symbolism of evil? But now there is a general unease abroad this time, whispers to the effect that these protagonists of faith might at the very least be guilty of criminal negligence in not adequately preparing for the potential dangers of an enormous crowd in frenzied rapture. There is even some audible murmuring to the effect that the grip of religion on the people of this land is reaching depths of suicidal imbecility. Among those elected to arrest the slippery slope towards scepticism is a doctor-priest. He dutifully appears on TV with a good reverend from the culpable church in a gesture of solidarity with one of the brethren under siege. Together they defend the faith and dispense demonology as a fable of causation with various degrees of hilarity. But the doctor-priest is not alone. He is one among many of our men and women of science, the intelligentsia and public figures who, in a vast conspiracy of wilful ignorance, have sworn fealty to self-styled "men of God" and abandoned the work of reason: work of pressing existential necessity, work for which this land stands in as desperate a need as air, water, light and, lest we forget, decent toilets.

    Every day, every week, hour after hour, men and women are glued to television sets, utterly mesmerized by the wondrous words and works of this consummate fraudster named T.B. Joshua, supposedly healing the sick and the infirm, making cripples walk and the blind see, dispensing copious gifts of food and money, thanks to his capacious heart and the evidently limitless blessings of prosperity gospel. The words are a tissue of laughable banalities, juvenile utterances, non-sequiturs and circular reasoning (God's will is true because God's will is good), delivered in weird, barely intelligible sentences. The works are transparently staged performances, the testimonies demonstrably extorted and fake. That does not stop the enchanted from scribbling down every word in rapt attention, voicing their unquestioning trust and obedience. It is an incredible and heart-wrenching spectacle to behold: men and women you would suspect of having some familiarity with the life of reason partaking in the mass abdication of common sense. A world-wise relative of some intellectual capabilities (or so I thought), a lawyer and former ambassador to boot, counsels me, in all seriousness, to take a stage-5-cancer-afflicted, completely enfeebled niece all the way from Ghana to Joshua's sanctuary of healing in Nigeria. He is certain that it is there alone and with his aid alone that this niece would be restored to health. I demur in silent disgust. The niece would presently die. My faithless inaction would not be forgotten. Had I complied...

But T.B. Joshua is a symptom of a calamitous malady that has descended upon this land, captured, occupied and colonized every sphere of existence, inducing a-near universal, catatonic surrender of critical intelligence to mind-boggling superstition and arrant quackery. Never mind the hypertrophy of the religious sphere in its own right. Never mind the plethora of churches and sects and denominations and tithe-devouring pastors that increases with exponential speed year in and year out: arguably the most prolific sector of the GDP. What we are witnessing is the death of the secular as such, the death of the secular as an idiom of life and in spheres of existence where it once enjoyed a relative autonomy and distinctiveness. The ordinary language of greeting, song and dance, the totality of everyday life and culture, has been cleansed of the taint of the secular. Enter Mammon's very own citadel, a bank, and you will be greeted with a solemn hymn on radio or television, with customers singing or humming along, evidently happy to acquiesce to this incursion of religion – and only one religion, Christianity – into the profane, this totalitarian erasure of differences among spheres of existence. There is no billboard, none of the famous inscriptions on the back of taxis and minibuses and lorries, no storefront, that does not feature an invocation of god's grace and a citation from the bible, book, chapter and verse. It is a display of assiduity that one indeed prays, yes prays, could make a peeking appearance in other areas of life, say, the workplace or the offices of public servants. But there too the elimination of the secular prevails and the call to prayer reigns. Footballers implore god, not to bless the game and let fairness triumph, but to favour their team. Strange is the just and loving god who upon the entreaties of one of the duelling teams condemns the other side to defeat even before the battle is joined. Not exactly a laudable model for an impartial judiciary. But no doubt, His ways are as inscrutable as His writ is ubiquitous. The football field is not exempt from the general extinction of the secular and the capricious power of a despotic divinity. True, these sites and spaces were not entirely free of symbols of the sacred in the past. But it is the overwhelming disproportion of the religious sign and reference – predominantly Christian – which is remarkable in today's Ghana. Almost entirely excised from the vocabulary of everyday life are secular idioms of admonition and exhortation, celebration and lamentation. Where these days is the taxi or mini-bus (trotro) on whose back shield we will find inscribed that distillation of despondency and inextinguishable hope made famous by the title of Ayi Kwei Armah's first novel, *The Beautyful Ones Are Not Yet Born*? Where is the language that reminds us of our human responsibility and agency, even, especially, in times of evidently insurmountable difficulties and warranted despair? Where have all our grandmothers' proverbs of possibility gone? Today the favoured inscription we encounter everywhere with monotonous regularity, at least in Akan, is *adom nkoaa, adom ara kwa*, only grace, grace freely given. We have here totalitarianism of the most insidious and intransigent kind, totalitarianism without political coercion.

Ato Sekyi-Otu

BLACK LIVES MATTER.
WHAT OF GHANAIAN HUMAN LIVES?

It is a fine morning in August 2020. At a street corner in Cape Coast in the central region of Ghana, a team of policemen beat to the pulp, mercilessly bloody a hapless young man supposedly guilty of violating some Covid-19 restrictions, although he appeared to be in full compliance, mask and all. The violence is delivered with an earnestness that makes the comportment of Derek Chauvin, George Floyd's killer – left hand cavalierly in his pocket as he knelt on Floyd's neck – a model of enlightened punishment. The bystanders just look on. There is no video recording of the ghastly affair by any onlooker. No audible outrage. No report of the incident in the local, to say nothing of the national, media the day after. No demonstrations and denunciations of police brutality. No questioning of the Public Order Act, the enabling instrument of police violence. What does it take for such savage deployment of power to call forth the people's resistance? The scene of this police brutality is adjacent to the Cape Coast Metropolitan Building where women and men were that morning exercising their quintessential civic democratic duty, registering to vote in the forthcoming national elections, reaffirming in so doing their status as inviolable persons and their rights as citizens. And it is within walking distance from "Cape Coast Castle," the obscene name for the demonic place where captured Africans were incarcerated before being exported to unknown destinations. Founding place of racial and colonial violence, the "Castle" is so close in physical space to the site of police brutality meted out to a free citizen that fine August morning, yet so far in lived time, it seems, to function as a mnemonic trigger, spark that work of "traumatic memory," which might incite fury with current exercises of violence sanctioned by our very own democratically appointed agents of the state. Forgotten connectedness, inaudible evidences of disapproval. When poet Kwadwo Opoku-Agyemang says of our relationship to the "castle" that "We kneel because it stands," he is speaking of the kowtowing of the spirit induced by the collective amnesia that permits the legacy of the edifice to persist, unrecognized, and makes the citizenry acquiesce to contemporary violations by the state and its security agencies without a murmur.

Elsewhere, say in the less docile nation of Nigeria, some of the protestors against police brutality in 2020 invoked the slogan of the American movement Black Lives Matter. But isn't the reason that black lives matter the fact that black lives are human lives? Isn't it because human lives matter even where and when those who incarnate them are not primarily thought of as black although their skin is black, that is to say, even where and when blackness is not the defining feature of their being?

LITTLE KINDNESSES, "ANTAGONISTIC TOTALITY"

The other day Menu Osei, son of our single-mother housecleaner, dropped by to say hello and to thank us. This is the first day of his first semester vacation from Kwame Nkrumah University of Science and Technology. We had bought him a camera he needed for his programme in Graphic Arts. Looking mature and proud, he sat down with us in the living room. His hardworking mother, although she is not forbidden to do so, never availed herself of that human privilege. Here we have our society's divisions deconstructed and reaffirmed at one and the same time, beyond small reparative acts of individual kindness. The unjust whole, the "antagonistic totality" as Theodor Adorno called it, remains untouched. That is why deconstruction, be it interpretation of texts and disclosure of their internal dissonances or the unfolding of ironic twists and complicities in the drama of social power, is not the revolution.

MEA CULPA

Speaking of complicities, here I am crafting these blues for the homeland and lament for its destitute children from my study at my residence situated up a hill in Brafoyaw, Cape Coast. If I avert my eyes from my immediate surroundings, that is to say, if I summon with sufficient dexterity the moral obtuseness of class indifference, from my window I can see the sea gratefully receiving the radiance of the sun, bringing renewed energies to an aged body and recalcitrant mind. But sometimes if I allow my eyes and those surroundings to touch even for a fleeting moment, then "the honesty's too much." Not, as in Canadian singer Daniel Hill's achingly beautiful ballad of 1977, because of the unbearable ecstasy of restrained passion unshackled, but rather the shameful recognition of scorching truths made invisible by the practice of ignorance. It is the accusing honesty of irony, the repressed irony upon which the life of contemplation rests. Only a few years back, in plain yet conveniently censored view of the little valley below my window were children playing in filthy sand and mud, stark naked, taking turns to defecate in the bush adjacent to their "home." To this day one out of five households has no toilet facilities. Open defecation is rampant. This, I assure you, is not some cultural survival, a lingering expression of primeval freedom. Let's not turn this repulsive habit into one more emblem of our traditions. We are talking of some six decades after "Independence." In his Solomonic sagacity our paramount chieftain is presiding over the building of an ornate national cathedral to honour a solemn vow he made to god, in sacrilegious indifference to the filth and misery hidden from the paths to the majestic edifice. He has pledged to see it completed before he leaves office in 2024, a shining legacy among the monumental achievements he wants posterity to remember him by. Forgive me, indulgent reader, for bringing up this obscene scandal yet again. It warrants repetition because it is so perfectly emblematic of the criminal inversion of necessities on the part of our would-be leaders: the prehistoric shithole and the ultramodern shrine. But here I go again pronouncing sanctimonious sentiments of outrage from my well-appointed residence a stone-throw away from scenes of abject destitution, living the irony of writing insurgent prose ensconced in a place of comfort in the vicinity of the grotesque. Too much to bear, I permit myself an expiatory thought: Irony without blinkers is the spark of the work of justice. Kalonji – bless his kind and seditious soul now in the company of the ancestors – added an exculpatory assurance: It's not as if, he used to say, I attained what I call my sinful comfort by exploiting other people's labour. I am not so sure, Kalonji, not sure at all, my brother. The supply chains of social evil are labyrinthine, their originating agents and complicit conscripts impossible to trace and set apart. But "shame is a revolutionary sentiment." So wrote the young Marx to Arnold Ruge in 1843. Yet another comforting shibboleth?

THE RAGE AND THE GRIEF

"Often, it is true, a man's heart rages and grieves when he sees his [homeland] juggling desperately with itself – an immense body in quest of its identity." Thus spoke Kassoumi in Yambo Ouloguem's unforgettable threnody for the African condition, *Bound to Violence*, composed in the very first days of our postcolonial life. It is indeed to a wild and whirling world that I nursed this irrepressible yearning to go back. What must it be like to return, I often wondered, not to an earthly paradise but the native cauldron? What must it be like to be able to rail, yell, holler and dare to hope from the homeland rather than the adopted homestead? I never imagined it will be sheer ecstasy. Perhaps more rewarding, even in the agony it is bound to exact? Remember that the bard of return is no panegyrist, no empiricist of the true, the good and the beautiful. He does not say of the native land that it *is* beautiful. Sworn nonetheless to "return to the deserted hideousness of your sores," the great poet of homecoming is a prodding prophet: "And here at the end of the dawn is my virile prayer that I hear neither the laughter nor the screams, my eyes fixed on this town which I *prophesy*, beautiful." I would drop but one word from that call – "virile," heraldic emblem of one-half of our species, menacing bane for the other. The rest of Césaire's call stands. The beautiful homeland is not yet born. All the same, "my eyes [are] fixed on this town," fixed on all that blights its promise even as they descry glimmers of a transfiguration in the distant horizon, one that is ours to bring into being by dint of our concerted endeavours. This is the prophetic injunction, the visionary agent's idea of home, a place not yet in existence, a place yet to be built. Therein lies the difference between nostalgia and utopia. *The Healers* calls our relation to the one "celebration," to the other "invocation." I have to keep that in mind as I approach homeland. Whoever undertakes the journey of return must keep that in mind. There is a reason, at least one compelling and overarching reason, you have elected to go back, to give up the comfort of the familiar, however fraught with thorny questions. No need, then, to paint the homestead you are leaving in colors of unremitting gloom. Or else, prompted by intimations of the folly of radical rupture, magnify the virtues of existence in the place and the condition we call exile. Here are two cautionary tales, conveying contending thoughts, told in untutored verse:

Exile's Reputed Rewards

There are days when the eyes are aroused
by the penumbra of exile.
Then they are granted epiphanies foreclosed
to those inured to the bliss of dwelling
where homestead and homeland are twin.
But often, much too often,
a deathly decisive darkness supervenes,
making havoc of the vaunted gifts.
 Damn it.
The wandering life is for dogs and gods.

The intrepid Edward Said preferred a different picture of exile, one evoked by Auerbach in his citation of Hugo of St. Victor's *Didascalion* and one which Said endorses in his celebrated *Orientalism*: "The man who finds his homeland sweet is still a tender beginner; he to whom every soil is as his native one is already strong; but he is perfect to whom the entire world is as a foreign land." Straining strength. Bitter bliss. Painful perfection.

HOMELAND'S BURDENED BLESSINGS

Gone, long gone or freshly yanked from earth
with equal finality
the beautiful ones,
those who nested a fledgling promise
at the joyful hearth.
Gone, the lot of them.
The last to go, treasured survivors from time's remorseless
iniquity:
Kwamena Kwansa, his ferocious will at work
till the very last hour,
still battling the chastening tenderness
that is our shared patrimony.
And Ama Yaniba,
her radiance undimmed by infirmity
till the last day.
Also gone, Adwoa Beduwa,
dearest-twin-three-weeks-younger:
Go figure.
They say it is your mother's child
who is your true sibling.
Love among the offspring of a many-pleasured father
is but – or do they say it is also? – a beautiful thing.
We confounded the futile ordering
of the beautiful and the true
in the magnificent tangle of our affections.
They called me Beloved.
In the forlorn mists of exile
that name often granted a consoling clarity;
to this day it wrestles the clouds.

What is left?
Friendships from the day before yesterday.
Today in their company,
after the fleeting mirth sparked by remembered thrills
and a thousand outrageous pranks,
a searing chasm stares.

ATO SEKYI-OTU

How emptied of living kinship our worlds.
Their world, cemented with FAITH,
ardent and implacable in word,
infinitely pliable under necessity's clever anvil.
And their endless rites of death!
Torrential grief vying
with unshackled extravagance,
the pomp and puffery of newly-minted opulence.
Upon this blessed plenitude of a life
not one jolting thought,
not a single perverse leaf of a book,
has, it seems, intruded since school days
to exact one anguished insomniac night.
My world, shorn of shrines but not of belief,
murmuring doubts and questions and hopes
alien to sated girths and sedate souls.

Is it for these gossamer strings of remembrance
that I yearn to return?
Cajoled by a nebulous nostalgia to forsake
bonds wrought here, without design,
but not without consequence?
To forsake my darlings.
This land that a self-deluding habit calls exile,
this is their land, and mine.
There, I said it.

To what end, then, this inchoate longing
after another time and place?
In order to collude in our disenfranchisement?
Aid and abet those who flaunt their purelaineity,
wrangling with red-faced ire or decorous duplicity
over their chosen terms of our admittance,
offering potent enemas to cleanse us free
of all the odious dross of our savage ancestries?
Hell, this land is our land,
no mere transient sojourn.

And yet and yet,
on a desolate night of icy sidewalks
and howling winds
echoing the fierce souls of the denizens,
the flickering lustre of homeland beckons.
Hmm.
All paths are traitorous paths.

THE TROUBLE WITH "DIASPORA"

You don't have to be a fancy deconstructionist of "origins" to ask if today the talk of "diaspora" and its constant companion "exile" still make any sense – that is, if they ever did, given the history of the present. But whether it is historically obsolete or "always already" nonsensical, what – beyond the purely scholastic disputations of the postmodernists – does the very thought of exile and diaspora mean for the practice of life. Doesn't it foster the indolence of fruitless prevarication, of vacating the work of being where you are, thanks to this futile fantasy of the perpetual return? And you know in your heart of hearts, don't you, that the vast majority of those who go on and on about going back will never do so, and that many of those who do will quickly come to realize that the homeness of the homeland is vastly overrated. Isn't it better, far better, for yourself and your dear ones, to commit mind and body to cultivating belonging, embracing it not as a gift but as a task, irrevocable task, perhaps even a labour of love?

ANTIPHONIES OF HOMECOMING

For Ernst Bloch and our very own Ayi Kwei, homecoming is the permanent revolution, the unending striving stirred by life in this unhomely world for a place not yet born. By contrast Heidegger's Hölderlin twins it with getting back to the homeland we once knew and makes it sound awfully terrific. What with all this sweet rhapsody on reunion with "the gentle spell of well-known things and the simple relations they bear to each other." The trouble with this song of return is not (only) that it smacks of pastoral primitivism, worse still, that it prefigures fascist tribalism, as the detectives of the Frankfurt School thundered in disgust; the trouble is that it is, well, a tad too simple and too sweet. The real world – homeland and every single homestead in this actually existing universe – deserves tunes that are somewhat more atonal, considerably less harmonic. No serene jubilation then. No *fontomfrom*, no drums of exultation. Too many horrors to enrage you; too many ogres to fill you with sorrow, here, there, everywhere. In imitation of the ancestors' kindness, let's just call them strange things of our world and the times.

IX

STRANGE THINGS OF THE WORLD

THE SOULS OF RIGHTWING BLACK FOLK

I am a black conservative. My name is Clarence Thomas. My name is Armstrong Williams. My name is Ward Connerly. My name is Alan West. My name is Robert Woodson. My name is Condoleezza Rice. My name is Thomas Sowell. My name is Shelby Steele. My name is Glenn Loury. Unlike those dandy race warriors of the campus Left, I was not born with a silver spoon in my black orifice. I am intimately familiar – not just in theory – with what the radicals' prophet Karl Marx called "the harsh school of labour." Knowing what it really means to start with nothing and, as befits Black Sisyphus, work your way up life's many forbidding hills, I have an acquired right granted by lived experience, not metaphysical calling, to be rightwing. More precisely, I have a hard-won reason, rather than a cushy birthright, to be a Reaganite, completely blown away by the Gipper's hilarious witticism according to which the most scary sentence in the English language (American) is the declaration: "I am from the government and I am here to help you." Never mind the fact that a vital organ of the American enterprise, the armaments industry, driver of perpetual war for profit (I mean for freedom), gets by with a little help from a friendly government every budget day without fear of betraying the creed. And never mind the fact that it is with public funds that, contrary to the canard, pharmaceutical companies, otherwise risk-averse, pay for the research and development programmes that engender the very products over which they then assert exclusive intellectual property rights. My name is John McWhorter. Born doubly blessed, endowed with class privilege and a preternatural intellect, I have, unlike my soul brother Glenn, a natural right to be rightwing, thereby bearing testimony to the truth that from different social circumstances adherence to kindred convictions is possible. I know Noam Chomsky. Noam Chomsky is a disciplinary kinsman of mine. But Noam Chomsky is no ideological friend of mine. Although I share with him opposition to so-called linguistic determinism, the thesis according to which the particular language you speak constrains how you think and what you think, I am otherwise no Chomskyean, committed to radical politics as a consequence of my linguistics: thereby bearing testimony to the truth that from kindred theoretic positions adherence to opposing political persuasions is possible. My name is Amy Holmes, fervent American-nationalist in spite of or rather because of my having an African for a father. My name is Paris Dennard (serious askari or risible figure of self-parody?), all wound up, ever-ready to serve. My name is Tim Scott, sole black Republican member of the US Senate. Watch me grinning sheepishly behind Trump whenever the occasion calls for it; hear me rapping rhapsodic of my clan's miraculous ascent "From Cotton to Congress," an ascent possible, need we add, only in America. Never mind the fact that the previous condition of servitude, the life of cotton-picking drudgery from which the clan heroically rose, was not of the clan's own making, hardly an object lesson in what the human will, particularly in its vaunted American species, can accomplish. My name is Herman Kain. Emblazoned with the mystical motto 999, I pledged to die for Trump and so I did after having unprotected consort with Covid-19 carriers at a Trump rave. My mission? To serve as black intercessor so that my people shall bear witness to his infinite goodness and be forgiven for their dissolute ways. My name is Vernon Jones, vehemently opposed to the teaching of that pernicious anti-American fake academic subject known as "Critical Race Theory," preferring the teaching of uncritical historical amnesia, a patriotic curriculum cleansed free of all knowledge and mention of white supremacy – and its consequences – as the constitutive principle of the American polity. My name is Larry Elder: Don't you dare degrade my identity, my Americanness unmodified, by calling me African American, *African* of all things in the animal kingdom, this repugnant reminder of the unarguable truth of polygenesis. Like the protagonist of that iconic scene of race-disaffiliation in Césaire's *Cahier*, I proclaim in no uncertain terms that "I [have] nothing in common with this monkey." And my adherence to libertarian philosophy is total, fundamentalist, inerrant in the retroactive application of its core tenet – freedom – even to the story of how black people got here: not through the organized crime of brutal force and seizure, but the exemplary result of the unregulated free market and its blessings at work. That is a tenet I will defend with a every fibre of my being, uphold in all cases, including opposition to state regulation of the means of controlling the lethal pandemic. I say (American) liberty or death and I mean it. And oh yes, lest we forget, my name is Dr Ben Carson, bearer of the healing message that the Middle Passage was an emigration route; Africans bound for the Americas not captured wretches but regular newcomers captivated by the "land of dreams and opportunity." Together we black conservatives belong to a new species of political oddities in America the beautiful. We loathe ideology and teach no doctrine save the twin principles of wilful historical amnesia and unencumbered egoism. We are the answer to the bewilderment once voiced by Justice A. Leon Higginbotham, Jr.: "I am at a loss to understand what is it that the so-called black conservatives are so anxious to conserve." So, let us now praise the precious things we wish to conserve: Slavery and its enduring legacy, the everlasting afterlife of slavery; the refusal to acknowledge, still less to recompense, centuries of unpaid labour; unrelieved poverty and misery in good times and in bad, be it in the midst of the most sustained economic boom in fifty years during the reign of Clinton the dissembler, or in the era of the Mesopotamian mayhem and the subprime catastrophe under the incumbency of Bush the arrogant and ignorant; ferocious unmasked assaults in the years 2000, 2004, 2008, 2012, 2016 and 2021 (and still counting) on the very right of African Americans to vote and to have their votes counted, more basically to have their votes made *countable*; unending threats to life and limb of young men living-while-black; the internecine violence and self-mutilating nihilism of a destitute and desperate youth, their evident renunciation of the very will to live. And the peerless gem of all, the crowning embodiment of things worth conserving: the unadorned anti-black racism of the cruel buffoon, Donald Trump. Shall I go on?

But perhaps there is reason in this unreason. Perhaps what may seem like a perverse devotion to a suicidal cause in fact answers to a profound need, a need that defines the African American predicament. At the dawn of the last century W.E.B. DuBois described that predicament in these celebrated words:

> It is a peculiar sensation, this double-consciousness, this sense of always looking at one's self through the eyes of others, of measuring one's soul by the tape of a world that looks on in amused contempt and pity. One ever feels this two-ness, – an American, a Negro; two souls, two thoughts, two unreconciled strivings; two warring ideals in one dark body, whose dogged strength alone keeps it from being torn asunder.

Perhaps by means of their bizarre allegiance black conservatives think to exorcise the wrenching ambiguity at the heart of African American existence. Adherence to the rightwing cause – this arranged marriage of ferocious tribalism and market fundamentalism consummated in evangelical frenzy – bespeaks a radical decision to rid the self of the tormenting incertitude Du Bois evoked. More than that, it is a decision that will bring the ultimate prize. Thanks to this act, Condoleezza and her soulmates can leave the caste of the dispossessed and the wretched; they will become one with the mystical body of the powerful. They thereby think to heal the congenital wound that afflicts existence-in-black in America: utter powerlessness. You can sense this need – a visceral, almost biological need as Nietzsche might say – in the rhetoric of American omnipotence breathlessly and constantly intoned by Colin Powell and Condoleezza Rice in their heyday. This is black power, of sorts: borrowed, vicarious, self-serving power. Not *Amandla Awethu*, not black *people's power* but power all the same. There is indeed reason in this apparent unreason. But as a famous German philosopher once said: "Reason has always existed but not always in rational form."

RIGHTWING BLACKS' NOTION OF POWER

Two decades ago some black conservatives wondered aloud why African Americans as a group were not beside themselves with joy at the ascendancy of Powell and Rice. Writing in the *Toronto Star* on 1 January 2001, a certain Debra Dickerson seemed utterly mystified by the manifest failure of African Americans to be thrilled by this veritable epiphany of "black power," particularly in the incarnation of Condoleezza Rice. Dickerson proffered an explanation for this absence of effusive celebration. In a breathtaking species of class narcissism and condescension, she averred that this was all because people like Condi belonged to a new category of black people. In effect they are too intellectually aberrant, too original, too – let's call a spade a spade – bright to be fully appreciated by the "family." The very academic specialties of members of this new privileged class proclaimed their internal exile from the family hearth. Condie – amazing grace – was and is an expert on Russia. Dickerson tells the touching story of another worthy and utterly idiosyncratic black scholar who is "fluent in French, Russian, Spanish and written German." To "the black Politburo," fierce sentinels of cultural enclosure, such specimens of a weird subspecies are dangerous. Or so Dickerson's reading of the black community's intellectual and affective bonds would have it. And so these few, these happy few, are "family members to weep with pride over, but who won't use their power as the family dictates." Condemned by their intellectual distinction to alienation from the black community, these oddities inevitably feel at home in the world of the Other, although Dickerson apparently and rather incongruously wants the black community to embrace them. I note that Cornel West has written on pragmatism, analytic philosophy, and any number of "traditionally non-black subjects" without being deemed a turncoat, racial traitor or secret agent. My deceased friend and high school mentor Kweku Garbrah, Professor of Classics at the University of Michigan, was a brilliant scholar in classical philology for five decades without suffering banishment from "the family." There must be another reason for the gnawing anguish of these new putative exemplars of "Black power" and for the less than effusive applause accorded their preternatural achievements. Could it be that ordinary black women and men do not subscribe to what Paul Gilroy calls "ethnic absolutism"? Could it be that they do not practice that knee-jerk tribalist reasoning – a habit regularly condemned by those very avowed conservative "individualists" – which asks us to cheer every instance of black elevation without a critical scrutiny of its provenance and purpose? Perhaps they can see through the perverse uses to which the "race card" can be put? Perhaps they know when the "successful sister" or "successful brother" signifies an accusing exception rather than an inspiring example? Perhaps they are dimly aware that "black power" comes in more than one hue? Perhaps they are tempted to heed David Levering Lewis's counsel. In a PBS *Newshour* interview on 24 January 2001, Lewis launched a barb unmistakably aimed at the shameless manner in which rightwing Machiavellians have twisted Martin Luther King's daring dream of moral life after racism – judging people "not by the colour of their skin but the content of their character" – how the American right have transmogrified MLK's prophetic demand and principle of hope into a duplicitous dogma of history-amnesiac, "race-blind" solipsism. "People of colour," Lewis offered, "must be judged by the content of their politics."

Some six years after she took the black community in America to task for being insufficiently enthusiastic about the elevation of Colin and Condie, the same Debra Dickerson would find Barack Obama, then presidential hopeful and all-time-exceptional-black-without-compare, insufficiently black because he was "not descended from West African slaves brought to America." In spite of his peerless credentials, Obama's *East* African antecedents (to say audibly nothing of his white mother) evidently made him less than an ideal candidate for unqualified black adulation. Was there a reversal here? Not really. The same "ethnic absolutism," previously dressed up as commitment to meritocracy, that led Dickerson to expect African Americans to rejoice in the vaunted accomplishments of Powell, Rice and other admirable freaks of the race would now lead her to deny Obama the badge of authenticity. But this, patient reader, is not the pits to which the souls of rightwing black folk can descend. Believe me, it actually gets worse, this rightwing-black understanding of power, the path to its attainment and the ends it serves.

JOHN RIDLEY'S BLACK PANTHEON

In a 2006 essay "The Manifesto of Ascendancy for the Modem American Nigger," John Ridley gave this black right understanding of power, shall we say, a certain moral clarity, placing in full view its delusional nature and characteristic solipsism, to say nothing of the pathetic poverty of its standard of excellence. The gospel according to Brother John? For eleven days in the spring of 2001, Condolezza Rice and Colin Powell "ruled America." Just how did this miraculous ascent to the summit of power by one black woman and one black man occur? By resolving with matchless intelligence a confrontation with China in the "Hainan Incident," when a US navy aircraft and a People's Republic of China interception fighter collided. The duo's role was in John Ridley's eyes "a crowning moment in our history," nothing less than "the high-water mark of black political power." Why dwell on the other three hundred and fifty-four days – to severely shrink the temporal frame – when the wondrous phenomenon of supreme black political power was a closely guarded secret? Espousing a nihilistic egocentrism indebted to Ayn Rand, Ridley excoriates "niggers" for forgetting what Powell and Rice personified: "All that matters is accomplishment. The very pinnacle of accomplishment is the ability to live and work without regard for the sentiments of others and with, as sister Rand would tell us, a selfish virtue." Sister Rand. Yes, you heard it right. For eleven days, during that dangerous confrontation "a black woman and a black man were in the position of speaking for America to the world." What matters was the unprecedented power the duo exercised in the nation's affairs and the unaided labour of mind and body that prepared them for their hour, I mean, their days of glory. It is these accomplishments and their enabling virtues that the "ascendant" black American should remember. Not Powell's day of infamy, his mendacity before the parliament of the world on 5 February 2003 regarding Iraq's alleged possession of Weapons of Mass Destruction, the testimony that this black pearl would subsequently claim to have been deceived into giving. Nor Condi's starring role in designing and justifying the invasion of Iraq, the curtain-raiser of the century's American-made infernos. No. It is those eleven luminous days of 2001 and the power wielded by the duo that should be carved into racial memory and guide "our collective ascension." It is that moment alone that should be memorialized and recast the two protagonists as incarnations of the "evolutionary brother and sister." The *"evolutionary brother and sister"*! A telling locution, albeit a malapropism. Ridley probably meant to say the "evolved brother and sister." If so, he was digging deep into the sordid sewage of colonialist racist taxonomy and its repugnant version of the doctrine of the "chain of being," the idea of the *évolués* to name the elect of the subject race: those curious freaks of white-supremacist teleology, the fortunate few salvaged from savagery by dint of arduous tutelage and patient moral hygiene. We have come to this. Aimé Césaire's Henri Christophe took imitations of European royal titles and symbols for proud insignia of national autonomy and racial power, "perfect replicas in black" of the white originals. Césaire called this drama of misrecognition and mimicry a tragedy, *The Tragedy of King Christophe*. Our rightwing brother today sees it all as divine comedy to be celebrated and emulated.

EXCEPTIONAL BLACKS AND THE AMERICAN IDEOLOGY

That exemplary high-achiever, George Walker Bush, put the matter with customary folksiness on the occasion of his appointment of Colin Powell and Condoleezza Rice to high office. He wanted to send a message "that people that work hard and make the right decisions in life can achieve anything in America." Naturally, the chief guest of honour at this celebration of the American Dream, Colin Powell, piously recited the catechism with all the exhilaration of a vulgar lore transformed by ritual repetition into an unassailable truth: "Finally, in the newspaper stories that will be written about this occasion, they will say that Colin Powell is the first African-American to ever hold the position of secretary of state. And I am glad they will say that, and I want it repeated. I want it repeated because I hope it will give inspiration to young African-Americans coming along, but beyond that all young Americans coming along, that no matter where you began in this society, with hard work and with dedication and with the opportunities that are presented by this society, there are no limitations upon you." The "race card," when played by the masters and their askaris is a perfectly legitimate device; more than that, it is a powerful talisman for conjuring away the demons of history.

Of Condoleezza it will be written that she grew up attending segregated schools in Alabama and that she rose from such forbidding beginnings to attain glory in the highest. On the way to the empyrean, she would have engraved on her heart and her mind the sturdiest emblem of the parvenu's creed: Never will I be found consorting with the sorry tribe of black losers, detestable reminders of the depths from which intelligent design – god's and mine working in concert – salvaged my appointed destiny. It is by dint of such resolve that she would rise to become tutor to Dubya the dauphin, prelude to being named National Security Adviser and subsequently Powell's successor as Secretary of State. In that capacity Rice would bring about nothing less than a momentous redesign of the chain of being according to the shared metaphysics of white supremacy and patriarchy: she, a black woman, black and a woman, would not only be teacher to the white President-elect but would also manage, with amazing grace, to reduce intricate questions of world affairs to – what else? – simple self-evident truths. Or as the grateful George would put it in his own guileless language: "[Condoleezza] can explain foreign policy matters to me in a way I can understand." Here is race put on full display the better to deny the open secret that it is the primal principle of social power in the city on the hill. Here is an appeal to race to end all appeals to race.

So black exception and Asian norm may with justice be called upon to shame and chastise your regular black loser. Revering Colin and Condie makes it permissible to despise ordinary African Americans. The worship of black divinities is the expiatory rite of anti-black racism, license to despise mortal black women and men. Right-wing black ideologues and their class-kinsfolk freely participate in this ritual; they are its willing votaries and happy beneficiaries.

LAMENT OF AN EXCEPTIONAL BLACK

Here is Darren Walker, President of Ford Foundation speaking on US television programme "Amanpour & Co," 12 June 2020: "We should be concerned, we capitalists, that the latest Pew survey of young people under the age of 39 is that only 52% believe that capitalism is the best way to organize an economy... That's very troubling." Really? Mr. Walker evidently belongs to that intriguing subspecies of black conservatives – the progressive conservatives.

RIGHTWING JEWS:
AN AUTOBIOGRAPHY OF SORROW
In memory of Mr Denton, my Classics teacher at Mfantsipim School

Quarry turned predator's aid, pariah transformed into the proselytizer's censorious acolyte: this is our regular rightwing black in the USA, in some bizarre quarters of the adopted homestead, Canada, and elsewhere in epicentres of the racial polity. It is also our rightwing Jew. And yet these two strange phenomena of contemporary history provoke in me, inexplicably, two different responses. Rightwing black folks make me angry; they fill me with livid scorn; they drive me to indescribable paroxysms of rage. Rightwing Jews? Rightwing Jews make me sad, unspeakably sad. Why? Is it because deep down in my heart, I prefer to see my erstwhile siblings in misery – to echo Frantz Fanon – still cowering with fear and abject powerlessness rather than strutting their stuff, walking the conquerors' walk? Or is my sorrow the consequence of a failure to appreciate certain irreducible differences between these communities of pain, their histories and conditions of existence? Is it the product of an even more fundamental and grievous failure to appreciate one irrefutable truth of the human condition: namely that, given the propitious opportunity we will, each and every one of us, every person and every people without exception, savour the sweet taste of power, one made all the more alluring by living memory of yesterday's abjection? Is that the human, all-too-human reality? I do not know. I do not know if I am ready to embrace that misanthropic conclusion. What I do know is that this irrational and utterly naive expectation of mine that Jews – all Jews – have to be better than this, that they are called upon to bear witness to the possibility of human goodness in all its infinite beauty and tragic inconstancy, that somehow they are incapable of such grotesque metamorphosis, this expectation of mine has a long personal history.

In hindsight it began with Mr. Denton, Percy Denton. He came in the late 1950s to Kwame Nkrumah's Ghana from South Africa, hounded by apartheid law and custom because he, a "white" man had committed the ghastly immorality of marrying a woman of Oriental origins. Some kind providential design – I will permit myself just this one visceral and uncensored concession to superstition – brought him, Mrs. Denton and their young son Jonathan to my secondary school, Mfantsipim School, Cape Coast. There, at that blessed school on Kwabotwe Hill, Mr. Denton taught Greek and Latin. I will not detain you, dear reader, with narrating the epic history of this famous school. In the tradition of the Ciceronian rhetoric I voraciously imbibed under the tutelage of Mr. Denton and other classics teachers, let me tell you what I will not say and do. No need for me, then, to inform the unknowing that Mfantsipim is Ghana's first secondary school, founded in 1876. That it survived and flourished through forbidding ordeals and impediments, kept alive at an iconic near-death moment of its early years by the sacrificial efforts of eight students justly memorialized as "The Faithful Eight." That it produced some of the most illustrious (one of our favourite epithets) names in our nation's history, indeed that "The School" (our modest self-designation) was a principal architect in the creation of the nation, "Mfantsipim in the making of Ghana," as the title of a book by one of our illustrious old boys, historian Albert Adu Boahen, has it. That we count among our old boys – let us now praise famous men – Kofi Abrefa Busia, Ghana's Prime Minister in the years 1969-1972 and father of noted academic and poet Abena Busia; Joseph Appiah, important lawyer-politician and father of renowned philosopher Kwame Anthony Appiah; Kofi Annan, former Secretary General of the United Nations, the first African to serve in that august office; before him, Alex Quaison-Sackey, the first African to hold the office of President of the UN's General Assembly; Mohamed Ibn Chambas, former President of Ecowas Commission; Kwame Gyekye, a major figure among African philosophers of our time; and Isaiah Blankson, the brilliant Aerospace Engineer, nicknamed "Speed Demon" by his colleagues at NASA.

And I will not rewrite my personal history by declaring that I always knew my school to be a nauseating nest for the sedulous mimicry of imperial culture and that I loathed it all. That would be a shameless tact of adjusting disconcerting facts of the past to accord with my present self-image as an insurgent Pan-Africanist socialist. The truth is that I loved it madly, every reverential, parroting bit of it. I loved it all. What am I saying? I was an exemplary product. Witness the fact that in Sixth Form I would be appointed the Head Prefect, an honour not customarily bestowed upon raging rebels and heretics. And to be fair, although the school's curriculum, certainly its arts curriculum, was overwhelmingly Europe-besotted, its ideological temper was not altogether oblivious to African necessities. To put it charitably, the school's soul was schizophrenic, a condition that is a perennial characteristic of avatars of the African Enlightenment: it would foster a thorough Europeanization of the African mind but for the purpose of Africa's advancement, perhaps even Africa's empowerment. Methodist discipline would nurture a native aristocracy elected to be torchbearers of a modern African civilization. Not unlike the archetypal mission of the intelligentsia of "latecomers" to modernity in other lands, except that this mission is here rendered far more dramatic, even epic, given received notions of African barbarism and ingrained African mental incapacities. The utterances of some late nineteenth and early twentieth century West African intellectuals, the tutelary spirits of my celebrated school, exuded this heady brew of race-apologetics and borrowed Enlightenment missionary zeal, one that, as philosopher Olúfémi Táíwò has brilliantly shown, welcomed the Enlightenment mission, precisely, by jettisoning the racist view of inherent African incapacities and embracing the work and artefacts of reason as a shared human enterprise. In our everyday life and on special commemorative occasions, we were required to honour that calling. So it was that on Speech and Prize-giving Day, clad in our resplendent *kentes* we would sing our Akan-language School Anthem, a rousing rendition in song of our motto *Dwen Hwɛ Kan*. The meaning of those founding words? Not "Think *and* Look Ahead," the common but mistaken English translation that severs the sentence into two parts and inserts the conjunction "and" between them, as if the second part describes a separate albeit supplementary activity, as if there is no necessary mutual implication of the two activities named. Rather, it is "Think Looking Ahead." Uniting thought and vision, the motto asks us to think "with a visionary eye," to borrow Bessie Head's quite apposite phrase. an invitation to visionary activity as the very essence of thinking, the call of futurity as the defining horizon of the mind's eye. The day after Speech Day, Sunday morning and Founders' Day, we firstlings of native enlightenment would march in our starched lily-white suits to the local Methodist Church in Cape Coast. And there, with equal piety and passion, we would sing the School Hymn "For All the Saints Who From Their Labours Rest." Nothing could be more emblematic of our enviable training in cultural ambidexterity than these alternating forms of song and apparel.

To this school with its ambiguous heritage, inflated sense of its historic and cosmic vocation, came Mr. Denton the South African as a classics teacher in the late 1950s. One day someone should undertake a comprehensive study of the mission of classical education in a colonized society such as the one I grew up in (although Barbara Goff has made an important start with her 2013 book *"Your Secret Language": Classics in the British Colonies of West Africa*). If it is true, as Oswyn Murray argued in a review article (*Times Literary Supplement* August 6, 1999), that "the classical tradition has a double heritage of conformism and liberation," then which habit of mind was cultivated by teacher and student of classics alike in colonial educational institutions? Was it the habit of obedience and, in the first place, allegiance to the empire and imperial culture thanks to a trained awe for its putative antecedents and, by entailment, for its contemporary legatees? Was it that quasi-religious sense of transfiguration, of cultural superiority by election, available to exemplary initiates? Or rather a critical intelligence encouraged to explore foundational questions of human existence as they were posed by other civilizations at signal moments of their gestation and efflorescence? In what direction did our teachers as rule take us?

My recollection, to put it delicately, is that of a mixed record. Of Mr. Denton, however, I have little doubt. And I was blessed, twice blessed. The beginning of Sixth Form in 1960 reduced the small tribe of classmates who had taken both Latin and Greek for the Cambridge School Leaving Certificate or the "O Levels" to one. I was left as the only boy in my class spurred by some inexplicable perversity to continue with Greek for the Cambridge Higher School Certificate or the "A Levels." So, not only would the erudite Mr. Denton teach me; while I would share him with others in Latin, I would be his sole pupil taking Greek in Sixth Form. In that privileged and enchanted solitude I pored over, with Mr. Denton's enthusiastic and exacting guidance, some of the most daunting and marvellous monuments of classical Greek literature (in the Greek originals, I must remind you, dear reader): Sophocles, Euripides, Xenophon, Plato, and the most formidable of all, Thucydides. Now, you have no idea what delayed gratification means unless and until you consecrated the prime time of your adolescence to the daily perusal and translation of a Thucydides sentence. After that formative fortification of the mind, to say nothing of mortification of the body, the labyrinths of postmodernist prose awaiting me in the distant future will, trust me, be lucidity incarnate.

The passion with which Mr. Denton conveyed the majesty of these texts, their ageless grandeur, still rings in my ears. That did not debar him from reminding me of the historical and political circumstances of these awesome texts, say, the famous funeral oration of Pericles in the second book of Thucydides' *History of the Peloponnesian War*, the prescribed prose text for the A Levels in 1960. Of the cant, self-glorification and claims of Athenian exceptionalism – claims destined to be echoed by future griots of empire – one utterance in Pericles' panegyric still rings true: "The secret of happiness is freedom and of freedom courage." Two decades before Edward Said, Mr. Denton would not gloss over questions of power and empire, of slavery and social evil, that occasioned these texts, questions that are echoed in the most sublime utterances they contain and will echo with undying regularity through times to come. Today's cultural fetishists and sentinels of Western Civilization could have learned a thing or two from Mr. Denton. They ask us to choose between reverence for the timeless splendour of cultural artefacts and a critical inspection of their historical occasion. They suppose that the sole alternative to the vulgar historicism of the radical sceptic is supine ancestor worship, an unthinking idolatry indistinguishable from cultural necrophilia. Mr. Denton, apartheid's child, *because* he was apartheid's child, it now seems to me, thought and taught otherwise, renounced the facile divisions of the mind and the world. With a conspiratorial twinkle in his gentle eyes he discerned in the interstices of these ancient texts and distant contexts the perennial human story of the ways of power, the fate of the despoiled and the possibility of social hope. Even as I learned to revere cultural monuments – including those of the people who ravaged Africa – Mr. Denton prepared me to appreciate later in life the wrenching truth of Walter Benjamin's famous words: "There is no document of civilization which is not at the same time a document of barbarism." Of the exalted "cultural treasures" we are educated to revere, that questioning and visionary Jew said that they have an origin that cannot be contemplated by the historical materialist without horror. It is an audacious intelligence that can hold the horror and the honour in precarious proximity. Such an intelligence Mr. Denton possessed.

Only one other imported cultural treasure came close to claiming the enthusiasm of Mr. Denton and, in this instance, Mrs. Denton as well. And that was cricket. It is impossible to convey the exhilaration with which Mr. and Mrs. Denton, especially Mrs. Denton, greeted the school's every victory at a cricket match, or the veritable gloom with which they enveloped us when we lost. The desiccated habit of emotional constipation practiced by the stiff-upper-lips and their Afro-Saxon mimes must have found these outbursts of unrestrained exuberance and lament by the Dentons too primitive, too Oriental, much too African. But we loved it. We sensed in it an unaffected manifestation of kinship. Classics and cricket: it seemed oddly fitting that these quintessential specimens of imperial culture were the things with which this alchemist of the soul would think to cultivate a sense of human solidarity.

I regret to say that I was no cricketer or any kind of sportsman for that matter. Oh, I did enjoy a fleeting episode of unheralded triumph in the 440 at intra-school track competitions. But that ended with an inglorious injury incurred at a meet in my second year. From that day I returned to my natural calling as a "waste pipe," the name bestowed by those blessed with a catholicity of talents upon those afflicted with a monomaniacal devotion to books: a calling that culminated in what I remember to this day as my finest hour – winning in Form Five the triple prize for Greek, Latin and French at the Speech and Prize Giving Day in November 1959. And so, alas, it was principally as a boy of the book that Mr. Denton knew me and transmitted to me the seductive splendour of borrowed cultural treasures, borrowed yet transformed in his curator's hands into shareable monuments of the human spirit. From what particular territory of human experience did Mr. Denton acquire this sense of place that transgresses place? It would be a few years before I would read Jean-Paul Sartre's controversial testimony in *Anti-Semite and Jew* regarding Jews as privileged protagonists of the universal, thanks, precisely, to the particularity thrust upon them. In my recollection, only once did Mr. Denton mention to me the fact of his being a Jew. It was the day after the staff performance of *The Merchant of Venice*, the drama in which the iniquitous lore of race is at once paraded and parodied. Mr. Denton had not attended the performance. I asked him why. He told me that he was a Jew.

Thanks to Mr. Denton's tutelage, I obtained distinctions in Greek and Latin in the Cambridge Higher School Leaving Certificate Examinations (the A-Levels) and got an admission to Harvard. Of course, he wrote one of the letters of recommendation for my application to that really illustrious institution. A year or so later I wrote to him from Harvard, reporting my growing embrace of a left political persuasion. That turn to a left understanding of the world was for me tantamount to anagnorisis, a word appropriately from Greek drama describing, as Ernst Bloch insisted, the shock of a startling world-disclosing and indeed life-transforming event, akin to what Sartre called "radical conversion." It came with a certain retroactive self-chastisement and a deep embarrassment regarding my past, the things I had learned not to see. The result was a profound reordering of my priorities. That took a self-inflicted toll on my studies. For the first time in my life, obtaining the highest grades was not a major preoccupation. I succumbed to the neophyte's cult of "relevance," considering that an infinitely more significant measure of a meaningful life than academic excellence. I did not excel at Harvard. I doubt that Mr. Denton would have approved of that outcome or endorsed it as the necessary price to pay for being rudely awakened from my lingering ignorance of the vortex of the world, a slumber that not even the intimations of political understanding stirred by his Aesopian reading of the classics with me had completely disturbed. All the same, in his reply to my letter, Mr. Denton signalled his approval of my turn to the left, but, all too familiar with the persecution of insurgent political commitments in his native South Africa, cautioned me to be careful about things I said in my letters.

Since those decisive years, I came to see the Jew as special friend in a world brimfull of black people's tormentors, more than that, as privileged witness of the possibility of human goodness. Henceforth, it seemed perfectly logical to me that Jews would be first among harbingers of the news that another world is ours to imagine and bring into being. That belief would survive the ascendance of a repugnant virus of black anti-Semitism (it exists, brothers and sisters, it exists, a repugnant virus cultivated by cretins for the perverse solace of the wretched, the identification of opposition to Israeli apartheid and the Boycott, Divestment and Sanctions movement with anti-Semitism being an entirely ignoble conflation). From that abiding conviction born of a formative bond recollected in gratitude to this: the unholy procession of David Horowitz; AIPEC; Stephen Miller, the iniquitous Donald Trump's insensate counsellor in the business of ridding the nation of impure breeds bleating at the gates; the insufferably arrogant Jared Kushner hectoring Palestinians, in the imperious accents of a bad headmaster, to renounce the irrational intransigence evidently lodged in their ethnic character, which repeatedly leads them to reject the kindest offer thrown at them, telling them to behave incongruously well for once and assent to their irreversible capitulation to the consequences of conquest. And the peerless gem of all, the phenomenon of Benjamin Netanyahu, his soul steadfastly steeled against irony, a Jew presiding over the formal design of a racist polity, eternally returning to power after every seemingly fatal discomfiture to finish the job with the help of allies even more guileless in their hateful views and cruel intentions. To say nothing of Netanyahu's worthy immediate successor, Naftali Bennett, racist without apologies, he of the priceless zinger, "I've killed many Arabs in my life and there's no problem with that." Consider the tell-tale designation, the collective indiscriminate branding of the enemy: "Arabs." It would be wicked enough if Bennett's sadistic pleasure were directed at a determinate populace, say, the Palestinian people, putative object of his animus; that would be a kind of macabre precision. But no, it is directed at a genus, "Arabs." What is the name we normally give to the execution of murderous hatred not of a specific individual or even a particular national community but a human (?) genus?

Is there no choice then, as these idolaters of force suppose, other than abject meekness or vengeful might, the erstwhile victim's first love of supremacy without restraint "when it disjoins remorse from power"? Is heartless egotism the sole alternative to suicidal compassion? It is painful, unspeakably painful, to hear their words and witness their deeds. It is as if they have sworn to transmogrify into something unrecognizable the character of a people Edward Said memorably called the "most morally complex people," a people made beautiful precisely by that especial complexity, confounding thereby the prejudice that equates beauty with simplicity, the untroubled elegance of the simple. Is that transmogrification – an ugly word befitting an ugly piece of work – the legacy this generation of hard right Jews, claiming to speak and act in the name of all Jews, want to bequeath to posterity? If we should meet someday in the land of the ancestors, Mr. Denton, how will I ever begin to convey to you this searing spectacle of those who with casual impudence spit on the prophetic injunction to repair the world, *tikhun olam*? The words with which Aeneas begins to tell Dido the story of Troy's calamity come to mind: "*Infandum, regina, iubes renovare dolorem*; unspeakable woe, oh queen, you bid me rehearse." Uttered in another place and time, Aeneas' gut-wrenching words, words I pored over with Mr. Denton's guidance over six decades ago, evoke the human encounter with catastrophe of shocking magnitude. Of the terrible things of this world and these times which, rather than enraging me, fill me with sorrow, profound sorrow, the sight of the rightwing Jew is the most unbearable to behold. Mr. Denton is the beginning of the reason why. If hindsight serves me right, I dare say that it is to his tutelage that my education in the tragic vicissitudes of all things of beauty owes what one of our pathfinders calls its "seed time."

But it just so happens that there are other human marvels of our time towards whom my sentiments are not riddled with such benign equivocation.

AYAAN HIRSHI ALI

She worked the Islamophobic halls of the Netherlands with, shall we say, indifferent results. So off she went to Washington DC. Why squander precious time and effort in a subordinate region of the West when New Rome's citadel beckons alluringly with the ultimate prize? The marriage of the imperial neo-cons and the vassal black convert. It is a consummation devoutly to be relished. There at the American Enterprise Institute – that celebrated house of care for the wretched of the earth – Ayaan would refurbish her tried and tested wares with limitless resources, hawk them to a nation made astonishingly credulous and incurious by its terminal narcissism, undergo beatification as a beleaguered truth-teller, appropriately tie the knot with principal hymnist of white supremacy's accomplishments and zealous griot of empire, and prosper. She would renounce Islamism for the idolatry of the West with soul and body. That is not, as she fancies herself to be, the way of the heretic. That is the method of the shrewd trader on the creedal stock exchange.

V.S. NAIPAUL, A BELATED NOTICE

Peerless craftsman of words and worlds. Also vulgar racist. Vulgar, reprehensible anti-African, anti-black racist. Blessed with a masterful pen thanks to which the vulgar is transfigured into the extraordinary, conventional calumnies turned – so say the eulogists – into truthful albeit rueful pictures of the human condition in its savage aspect. I am asked to adore the radiant art and to ignore the rancid racism. Hell no. The art is the thing. I cannot manage that wondrous separation of the faculties that would allow me to savour, with Naipaul kinsman and praise-singer Neil Bissondath, "the finest chocolates" contained in Sir Vidia's well-wrought urn while the overpowering stench of his racism assails my nostrils. No doubt, this is because I am one of those "infies," all smell and no judgment, whom Sir ("I cannot do a tribal dance") Vidia scorned and loathed with such Aryan intensity.

FAREED ZAKARIA

No doubt. he fancies himself to be middle-of-the-road in political persuasion, unencumbered by the silly duty to "take sides" in the wrangles of the day, his sole mission being "to explain what I think is happening on the ground," that is to say, from the enlightened salons of New York. But he is no radical neutral of the type Dante consigns to the most disagreeable quarters in hell. He did not hesitate to take sides in his formative years at Yale, joining the Party of the Right and opposing the anti-apartheid disinvestment movement. And he supported the invasion of Iraq before he became a critic not indeed of the occupation in principle, but of how it was conducted: disappointed with the means, unrepelled by the ends. He calls his weekly CNN programme "The Global Public Sphere" (GPS). *Global.* You can't tell that from the issues and topics he features on his show, to say nothing of the cast of characters who appear on it. Those topics are relentlessly Western-centric. The principal members appearing with insufferable regularity are: Zanny Minton Beddoes, Anne Applebaum, Richard Hass, Niall Ferguson, Thomas Friedman, Bernard Henri-Lévy, Anne-Marie Slaughter – not exactly a cast of characters committed to the necessity of a radical transformation in the order of things. And they are almost always an all-white cast, relentlessly all-white. Has Fareed Zakaria ever heard of Cornel West? Of any Black thinker, analyst, cultural and political figure, particularly a seditious one? Do African thinkers, women and men, exist? Should the rare black character be permitted to intrude upon this proscenium of whiteness, she is rigorously typecast, her dramatic role pre-set, confined to a designated performance. Not to join in a conversation concerning the world economy and international affairs, the "threat" of China or the shenanigans of Putin "the killer," or some shared national preoccupations, still less some shared predicaments confronting the human condition today. Heavens no. Obedient to the rules of pure epistemic apartheid, that black recruit is there to fulfil one and only one purpose: to serve as native informer regarding race matters in America, more specifically, the present state and prehistory of race matters. So it is that in a 2021 Fourth of July episode devoted to the "State of America," Zakaria predictably hauls in black Harvard Professor of History and Law, Annette Gordon-Reed, to take care of the black history business of the American enterprise. Black scholars, thinkers and analysts evidently can't jump intellectually beyond race matters, more precisely, beyond black things. *Et tu* Fareed?

Is Professor Gordon-Reed destined to be a visiting *black* star in your show, her allotted role ordained by a pre-existing script? Does she have to be?

DINESH D'SOUZA

Like Fareed Zakaria, Dinesh D'Souza came to the United States from India. But he is utterly and proudly devoid of Zakaria's unctuous civility and skewed neutrality. America has been mighty good to him. In gratitude for what America has done for him and fidelity to what he can do for America, he has acquired high competence in the most American of American sports, *the* quintessential American sport, antiBlack racism. His opening starring jersey came in the form of a criticism of the "culture of dependency" in which black Americans are allegedly mired. Presently, he will drop the coded language, take off the culturalist veil, get right into the rancid gutter and spew unadulterated racist bile and undisguised contempt for Obama, his African antecedents and the dreadful political history that allegedly birthed him and infected him with the congenital hatred of white people. Perverse self-loathing, it must be, since a cruel fate contrived to give him a white mother. Well done, Dinesh, well done.

COLOURS OF ANTI-BLACK RACISM

But the reprehensible D'Souza is no anomaly. He is but the metastasis of a diseased norm. What, after all, is anti-black-racism? Is it not the required rite of passage into that perfect union which is the United States of America and other locations of the racial polity of the world? This is the undeniable truth of Frank Wilderson's dismal Afropessimist report (America being for Wilderson no more and no less than a special instantiation of a global "political ontology"). Such is the psychopathology of belonging in the racial polity in its world-historical formations. Particularly in the United States. Anti-black-racism is the certificate of incorporation even for non-white immigrants, particularly non-white immigrants. Especially for Asian immigrants, the open secret of their coveted status as "model immigrants," to say nothing of the offspring of those immigrants. All this, of course, before Covid-19 was named the "Chinese virus," brought guilt by imputed genealogical association upon the heads of all Asian Americans, tarred them with the same demonizing brush, whether they were of South Asian or Chinese origin, and in the process insinuated a certain discordant note into the hybrid Orientalism – part admiring, part resentful – of yesterday's ethnocultural classifications in American public culture. But don't tell me it is purely principled commitment to political doctrine that makes Nikki Haley (née Rimrata Randhawa) such a strident American nationalist, spurs her hard-line stance on immigration, fires her perfervid Zionism and visceral contempt for the very idea that Palestinian lives matter, inspires her bad headmistress hectoring of United Nations representatives from the Global South who would not vote as America dictates, letting them know that their votes would be remembered, and threatening them with withdrawal of American "aid" for being insufferably uppity. You have to be hopelessly ignorant of the genealogy of morals and political attachments in the USA, if you think all this is due to pure albeit over-zealous conviction. You must know nothing about the half-hidden drive behind the passionate intensity oozing from the eyes of characters like Randhawa-Haley – this urge to perform symbolic acts of "passing" through disavowal of kinship with black people and other peoples of colour, their needs and their cries. But the Haley syndrome is not the weirdest of the forms which the psychopathology of belonging in the racial polity assumes. Now, this one is bizarre, really bizarre, laughable if it was not so perverse: For us immigrants from the African continent also, anti-black-racism is the mandatory rite of passage, anti-black-racism in the special subspecies of contempt for African Americans (aka "our brothers and sisters"), contempt dictated by acceptance of white supremacy's taxonomic lore and the dogged effort to be exempted from that lore. I have heard this said more than once: "I'd rather my daughter married a white man than one of those black Americans." So you see, we immigrants of colour, all of us, are super-spreaders of this contagious malady that is anti-black-racism in all its prodigal and virulent mutations. African immigrants are no exception. And here is why. I mean, how do you prove, beyond all reasonable doubt, that there is nothing different about you, nothing different according to the American law of being, except by proving how radically different you are from those whose abjection is the primal and continual foundation of that national law of being? And who better to show that race does not matter than other people of colour? Who better to demonstrate irrefutably that to attain the American dream all you need, as John Locke famously put it, is the labour of your body and the work of your hands, and that the only losers are those who fail to live by this creed? If you can find some men and women who happen to be black or persons of colour but who can testify, by virtue of their accomplishments, to this self-evident truth, so much the better. Such is the dramatic role assigned to black demigods in a society defined by the damnation of black people. Amazing individual exceptions to the general rule of black ineptitude, they join those Asian high-achievers – high achievers, this time by collective right, we all know – as walking verifications of the principle that dogged unaided effort will always trump history's alleged impediments. It is not progenies of history as such who are doomed to fail. It is only prisoners of historical determinism as a living creed, or rather a life-enervating belief, who keep invoking the perpetual afterlife of slavery and racial apartheid as disabling facts of existence for black people in the United States of America. Thus it is that Asian model immigrants, exceptional black Americans and regular African newcomers, through studied strategies of disidentification, serve as earnest enablers of white supremacy, at once accomplices and beneficiaries of racism's collectivist logic and contrastive schemes. In the multiracial societies of the Global North, such disavowals of filiation with blackness and invidious attestations of difference in the service of white supremacy are normative.

ANTIBLACK RACISM'S KALEIDOSCOPE

The consequences of white supremacy for the ways members of communities of colour see themselves and one another in the process of forging their civic and moral status are indeed bizarre, even tragicomic. They are evident in the psychopathology of belonging and identification that drives antiblack racism and fuels undercurrents of reciprocal antipathy between these communities in the multiracial societies of the Global North – particularly Britain and the United States – and in South Africa. There, that psychopathology is complicated by apartheid's system of societal stratification, one that places Asians in the middle rung of social power and blacks at the bottom. Asian antiblack racism is the toxic fruit of this societal ordering. So is black anti-Asian racism. Interracial violence in Durban in 1949 and in Phoenix during the so-called "food riots" in 2021 are iconic dates in the metastasis of the twin pathogens, the one engendered by a social ordering obedient to white supremacy's hierarchic taxonomy of human kinds, the other fuelled by the ressentiment of those placed at the bottom of that scheme.

What then – counting the strange things of our time – about the curious phenomenon of transatlantic formations of antiblackness among people of colour in, say, "multiracial" Britain? The story of Kwasi Kwarteng, the supremely accomplished son of Ghanaian immigrants to the United Kingdom who chose service to the dual powers of white supremacy and capital, became Britain's Chancellor of the Exchequer in the summer of 2022, rolled out policies pleasing, he was certain, to the gods, and in the end was ignominiously sacrificed and sacked, is an instructive story. It is a case study in the complex epidemiology of antiblackness, its peculiar and peculiarly aggressive variant as a self-consuming and internecine malady, and the devastating consequences when it is conjoined with class ambition and animus propelled by the desire to live in accordance with the laws of white supremacy. It is a story that warrants a special look.

X

KWARTENG'S TALE

PROLOGUE

It is tempting to echo a line from a poem by Derek Walcott, as though it accurately captures the saga of Kwasi Kwarteng: "Deciduous beauty prospered and is gone." Alas, Walcott's elegiac idea of the decay that awaits every thing of beauty in its due time is not quite a fitting description of Kwarteng's story. It can hardly be said of his public life that it flourished in its appointed season and withered, inexorably, in the fulness of time. One day we watch him "bestride the narrow world like a colossus," son of immigrants from Africa of all places, berating members of the "mother of parliaments" concerning the fatal misdirection of the nation's affairs in recent times and prescribing hard and bitter remedies necessary for its regeneration – to the delight of an authoritative voice of the right, *The Telegraph*, utterly mesmerized by the substance and form of Kwarteng's speech with its "stunning neo-Reaganite peroration." The symbolism alone is priceless, a reversal of roles of epic proportions pertaining to the standard protagonists of historical action in the world built by empire: offspring of Britannia's former wards recast as the censorious and civilizing master. Kwasi was equal to the occasion. It was his finest hour. Next day, lo and behold, he is unceremoniously deposed, his momentous appearance on the stage of British history over, his grand design in ruins. Such an abrupt change of fortune requires a considered response, one a little more edifying than what we were offered by interested commentators in the land from which our ill-fated hero's parents hailed, Ghana. To a prominent member of the local cabal of Thatcherite soulmates, Gabby Otchere-Darko –

patrician by artifice, reputed to be the sitting president's "brain' and later day Rasputin – Kwarteng was the undeserving scapegoat for the repudiation of an ideologically correct economic policy, scapegoat, however, who is destined to rise again, Phoenix-like, and ascend to the highest office in the very near future. Years earlier, Otchere-Darko wept when Margaret Thatcher died, extolling that wicked enemy of working people and their supportive unions as the embodiment of an endangered tradition, the tradition of unyielding conviction now in mortal combat with the tepid politics of compromise. Appropriately, he was joined in his grief by kinsman, fellow Thatcher admirer and future president Nana Akufo-Addo. Once more, our dynastic clan of homegrown Thatcherite-Reaganite zealots evidently assembled at the family hearth when Kwarteng crashed, for them, no doubt, the fate of a "misunderstood genius," as the Economist, no flaming left-wing paper, wryly quipped. And Finance minister Ken Ofori-Ata, yet another kinsman and scion of the hybrid tradition of market fundamentalism and ethno-nepotism, would lament, in his insufferable choirboy solemnity, the cruel sacking of Kwasi the "Ghanaian" truth-teller. All too predictably, this god-intoxicated, abysmally failed manager of our nation's earthly treasure, would console Kwarteng by imploring him to see in his travails the beneficent workings of a divine plan. But not everyone was prepared to leave it all up to providential design as an explanation for Kwasi's misfortune. According to the race-reductionist school of conspiracy theory, it was nefarious white racists who set him up for catastrophe. Others in the parental homeland, seeking vicarious glory in the accomplishments of the offspring of a native son in the colonial master's land, kept it simple, really simple. I am speaking of those who see themselves, other people, and everything in human affairs through the lens of the "tribe" to which you belong. From the beginning what mattered to these people, what made them exceedingly proud of this eminent descendant is not the fact, or better, the lived experience, of his blackness, still less the content of his character and the principles he holds dear. What mattered is the "tribe" from which his blessed parents hailed. Since the father is Akyem and the mother Asante, which of these two "tribes" can legitimately claim him as their very own, ancestral source of his virtues, his genius and his feats? This is the gripping debate staged in the Ghanaian media the moment the phenomenon of Kwasi Kwarteng burst upon a nation needy for infantile distractions. And when the precipitous fall came, the same deep dispute regarding tribal genealogy persisted, albeit in less celebratory accents. What is accountable for the fallen star's errors, the errors that became the reason or the pretext for his fall? His Akyem genes or his Asante bloodline? Tribe. This is the language, the language of racist colonialist ethnology and classification of "the natives," in which we explain the provenance of the good and the bad, apportion praise and blame in human affairs, nearly seven decades after we allegedly gained independence and mastery of how we appraise human things. In the end, there is little to choose between the race reductionism that drives the "wicked-white-people" conspiracy theory, or the admixture of shared Thatcherite dogma and Christian theodicy that motivates Otchere-Darko's and Ofori-Ata's faith in Kwarteng's ordained destiny, or the primitive tribalism of those beating the drums of atavistic attachments in behalf of every cause and everything under the sun. But are the only possible responses to the dénouement of the Kwarteng saga tears or jeers, the saccharine elegy of the naïve or the callous schadenfreude of race-firsters thrilled by the spectacle of the traitorous brother's ass comprehensively fucked? Surely, another way of responding to the rise and fall, the feats and foibles, of significant figures of the new African diaspora is possible – if that very name "diaspora," diaspora in the twenty-first century, makes any sense at all. A first step towards that necessary reappraisal is to take a clinical look at what motivates the politics of the company to which the Kwasi Kwartengs of contemporary history belong, the company of hard right black ideologues adorning today's political landscape. I have in mind a sketch of what Fanon might have called a psycho-existential "sociogeny" of their political outlook and ideological commitments, the inner strivings, needs and impulses from which they spring, the subterranean roots of this curious phenomenon of black rightwing political formations in our time. What follows, then, is a contribution to an answer to the question posed by Yuri Prasad in *Socialist Worker* (15 July, 2022) as he considered the presence of so many black and Asian candidates in the 2022 British Conservative Party leadership contest: "What's behind the rise of black reactionaries?" If the answer suggested here sounds rather "idealist" to a Marxist ear, let us just say that it is intended to supplement rather than replace an integral materialist interpretation, one that attends to things in the territory of the spirit. A materialism that does not attend to that territory is an incomplete materialism. For is it not here that our responses to the dictates and depredations of social power find expression in so many common and rival impulses towards acquiescence and collaboration, refusal and resistance? I am referring to identifiable forms of that fraught combination of reactions to the material and moral conditions of existence whose historically Black American archetypes W.E.B. DuBois evoked in the celebrated opening essay of *The Souls of Black Folk*, "Of Our Spiritual Strivings." I will sketch a picture of the ways in which for black elites – the class from which Prasad's "reactionary blacks" hail – that existential predicament and the "strivings" which define it are marked by a specific gravity.

LOGIC OF A WORLD

If it is true that white supremacy is a global order, it is also evident that its characteristic consequences – psycho-existential and socio-political, ideological and discursive – are registered in their most acute forms in those societies whose defining feature is the presence of multiracial communities. Products of slavery, empire, settler colonialism, indentured labour and emigration at the behest of necessity, it is in these societies that members of the constituent communities form perceptions of themselves and one another, but also forge plans and prospects of life, in accordance with the hierarchic taxonomy – "the great chain of being" – that is white supremacy's presupposition and invention, its major premise and arranged inference. In this scheme black people are everywhere at the bottom, their plans and prospects of life accordingly constrained by that position. As such they are, as Afropessimists tell us, the designated species by reference to which members of all the constituent communities – including black people! – take a measure of their being, define themselves by negation, that is to say, show and tell who and what they are *not*, entertain plans and prospects of life in relation to that contrastive scheme. This is the social metaphysics – the perverse logic of a perverse world – which, to various degrees of conscious awareness or tacit knowledge, conditions the conduct of representative actors from these communities and in so many subtle ways govern their political outlook and practice. The politics of our far right brothers and sisters is no exception: it is a consequence of one among the ways in which each and every one of these communities, as a whole and as groups, classes and individuals within them, respond to the material and moral conditions of their existence in light of the hopes and fears spawned by the social metaphysics just adumbrated.

In these multiracial societies, then, black life is the negative criterion in contradistinction to which humanness is appraised and awarded. Blackness signifies all that a deserving claimant to authentic humanness and so to membership in the moral community should not be, should disavow and renounce, or at the very least, repress. For the black person in these societies to dare to be such a claimant in defiance of the formal prohibition, is thus to subject life to an essentially contradictory ethics of aspiration, one that at once demands that you slay the blackness in you and at the same time, precisely because it is race-based and bound by its foundational determinism, fully expects you to fail in doing so. No individual exceptions are in principle permitted, no exculpatory evidence of uniqueness is allowed to tamper with racism's defining law. All the same our invincible humanness being the way it is, we will not acquiesce to this prohibition without resistance of one kind or the other, in the service of this end or the other. Whoever perversely insists on such an affirmation of individuality in the teeth of racist culture's constitutive collectivism, its "nothing-personal" way of perception, will do so with a certain aggressiveness: such is the neurosis that is peculiar to moral life in an antiblack racist culture and vitiates the ordinary human enterprise of individuation. That aggressiveness is particularly intrinsic to the conduct of the black elite, the class whose members possess the desire and the resources to stake a credible claim to individuality. Alas, it is also the class whose members characteristically direct this will to individuality, this salutary refusal of racism's repressive collectivism, into a ferocious egoism. If the claimant to distinctiveness happens to be in reality or in his own eyes blessed with extraordinary abilities and moral resources, then there is an added edge to that aggressiveness. He will let it be known in no uncertain terms that he is by miles the smartest person in the room, the very best the culture can produce, superior to those who, damn it, claim a natural right to recognition of excellence as a white privilege. And that surplus aggressiveness will be directed not only at the inveterate white racist ever ready to spit on our hero's vaunted uniqueness and send him back to the herd from which he so badly wishes to dissociate himself. It will be visited, with far more grievous consequences, on everyday black people whom our exceptional black holds in withering contempt and cringes at the very thought of ever being confused with any specimen of the sorry lot. Our exceptional black is perforce a monstrous narcissist. Inordinately enamoured of himself and the feats he has accomplished, needless to say, by his unaided efforts, he is mercilessly censorious and cruel towards the generality of black people for failing to rise above their lot, thanks to their dissolute ways and a thousand turpitudes they inherited from shiftless forebears and will pass on to their children and their children's children; in a word, for condemning themselves to a wretched life of their own making. This way, the exceptional black aids and abets antiblack racism with the spurious solicitude of "tough love." Such is the psychopathology of excellence which afflicts a great number of members of the black elite in racist culture. And such, in the hypertrophic form exhibited by the Kwasi Kwartengs of the world, is the destructive hubris demanded of themselves and the internecine damage it wreaks upon the communities with which they are, willy-nilly, associated.

How do these psycho-existential conditions define, and are defined by, relations with other subordinate communities, in particular, communities of colour, each of them crafting ingenuous ways – often injurious to the welfare of another such community – of breaching the walls white supremacy built; all of them caught, as collective entities and as classes and individuals within them, in a strange struggle for recognition, a vicious rankings rivalry, one that consists in a competition for a superior place in the hierarchic order of being which is white supremacy's gift to the metaphysics of the social world? What in particular would it mean for the black elite, the class in the racial polity who embody a condensation of the psycho-existential conflict it instigates, what would it mean for the elite to carry symptoms of that inner turmoil into the public realm? More specifically, what would be the consequences should a fortunate few among this elite bring the strife of the spirit at the core of their being into public life, and – Lord have mercy – into the corridors of power? We have reason to fear that from those heights they will unleash upon an unsuspecting citizenry, particularly the most vulnerable among them, decisions, plans and policies emanating not from the voice of prudence, not even from the cold sobriety of rational interests dear to the ethics of political economy, but rather from the compulsive urge to prove the negative, to show and tell who you are not, what species of sentient beings with what depraved habits and wasteful needs you do not belong to, in fine, what you dread ever being mistaken for: black. Black, of course, in the debased way produced by the depredations of racist culture, the only way of being black known to the destroyers and the defeated. Of the idea that another way of being black is possible, our exceptional black, bent on self-exemption from the general damnation, in a desperate flight from a terrible curse, is wilfully ignorant. I mean the idea of being black neither as decreed by white supremacy's lore, nor as dictated by the primitive solidarity of skin, but rather being black in virtue of a willed and insurgent kinship with all those who, as the bard, Césaire, enjoined, know the darkest corners of the "geography of suffering" and are sworn to work in the service of hope that tomorrow there will be a clearing. Kwarteng's saga is an allegory of a trained refusal to hear the call to this other way of existence in black.

A METEOR'S CONSTELLATION

In the public realm, a meteor owes its singular radiance to the constellation out of which it bursts, the company of sociohistorical forms and forces that are at once the constraining and enabling condition of its appearance. So it is with Kwarteng's story, the astonishing ascension and the spectacular fall, product of a shared constellation of motive forces which shape historical existence.

It is the summer of 2022, and the contest to replace Boris the Boor as leader of the British Conservative Party and so as Prime Minister comes down to three candidates. One of the three, Rishi Sunak, offers a robust response to the charge that he is a man of enormous wealth and privilege hopelessly out of touch with the agonies of everyday people. Flaunting that opulence and privilege without apology, Sunak proffered as his unimpeachable credentials and fitness for the office his personal history as a child of hardworking immigrants of Indian origins from Kenya, parents from whom he acquired the habit of self-reliance and unaided striving (not for them, needless to add, parasitic dependence on the public-purse- devouring dole). What do you think the clever Sunak was up to with this edifying recollection of his moral education? Who do you suppose he had in mind and wanted the good (white) people of UK to remember as the less deserving sort of immigrants, those inured to habits not readily consonant with the austere norms of the national culture? This is subtle antiblackness, the antiblackness of silent dissociation and implied contrast in the service of proofs of authentic Britishness. And then there is Priti Patel, another child of immigrants from East Africa, also of South Asian origin. Patel has no time whatsoever for decorous subtlety. She prefers to proclaim with guileless belligerence her Britishness unmodified, uncontaminated by hyphenated designations, particularly those alluding to lands of origin and ethnicities without honour. Performing the requisite rites of conspicuous antiblackness in the form of self-definition by assertive negation (I am *not* in any shape or manner one of those people), she blasts post-George Floyd Black Lives Matter demonstrations as "dreadful." And she dismisses the accompanying symbolism of solidarity, the practice by athletes of "taking the knee," as an inconsequential "gesture politics." Not for her such kneejerk expressions of kinship with other people of colour, least of all black people and their plight, for the simple reason that she is not, and must not be seen to be, one of them. More profoundly, she is citizen Patel blessed with what political philosopher Michael Sandel used to call the "unencumbered self," unencumbered, that is, with any ethno-racial attachments save pure Britishness. Such is her perverse version of existential freedom. As Home Secretary, she had to be hard on "illegal" migrants, signing on to the callous policy of sending asylum seekers to a third country, Rwanda, in contravention of international law. But for sheer ferocity of venom and contempt for mere mortals, Suella Braverman, yet another child of immigrants from Kenya with Indian ancestry, has no equal. Holy warrior against a diabolical enemy called "cultural Marxism," she admits to harbouring a "dream" and an "obsession" with sending cross-Channel migrants and asylum seekers also to Rwanda. Why this intense antipathy towards these wretches? Is it because you are sworn to exorcizing all disconcerting reminders of who and what you desperately wish not to be or be seen to be, the moral status that would surely be yours but for the grace of the gods? Is that the secret fear that drives the cruelty of the reprehensible Patels and Bravermans of this inverted world?

But the offspring of East African immigrants of South Asian origin – no doubt scarred by searing memories of Idi Amin the brute transformed into the generic African and sufficient reason for the temptation of undifferentiated antipathy – are by no means alone in representing transatlantic formations of serviceable antiblackness, be it oblique and covert or undisguised and aggressive. The epidemiology of antiblackness is a strange and complex thing. South Asian immigrants and their offspring do not own the patent for dog-whistle antiblackness as a constant companion of right-wing politics. Thanks to a perverse logic, that caste of miscreants includes some seemingly unusual suspects, black people, black people labouring under some variant of the Patel syndrome: living with the anxiogenic possibility of mistaken identification, the dread of being seen as kinsman of the blacks, if not indeed one of them, that unthinkable disaster of misrecognition. And what can be a more credible demonstration that you are no part of that species of failed humanity – a people in perpetual need of public succour, a collective drain on national resources – what can be a firmer proof of being anything but black, even if visibly sporting a black skin, than embracing the hardest of hard right politics mated with the economics of malevolent neglect and a disciplinary morality of bootstraps self-reliance, exactly what black people are notoriously allergic to? Think of that: life lived in the grip of such a reputation, a reputation congealed in social consciousness prior to the appearance of any concrete individual member of an entire human(?) population, an ascriptive essence that, in cruel mockery of Sartre, precedes existence. What will it take to contradict such a reputation so that life, intercepted by that reputation, can go on or rather can begin again? To stake a claim to exemption from that tyrannizing perception requires salvation by works and by faith, demonstrable commitment to the articles of the dominant ideology with a ferocity far exceeding what is expected of regular believers, that is to say, believers blessed with the effortless credibility of whiteness. No wonder, then, that the extreme hard-right faction of the British Conservative Party, that band of neoliberalism's looniest votaries, features accomplished descendants of black African immigrants. They lead the pack of zealots keen on eviscerating the state, demanding deregulation, axing taxes for the wealthy the better to foster "growth," and jettisoning "inflationary" social support programs. That black people are, of course, known to be principal beneficiaries of these programs – their women being "welfare queens" according to the iconography of Reagan's America – is a defining and sufficient reason for their demonization and rejection on the part of those haunted by the anxiety of blackness, consumed by the desire to prove how unblack they are, thanks to the capacities and virtues they have valiantly acquired and arduously cultivated. This is the murky provenance of the sadistic solipsistic individualism which informs consequential choices regarding vital matters of public policy. This is the stuff our black protagonists of the hard right cause are made of, the genealogy of the cruel ethics of political economy they will let loose upon society and, above all, wield as a shaming cudgel against everyday black people.

In this circle of the new moral overseers embodying a toxic fusion of libertarian fundamentalism and the antiblackness of disaffiliation is to be found the strident Kemi Badenoch, daughter of Nigerian immigrants, and the inimitable Kwasi Kwarteng, chief prosecutor, among the bill of indictable wrongs, of those "inflationary" social programmes inspired by a misguided redistributionist ideology inimical to "growth" and intended for the illicit comfort of all those swarming parasites of the world. But Kwarteng's intellectual and socio-political outlook is nothing if not a comprehensive body of interconnected parts. Concurring with Priti Patel on the inconsequence of symbolic gestures, the patrician Kwarteng would not deign to "take the knee" in memory of George Floyd and other victims of racist violence, preferring, as is his wont, to do things productive of tangible results. He would presumably count among those fine and tangible things his role as designated messenger of the news that Great Britain is not a racist country, notwithstanding the fate of the Windrush Generation, people from the Caribbean brought to Britain to work in her hour of need – a time of labour shortages in the post-war years – but deemed unworthy of the gift of citizenship. In the same spirit of depreciating "white guilt" is Kwarteng's less than fervent antipathy towards Britain's imperial past. He is on record as being a "nuanced" historian of empire and colonialism, unlike those misguided demonologists of the white man's burden, those Marxists and followers of the Black radical tradition such as Black Lives Matter. Today it must be a white soul of extraordinary and perverse fortitude who will speak in praise of the good deeds of empire and colonialism without blushing. With the testimony of a white panegyrist of empire such as Niall Ferguson discredited from the start, pronounced unreliable by filiation, who is better placed than a black scholar of African origin, enlightened kinsman or rather distant relative of *les damnés de la terre*, to set the record straight, rectify the "cartoon-like view" and unthinking moral absolutism of vulgar anti-imperialists, and stake a decent *via media* between glorification and imprecation, between Kipling and Fanon? To be sure, Kwarteng's admiration for the execution of the imperial project is not unmixed. He criticizes the "anarchic individualism" that allegedly drove the conduct and actions of a great many colonial administrators. This may seem odd: a denunciation of "individualism" by a follower of "there-is-no-such-thing-as-society" Margaret Thatcher, a true believer who elsewhere states the defining creed of today's British conservatives: "We believe in markets, we believe in individual responsibility, we believe in the ingenuity of individuals to come up with ideas that can transform society." These two stances seem incongruous until you notice the point of Kwarteng's criticism of "individualism." What he laments is not Lockean individualism, the kind of individualism born of the idea of self-ownership and eminently conducive to the moral psychology and ethics of market society. Rather, it is the unbridled egocentrism that leads the new colonial administrator on the ground to think to dismantle the work of predecessors and to commence everything *ex nihilo*. The result was the pursuit of goals unmoored from any directive authority. That form of individualism, Kwarteng thinks, was detrimental to the needed structure, cohesiveness and continuity of the imperial enterprise. In a word, it sabotaged the efficacy of the work of empire. Kwarteng's criticism of the imperial enterprise, then, is not a criticism of the fundamental wrongness of its ends. Rather, it is a consequentialist judgment, a criticism of deleterious outcomes resulting from the methods, procedures and characteristic styles of administrators. That is what makes Kwarteng's a "nuanced" assessment of empire, one purged equally of anger and adulation, *sine ira et studio*, as Kwarteng, the first-class Cambridge classicist might recite from his Tacitus. In support of this well-tempered view of empire and colonialism, he invokes the attitude of Africans who express fond nostalgia for the good old colonial days. A rather skewed verdict derived from an unrepresentative polling, one that mistakes for the judgment of the people as whole the opinions of imperialism's local collaborators, beneficiaries and co-religionists, those for whom the ending of colonial rule was always going to be a political and spiritual catastrophe; but also, let it be said, the sentiment of those, with or without historical memory, for whom the postcolonial condition is not so much a tragedy but rather a farce, utterly undeserving even of mournful albeit redeeming remembrance of oaths traduced and promises not kept. Such voices of nostalgia for the white man provoked by disenchantment with independence – sometimes tinged with a certain defeatist Africa-pessimism and hints of radical antiblackness – do indeed exist. All the same, victims of torture at the hands of British forces in Kenya during the "Emergency" might have a historical memory somewhat different from Kwarteng's purveyors of nostalgia for the glory that was Pax Britannia. Let's just say that Kwarteng's "nuanced" verdict on empire is part of the arsenal he deploys for the burden of proving his non-compliance with normative blackness, with intellectual and political positions predicated of the fact of blackness.

For being so admirably devoid of animus concerning the history of the present, so sensible, bright and right, passionately committed to the depreciation of white guilt in race matters and Thatcherism in political economy, Kwarteng was duly rewarded with the august office of Chancellor of the Exchequer in the new Prime Minister Liz Truss's government. Convention would predictably confer on him the degraded accolade that passes for meritocratic recognition in a white supremacist world and call him the first black this and the first black that. Convention would thereby conflate the trivial fact of Kwarteng's skin colour with ethical filiation with what Fanon called "the lived experience of the Black," to say nothing of an insurgent kinship with that lived experience. Before jumping for joy in a kneejerk celebration of the accomplishments of a black man, we ought to have seen the innards of his thought and his convictions. If we should find fault with a Kwasi Kwarteng, we should do so not because he is not "Black enough," and not because he espouses beliefs and causes a black person or public figure is not supposed to espouse. To that charge Kwarteng has a countersuit ready-made for us: the charge of identity politics. That is the accusation levelled by those who own and take for granted the dominant forms of identity, and represent them as being natural, devoid of invidious presuppositions, generous in their civic and cultural geography, in no way exclusionary. That of course is bullshit. But yes, we should spurn Kwarteng's politics and policies not because they depart from some norm, scripted by the tyrannical identity politics politburo, of what a black political figure or public intellectual must espouse. That is Kwarteng's preferred interpretation of the hostility of "the left" towards people like him. We must steadfastly avoid offering him and others like him any quarter for that subterfuge by staying clear of the slightest whiff of race-reductionism in our brief against what he stands for. We should spurn his politics and policies for the simple reason that they are repugnant and sadistic, absolutely detrimental to the health of human beings, irrespective of the race of the person who upholds or prescribes them. That is necessary and sufficient reason for detesting the Kwasi Kwartengs of our time. That is enough justification for refraining from beating the people's drums of jubilation the higher they rise or singing the ancestors' songs of lamentation the harder they fall.

THE FALL

20 September, 2022. A future biographer of Kwasi Kwarteng may recall that date as the beginning of the end, the moment when omens presaging his fall appeared. It is the final day of ten days of majestic solemnity, the day of the funeral service for Elizabeth ER at Westminster Abbey. Naturally, among the assembled potentates is the new Chancellor of the Exchequer, Kwasi Kwarteng. A cruel television camera catches him committing an act of supreme impiety: speaking on the phone, shuffling in his seat and laughing while the civilized world wept. The picture is greeted with horror, outrage and disdain. Only a bastard Brit could inflict such savage ignominy upon the last rite of mourning the beloved monarch. Among the many searing reactions on social media is a tweet calling this native pearl of His Majesty's newly-minted government "Ghanaian." For Kwarteng, that must have been "the most unkindest cut of all." A kind voice from the parental homeland put it all down to the African tradition of mingling profound grief with exuberant celebration of the life of the departed, a tradition presumably engraved on Kwarteng's cultural unconscious and vying with his manifest

dream of a self entirely fashioned in England, cleansed free of every trace of barbaric alien ancestry. Instinctively prompted by that repressed but returning cultural memory, this generous voice wants to plead, Kwasi faithfully joined in the sustained sombre rites of reverence for nine days and on the tenth day, to echo the famous lyricist of Negritude, he laughed the great Black laugh. Whether it is meant as damning evidence or as exculpatory plea, what each of the two reactions implies is this: at his finest hour, a life devoted to disencumbering the self of eccentric attachments, particularly racial identity – "Pay no attention to my black skin, the sun did it" – that life is now rudely reminded of the very kinships it worked so sedulously to disavow. Here is an analogy, with a difference: It did not escape notice at the time that upon returning to Canada in disgrace in the aftermath of the doping scandal at the 1988 Seoul Olympics, Ben Johnson went from being Canadian to Jamaican-Canadian to Jamaican to simply black. Unlike Kwarteng the pure Briton, Ben Johnson was not known in his days of glory for endeavouring to make his ancestral origins inconsequential and to keep his blackness a closely guarded secret, or rather a thing hidden in plain sight. The question was whether Kwarteng, after all his strenuous and rewarding efforts, would suffer the same fate, undergo symbolic ostracism in the form of rude reminders of his savage ancestry and indelible blackness every time he committed a gaffe no truly true blood would ever commit, or, heavens forbid, if he ever made a major mistake in public policy.

The answer to that question – would Kwasi's status undergo serial demotion from Brit unhyphenated to black unmodified? – came more quickly than the most cynical observer imagined. From the moment he presented his disastrous 23 September "mini-budget" inspired by hard right dogma, references to his ancestry and blackness multiplied. And it got worse. An article in the *Mirror* reporting Kwarteng's defence of his budget to the effect that "he had to do something different" used the picture of a different man, a different black man. An innocent case of mistaken identity or, as some outraged readers suspected, the outcome, be it calculated or inadvertent, of the old racist culture of perception according to which all black people look alike. All that dogged labour of demonstrating your distinctiveness, of being different (with regard to normative blackness) and of doing something different (with regard to received economic thought and policy), all that labour, it seems, had come to naught. Kwarteng's protest to the newspaper "That's not me" was entirely in order. However, the protest is significant in complex ways, not all of them deserving of our unmixed sympathy and support. Beyond the specific instance of the image in the *Mirror* and Kwarteng's reaction, "That's not me," is in principle more than a case of correcting mistaken identity. In the simplest yet profoundest sense, it is a protest against racism's totalitarian collectivism, its defining habit, in Fanon's words, of "putting all blacks in the same bag." In the hands of Kwarteng and members of his caste, however, this is by no means an inclusive and egalitarian affirmation of the human principle of individuality, the benign paradox of one person affirming individuality in behalf of each and every member of a group. Rather, it is one man's solitary assertion of his singularity, his right to exemption from the collective curse that white supremacy inflicts on everyone born black. It is difficult to see how we can, in the name of antiracist individualism, give unalloyed support for such solipsistic and invidious exceptionalism. As for Kwarteng demonstrating his distinctiveness by doing "something different" with regard to economic policy, he did so alright: by proposing measures taken straight out of the canonical textbook of so-called trickle-down economics, different only in that they represented the most extreme form of that species of economic doctrine and practice. That the Honourable Kwarteng was seen attending a champagne reception with hedge fund managers – potential beneficiaries of his plutocrats-friendly budget – shortly after he delivered it, was hardly a brilliant demonstration of radical difference in the ethics of political economy, or for that matter, of mundane prudence. As it turned out, Kwarteng would jettison the most egregiously odious part of the budget, the part which awarded outrageous tax cuts to the wealthiest of the land, after uproar from the public, turbulence in "the markets," and harsh criticism even from members of the Conservative establishment. That would be followed in short order by his inglorious sacking, the appointment of a new chancellor and the comprehensive scrapping of the proposals Kwarteng had crafted with the imprimatur of the prime minister – and in no time at all the resignation of Liz Truss herself as prime minister.

But the Kwasi Kwartengs of our time are an object lesson in the genealogy of the politics and political convictions of black elites in epicentres of the racial polity, a lesson that may temper our enthusiasm for every instance of black eminence. Desperate for vicarious glory, we rush to cheer black icons in public affairs. We succumb to this adolescent lure of seeing ourselves in those at the apex of power. But could it be that this place of power is the stage on which is enacted a veritable inner strife with damaging consequences. Here the Kwartengs of a system of racial hierarchy live out the fraught impulses and drives of their being: pride and anxiety. Pride in their accredited excellence, anxiety of authenticity that constrains them to be constantly and obsessively exhibiting their credentials, their loyalty to the rules and beliefs of the ruling caste. And they must do so by outdoing scions of the establishment in the inerrancy of conviction and intensity of commitment to requisite action. The result is ironic. In the sacred name of individuality, they furiously object to the presumption that, because they are black, they must conduct themselves the same way, espouse the same political positions, more specifically, positions on the left, more reductively still, that they should be preoccupied with race matters or predominantly, if not exclusively, with race matters. No one, Kwasi Kwarteng protests, expects all Chinese to hold the same views. Is it not the hallmark of racism, antiblack racism in particular, to expect such herd unanimity from black public figures, a perverse application of the "they all look alike" rule to the sphere of political belief? Who among us will object to that objection? Who indeed? Except that there is a near monotonous unanimity to the positions and stances our rightwing black folk do espouse. To a person they rail against the "welfare state," and for motives I have suggested. To a person they deny that their country is foundationally racist or that the social condition of black people has anything to do with racism, with one of them, the bellicose Kemi Badenoch, going so far as demanding legal action against anyone who teaches such pernicious ideas – the associated idea of "white privilege" among them – in schools. To a person they detest Critical Race Theory, a hopelessly caricatured version of it, with a venom worthy of the most retrograde of US Republicans. To a person they detest Black Lives Matter with equal passion. To a person, they supported Brexit in the name of a cherished national sovereignty endangered by intrusive restrictions and regulations from a "social Europe" and its unelected bureaucrats. To a person they, children of immigrants, take the hardest line on immigration, with one of their leading lights, the acerbic Suella Braverman owning up to having a "dream," an "obsession" with sending "illegal" migrants off to Rwanda, a country with a regime not known for being a friend of human rights, a dream duly fulfilled when soulmate Priti Patel came to hold the office of Home Secretary. We have to ask: To what peculiar species of the animal kingdom must a person belong so that for such a person the expulsion of desperate asylum seekers from British shores is a paramount matter of public policy, more than that, to echo Hamlet, "it is a consummation devoutly to be wished"? What inner demons must be baying at her, goading her to embrace such a perfectly wicked design on pain of being or appearing to be insufficiently committed to keeping Britain pure? Needless to say, perfervid market fundamentalism is the shared foundational creed of all members of this family. Altogether, they are without exception under some inner duress to outright the white right, outbid everyone in the fervour of their patriotism and fidelity to the national culture. There is little distinguishing these apostles of individual distinctiveness in matters of overarching doctrine or public policy. So much for the right to be different in the name of which they lambast the "left" for their alleged expectation that all black political figures will espouse the same causes. It turns out that our black right political figures and other rightwing people of colour do share practically identical positions on a whole range of issues, just not the positions the left endorse. That is not surprising, given the shared impulses which drive the politics of our representative protagonists.

From these shared impulses emanate not only the unvarying substance of the positions figures of the black right hold, but also the especial certitude and heedless fanaticism with which they promulgate vital public policies. After the fiasco of the mini-budget, a Conservative colleague would say of Kwarteng that "he doesn't tend to change ideology...Kwasi is a zealot." In tacit agreement with the view of American social activist Rashad Robinson according to which "budgets are moral documents," Scotland's First Minister Nicola Sturgeon described the mini-budget as "a morally abhorrent disaster." Presently, Jeremy Hunt, Kwarteng's successor and designated cleaning-gentleman in the wake of a fortnight of wilful wreckage, would dare to say what our apostle of "growth" would not dream of saying: "It was wrong to cut the top rate of tax for the very highest earners at a time where we're going to have to be asking for sacrifices from everyone to get through a very difficult period." This was in sharp contrast to Kwarteng's unrepentant assertion that his and Truss' "vision" was unimpeachable, the only problem being the haste with which it was unfurled and the manner in which it was communicated. Heeding prodding voices from the inner recesses of a mind possessed, Kwarteng is a walking refutation of the myth that "ideology" is the preferred prison-house of the left whereas those on the right are impelled by conviction tempered with common sense – just as Americans fervently devoted to their nation are patriots and others similarly disposed toward their country are nationalists.

Consider in this regard the 2012 programmatic document *Britannia Unchained* co-authored by Kwarteng and fellow members of the hard right club, the "Free Enterprise Group," Truss, Patel, Rabb and Skidmore. Here is a notorious, oft-cited passage: "The British are among the worst idlers in the world. We work among the lowest hours (sic), we retire early and our productivity is low." Among the chains to be cast off Britannia's incapacitated body and the national economy are "excessive protections" offered to workers. As one commentator observed, this view would appear to support "fire at will" laws in parts of the US, and the crushing of the hard-won rights of working people, what neoliberal newspeak calls "reforms" and "liberalizing labour markets," in short, a return to the golden age of life without these rights. Kwarteng and Co's slanderous strictures on working people are in fact the recognizable products of pure and patented neoliberal dogma. Pure because uncontaminated by any actual knowledge (or is it calculated ignorance?) of the actual habits and conditions of the working class. And patented because they are the standard criticisms wherever and whenever neoliberalism encounters established or new restrictions and regulations instituted to place the most minimal restraints on the rule of capital. For corroboration I pick at random the heading of a *Wall Street Journal* article of 7 December, 2006: "Indonesia chained by labour law." The writer is referring to Indonesia's 2003 labour law enacted in the aftermath of massive loss of jobs by Indonesian workers during the Asian financial crisis of the time, a law which "require[d] that dismissed workers receive up to seven years in severance pay." You only have to notice the affinities between the language of the *Wall Street Journal* article and that of Kwarteng and Co's case against "excessive protections" granted idling British workers to conclude that there is nothing peculiarly British about the defects ascribed to British workers or the allegedly deleterious protections they are said to enjoy. According to the Orwellian inversion of meaning uniting the language of the Wall Street Journal article and that of Kwarteng and his co-authors, a little slackening of the masters' grip on the workers' necks is tantamount to the imposition of chains; freedom must mean the uncontested perpetuation or restoration of that grip. The regime of US antebellum slave labour and its refinements under the rubric of "reforms," from Reconstruction to the age of neoliberalism, must be accounted the paradigm of liberty.

But if Kwarteng and company speak the common language of neoliberal anti-worker slander, that language also reeks of all too familiar racist tropes which depict black people as indolent and shiftless welfare bums and queens, a collective drain on the public purse. It is easy to discern elective affinities between racist tropes justifying slashing social benefits and disparaging representations of working people's habits to justify opposition to rights-friendly laws and the relocation of factories to "alternative production sites" where the tyrannical freedom of the owners still reigns. There is mutual discursive transference between the condemnation of black peoples' utter lack of the virtues and tendentious pictures of workers' habits and their responsibility for the low level of productivity in the national economy. Listening to these interchangeable strictures, it would seem that in the imagination of people on the extreme right, workers are the black people of class society. Character assassination of working people and antiblack racist mythology are thus defining elements of the dominant social consciousness and worldview. For the caste of right wing blacks in particular, this worldview is grist for the ideological mill they will forge and bring to the public sphere. That perceptual language is the pernicious baggage they will carry with them, and the reason, to repeat, is this: By virtue of our very existence, black people are a priori profiled, prime suspects as enemies of all that a healthy material and moral economy must embody and protect. Labouring under this collective suspicion, all who aspire to pursue the normal human task of individuation, to say nothing of excellence, must do so in an abnormal way: They are driven by this compulsive need to live life as a daily routine of self-definition by negation, to show and tell who and what they are *not*, forever called upon to enact their exceptionalism – a fretful, Sisyphean struggle for the recognition of distinctiveness. Race disavowal, making manifest the fact of your non-blackness, is the rite they must of necessity perform if they are to succeed. Class is the thing with which our self-created patricians think to defeat the arranged fatalism of race in their own eyes and in the judgment of white people. In their psyche, then, an urgent need for race disavowal interacts with an overwrought class consciousness as complementary pathogens to produce a poisonous effect: a triumphalist and invidious claim of hard work, unaided striving and merited privilege; a censorious and punitive stance towards everyday black people, shaming and blaming them and their vices, not some accumulated "white wrongs," for their wretched conditions of existence, They thus invest in the power and paraphernalia of class – self-presentation, speech, profession of ideological faith – with the same ferocity and absolutism with which they enact their disavowal of race, and to the degree that they do. This is the morbid source of the insensate class narcissism that makes Kwasi Kwarteng go partying with opulent potentates of the City minutes after delivering his atrocious budget and while people went distraught over astronomical increases in their mortgages triggered by that budget. This is what drives him to declare in haughty accents that "there is more to come," more drastic slashing of taxes in behalf of the wealthy at the very moment when the less well-off screamed foul with the unfurling of the first round of cuts; and even as the very putative allies called the "markets," demurred with audible "turbulence." Beyond punitive economic policy, this toxic admixture of race renunciation and class animus is the root of other bizarre but complementary stances, say, the hyperbolic nationalism that makes Kemi Badenoch, another grateful black product of empire, such a vociferous hymnist of Britannia's exceptionalism, infinitely more concerned with the conservation of "our British values" than the survival of Black Lives.

Presently, Kwarteng would undergo a swift transformation from extraordinary genius to an idiot savant in unthinking thrall to dogma, one so extreme as to invite the revulsion of the very people whose recognition, beneath all that bluster and puffery, he so devoutly craved. But such manic extremism is more than a purely personal idiosyncrasy. The Conservatives pat themselves as a party for being second to none in the number of members of racial minorities they have elevated to the highest offices. They may be less inclined to gloat if they knew what they were getting, if they understood what in particular motivates these admirable black gems and the phenomenon they represent: a caste for whom public life is the continuation of psycho-existential strife by other means and social and political power a resource to be harnessed in the service of impelling needs and impulses of the spirit engendered by history. The dubious gift they bring to party and nation akike is a fanaticism bred of the fatal interaction of twin pathogens: race disavowal and class animus gone utterly berserk. Ultimately, it is the plebeians of society who pay most dearly for the consequences of the subterranean drama at the heart of this reactionary politics. In the life of the postimperial multiracial polity, the caste of rightwing blacks may very well be the most toxic presence of all. That is why a deep analysis of their desires and deeds is necessary. The slightest empathy for their foolishness is otherwise impossible to justify. So is a hearty cheer for the fate of one hapless figure among them. It is certainly difficult to extend to him the conciliatory generosity of Walcott's poetic voice: "All in compassion ends."

But if in that spirit of unblinkered understanding, you are inclined to further probe with sardonic eyes the tortuous strife raging in the souls of our rightwing black folk, you may be tempted to entertain the following thought, a pure phantasm of the dramaturgical imagination: Can it be that this race abjuring and class fixated man contrived to be made a principal minister in His Majesty's government in order to preside over the disarray of the economic life of the realm? Was that always the subconscious design of this black man who seemed so reluctant to be a black man? In retrospect, was his irreverent behaviour at the Queen's funeral a delayed manifestation of a long smouldering rage and self-chastisement, an inner revulsion with the artifice of pure Britishness he wore with such consummate dexterity, and a belated premonition of far more consequential acts of reactive vengeance to come? Wouldn't that be the most bitter of bitter ironies, or the cruellest form of poetic justice? It is a thought too devilish to harbour and too compelling to dismiss.

EPILOGUE

Against the foregoing exercise in what-if speculation stands an immovable fact: Kwarteng fell and with him fell Liz Truss and her government and all the sturdiest warriors on the extreme right phalanx of the British Conservative party. In the aftermath, Rishi Sunak, another "man of colour," accomplished child of East African immigrants of Indian origin, would become prime minister. Like Kwasi, Sunak had long elected to dwell in the masters' house, but with discernibly less obsequious pride and abject enthusiasm. And Sunak would keep Jeremy Hunt as chancellor, a man no less faithful in ideology but considerably less impetuous in its application than his predecessor. His class standing made impregnable by the grace of whiteness, in absolutely no danger of ever being mistaken for a tribune of the damned of the earth, Hunt is able to temper fidelity to ideology –

"commitment to principle" in polite language – with a prudence born of what Machiavelli called the "effectual truth of the matter." Kwarteng was not so blessed, or rather, by choice and habit he denied himself that chastening ability. Labouring, like others of his caste, under an existential insecurity of his own making, he exuded an unbridled zeal fuelled by the need to answer the embarrassment of race with the weapon of class made all the more relentless by dogma. He was thereby led to unleash upon a populace living in dire times the most heartless policies crafted in recent memory, exceeding in their severity the conservative tradition of social cruelty with a human face adorned with the livery of noblesse oblige. For those of his class and party unencumbered with the anxieties gnawing at Kwarteng and people of his caste, the excess was too much. And so, Hunt and Sunak promptly set about comprehensively dismantling Kwasi's vaunted salvific proposals, and in the process consigned his public life to precocious anonymity. The upshot is that in the rankings rivalry on the ladder of being fought among subject races for the narcissistic pleasure and power of white supremacy, in that veritable cockfight, some in South Asian communities would declare victory, to the chagrin of misguided Africans desperate for vicarious glory, particularly the kente nationalists of Ghana, more precisely, Asante and Akyem fetishists of the tribe. It is the sweet victory of the elite of one subject people over the elite of another subject people in one local corner of this inverted world. But white supremacy endures. So does capital's dominion and the class in whose behalf it works. They must fall and fall together or they won't fall at all. What will it take to hasten that day?

XI

PEEVES AND DREAMS, AT LARGE

AFTER 9/11:
SOPHISTIC ANALYTICS, TREACHEROUS TAXONOMIES

We suppose ourselves to possess unqualified scientific knowledge of a thing, as opposed to knowing it in the accidental way in which the sophist knows, when we think that we know the cause on which the fact depends, as the cause of that fact and of no other, and, further, that the fact could not be other than it is.
—Aristotle, *Posterior Analytics*

Let us now savour specimens of global public wisdom after 9/11.

The news that a suspect in the 7 July, 2005 London tube terrorist bombing was a recent Leeds University PhD graduate in biochemistry caused some astonishment. How did that jive with Samuel Huntington's morbid diagnosis, the "clash of civilizations" account of this season of disorder? If it is true that such a person hates "our" values, "our" culture and modernity itself, as official wisdom and its epigones would have it, then biochemistry must be an occult lore, some bizarre Oriental ritual.

Likewise Hamdi Issac, a suspect in the failed 21 July sequel. An article by a certain Colin Freeze in the *Toronto Globe and Mail*, 2 August, 2005, had this to say:

> Hamdi Issac's lawyer has said that the July 21 attacks, in which her client is accused of taking

part, were a response to the U.S. war in Iraq and Britain's participation in it. One irony is that Hamdi Issac is said to have been in love with the West in the early 1990s. "He was obsessed with America. It was his dream. The music, Hip-hop," an Italian ex-girlfriend of his told the Italian newspaper La Republica. "He dressed rapper-style. Trousers with dropped crotch and a basketball vest. He drank alcohol: beer. He danced really well."

The "irony" is entirely the product of an imprisoning Orientalist imagination, one buttressed by a refusal to take seriously the political and, dare I say, the human, all-too-human, reasons for violence. The "irony" comes from this calculated blindness to the secular sources of sacred fury. As if only a lifelong residence in some infernal *madrassa* or else a radical conversion from the satanic and sybaritic lures of the decadent West would spawn the anger and the urge to commit terrorist violence. As if there is no reason on earth to be mightily pissed off with the barbaric treatment of the Palestinian people, the illicit annexation of their lands, the unending incineration of their homes, the craven and disgraceful acquiescence of the chieftains of the Arab world, the criminal silence of the peoples and leaders of the "international community."

ECCENTRIC AFFINITIES, AMORPHOUS ANTIPATHIES

I could not abide Churchill. I used to admire De Gaulle, secretly, so much so that in graduate school I wrote two papers on him, one on the animating principles of his foreign policy, the other on the conceptual resonances of his political thought. Read the text of a Charles De Gaulle pronouncement at a press conference, a once in a year laconic and limpid statement of national purpose in world affairs occasioned by a specific event or crisis. And then listen to a recent specimen of the American variety in all its vulgar and vacuous garrulity. You have before you a vivid measure of the decline of the West, its precipitous decline. Encountering the literary monument that is his *War Memoirs* did little to diminish my forbidden admiration for the General. That work – forgive me for invoking it a second time in these observations – famously opens with an utterance of universal appeal, a cheeky evocation of a political community's essence not as present fact but as magnificent possibility, one that abides despite its people's recurring failure to live up to it: "All my life I have had a certain *idea* of France... Instinctively I have the feeling that Providence created her either for complete successes or for exemplary misfortunes. If, in spite of this, mediocrity shows in her acts and deeds, it strikes me as an absurd anomaly, to be imputed to the faults of Frenchmen, not to the genius of the land." Upon reading those words I asked myself wistfully: Why can't we Africans apprehend Africa and the African condition that way, that is to say, not as this fallen fact, this execrable existing reality, but, according to Fanon's visionary challenge, as "*this Africa to come*," an imagined possibility, and summon the audacity conjured by that imagination to cultivate our native promise? De Gaulle's rhetoric of ideality, not the substance of his creed, not the specific myth of France which would seduce even the young Fanon to his chagrin, cajole him into fighting for the liberty of the racist republic, that rhetoric – with its stubborn, impertinent, even tragic irrealism – that seemed to me to be a shareable goad in a way Churchill's done-this-done-that celebratory Anglo-Saxonism could never be. Antithetical attitudes to two emblematic figures of empire and iconic agents Africa's woes.

★★★

I adore Marley and Mozart, Johann Sebastian and Nina Simone, Papa Wembe and Papa Haydn. I am not overly enamoured of rap, except when it comes with a sweet intermittent song. I detest country music and that species of indecipherable cacophony known as hard rock. Aretha's rendition of *A Change is Gonna Come* (with all due respect for Sam Cooke's original) and the second movement of the *Emperor* equally move me to joyful tears. It was thanks to our shared delight listening to an unbearably beautiful phrase in that second movement that Kofi Ansah and I bonded and became instant friends one afternoon at Saltpong, long before I knew anything about his views on religion and politics – they turned out to be, as they say, progressive. Kofi often jokes that awaiting the oceanic majesty that is the second movement, he finds the first a little too long. I know the feeling, my brother, I know the feeling. Yes, my soul serenades with Wolfgang Amadeus. But for that mystic tremor of the whole being and haunting promise of repose, Ludwig is incomparable. So I thank my stars that I came to relearn love of the variegated forms of the beautiful. For there was a time in my life – a mercifully brief period – when, in a pathetic aping of apartheid ways of loving and loathing human things, I refused to listen to European classical music. That, ladies and gentlemen, was my monumental contribution to the anti-imperialist cultural struggle. Hell, if Louis Farrakhan can shock detractors, gloriously confound accusations of anti-Semitism and hatred of white people, and perform Mendelson's and Beethoven's Concertos for Violin without the slightest twinge of embarrassment – oops, I almost said, without blushing – then everything is possible. "*Homo sum; humani a me nihil alienum puto*. I am human; I consider nothing human to be alien to me." That is Terence's aphorism dear to Marx and good enough for me. Still, why do I have to like that insufferable jingoist Elgar's *Enigma Variations*? Verily, verily, the ways of taste set free from wilful and fearful ignorance are utterly perverse, gloriously unruly. I must confess to unatonable aesthetic perfidies.

★★★

In defiance of the African norm sedimented in our lives for eons, I adhere neither to Christianity nor Islam. In my eyes they are twin supreme and supremacist superstitions, twin creeds of the invaders, creeds marshalled to justify our enslavement and to mollify its primal and persistent terrors. But they are not just Africa's bane. Everywhere they reign, they work to confiscate our human powers.

★★★

"To be radical," wrote Marx, "is to grasp things by the root." I am not religious, if by religion you mean trained obeisance to a despotic divinity of our own invention, one who like his terrestrial copies or rather authors, is by turns gratuitously benevolent and capriciously punitive. I am religious if you have in mind one possible meaning conjured by the root, *re-ligio*: the task of binding anew the ties undone by the divisions history has handed to us. The oath we swear to cultivate the earthly excellences of our being. Reverence for life and all living beings, but not in the sophistic manner dear to the misanthropic votaries of the "pro-life" heresy who respect single mothers less because they love motherhood more, condemn the bodies of the destitute to lifeless suffering the better to save their precious souls. Not if being religious means communion with Mike Pompeo who so loves (the idea of) the sanctity of life that he sends his precious gifts of boycotts, embargos and sanctions to the peoples of Iran and Venezuela, hellbent on exerting "maximum pressure," that is to say, sworn to condemn them to starvation, disease and death even in this cruel season of the plague, unless their nations' leaders do America's bidding. And not if religion comes with sharing a blessed bowl of fufu and groundnut soup or a sizzling dish of jollof rice (in lieu of breaking boring bread) with Jeff Sessions, that exemplary evangelical Christian whose idea of doctrinal inerrancy is to faithfully enforce the rule of yanking children of "illegal" migrants from their parents' bosoms and invoke Holy Scripture, Romans 13, in defence of that fine policy. Yes to "religion," if it means our solemn commitment to the concerted work of re-enchanting the human condition from the moment we recognize, with Bessie Head, that "the basic error is the relegation of all things holy to some unseen Being in the sky." In the spirit of that repatriation of the holy to earth and resistance to all that stands in the way, I can hear, with Hannah Arendt, the shareable significance of the news of Jesus as augury of new beginnings: the profound meaning she invited us to see in the Augustinian maxim: "*initium ergo ut esset, creatus est homo,*" "that s/he may be a beginning was the human being created;" the birthing of the extraordinary in the ordinary seasons of human time, the embryonic holiness of all newly born, and the call to make our existence live up to that promissory essence by dint of our self-originating acts. Likewise, the resurrection, that kindred image of the possibility of starting anew, not as a discrete and singular event but as the recurring miracle of human action, as the practice Walter Mignolo calls "re-existence." *Re-existence*. What a perfect word for what is to be done, exact name for the exacting work at hand. Can there possibly be a more fitting description of what is at stake in the enterprise of revivifying a land, Africa, which Goran Therborn calls "a continent of sorrow," a more apposite name for "this Africa to come"? Pity that, despite such shareable affinities in intimations of radical hope latent in her thinking, we must curse the discerning Arendt as a detestable anti-black-African-racist, excluding as she did Africans and the African condition from the common predicaments and prospects of the human condition. But I will not cancel her work. How on earth shall we ever know what is pernicious in her teaching if we do not read her work? Baffling.

★★★

As the foregoing confessional report shows, such is the admixture of eccentric affinities and amorphous antipathies that defines my life. So, into which procrustean bed are you going to force my body and contort my spirit? Where on the apartheid map you insist on fitting and arranging humanity's protean forms, unruly desires, aberrant allegiances, prodigal varieties of shared attachments, where on earth are you going to place me? "*Où me situer? Ou, si vous préférez: où me fourrer?*" Thus exclaimed Frantz Fanon with some exasperation, as he proclaimed his refusal of all tyrannizing enclosures. You may say Fanon was a dreamer, but he was not and would not be the only one.

So let us listen to the "final prayer" of the young doctor of the soul. By all means let us heed Frantz Fanon's call to keep our hearts and minds open to whatever enriches the human condition. But venerating life-mangling ogres of our troubled times? Naming the vital organs of our society after them? I doubt that even Frantz the Magnanimous meant to invite such indiscriminate generosity into the capacious space he encouraged us to grant our moral consciousness. You know what I am saying? The following observation will hopefully clarify what I mean.

ON FIRST SEEING GEORGE WALKER BUSH HIGHWAY IN ACCRA: A REPORT ON NAUSEA

I knew it existed. I knew because I had read about it and been told by credible witnesses that it existed, although I had yet to see it. If enigma, as I say elsewhere, names things seen but unknown, nausea – to slightly stretch Sartre – is the sensation provoked by encounter with the terrible being of something known by hearsay but hitherto unseen; something you wished and hoped against hope did not exist, and is now seen for the first time in all its awful, excruciatingly painful but undeniable, reality. So it was upon first seeing George Walker Bush Highway in Accra with my very own eyes, *mara me enyiwa kaagani*, as the expression for radical what-you-see-is-what-you-get empiricism in one Ghanaian idiom has it. Now there it was: a major artery of our national capital's life named after the architect of the empire's most demonic deeds in recent history, the one who laid bare America's heart of darkness with unrestrained terror and thuggish swaggering pride. "George Bush Highway in Africa! I'll be damned," the moronic George might have said with that infuriating snicker of his. The war criminal sanctified. The one who thought Katrina was Third World stuff, a quintessential African calamity, a chieftain abysmally ignorant of the depths of destitution existing within the borders of his country, a pathetic object of derision in his own land, honoured, what am I saying, beatified – where else? – in penurious and mendicant Africa. All the clichés, their perverse versions, are apposite here: the prophet scorned and unheeded in his own land, his true worth condemned to be discovered elsewhere. What's one more instance of the lucky reversal of fame and fortune, of words and meanings, a reversal that has been the hallmark of this character's life? It is fitting, is it not, that it is right here in Africa, wretched Africa, that he would trade places and reputations?

Was it not George Walker Bush who presided over the most profound renaming of things in the moral landscape, a radical transvaluation of values in ways that would have made Nietzsche envious and livid with a sense of underachievement? Under Bush's watch in the aftermath of 9/11, a revolution in ethics as we know it became mandatory public policy. It went something like this: I say that the American slaughter of Iraqis was as reprehensible as atrocities committed by suicide bombers and the like. I say that Saddam Hussein's gassing of Kurds in 1988 was no more ghastly than Americans' unleashing "agent orange" on Vietnam, Cambodia and Laos from 1961 to 1971. I say with Malcolm X that "wrong is wrong no matter who does it or says it." I say that ethnic chauvinism in my homeland shares a pernicious logic and unsavoury consequences with white supremacy and anti-black racism in the United States. I say with Frantz Fanon, against Octavo Manonni, that "all forms of exploitation are identical because all of them are applied against the same 'object': the human being." I say with Socrates against Polemarchus that "in no case is it just to harm anyone." In no case. You would think that I am a spirit companion of the most recalcitrant moral universalist who ever walked one corner of this bitter earth. A *left* universalist, yes, but indubitably a universalist. But not according to the revolution in ethics proclaimed into being, together with "regime change," by the new masters of the world and the word. No, I stand accused of asserting a "moral equivalence" between ghastly acts committed against human beings irrespective of the creedal auspices and political credentials of the regimes or groups or individuals that committed those acts. So I am guilty of "moral relativism," I who in defiance of the fashionable agnostics' creeds of our time entertain the possibility of rationally warranted common standards for judging human conduct. I am a moral relativist *because* I discern universals in ostensible particulars – in this instance, universals of the abominable kind, to be sure. I am a moral relativist because, rather than averring that to each our own in matters of good and evil, I say let us meet at a conversation of judgment in the hope that, given our kindred human needs, hopes and dreams, a shareable measure can be ours. In this new topsy-turvy world, Bush, Blair, Bennett and Bolton, the children of Thrasymachus – he whom Socrates subdued with withering reasoning – became the true friends of the ethical universal, in possession of "moral clarity." Why? Because they had the effrontery to call *their* case and *their* cause just and the power to enforce that verdict. Fuck me! "Fuck me pink," as dearest Derek Cohen loves to say with peerless Shakespearean eloquence (Derek can say and mean "pink;" *I* can't for obvious reasons; universalism, even in colourful expressions of moral outrage, has its material limits – you know what I'm saying?). But on first seeing George Walker Bush Highway in Accra, this repugnant exaltation of the empire's Luciferian prince into a satrapy's magnanimous benefactor and moral laureate, I thought of the inverted πworld of ethics that came into being under his reign. Fortunate the life and the times in which miracles such as this are possible. Weep, weep for the hapless homeland upon whose vital pathways such monstrous marvels are permitted to stand.

#MUST FALL: ETHICS WITH BORDERS (OF TIME)

George Bush is living memory, not some grotesque ogre of times past presumably exempt from today's exacting standards of critical judgment. It should not be a scandal, even here in comatose Ghana, to demand the immediate removal of his ignoble name from our highways. It shouldn't be, so fresh is the record of his gory mission accomplished compared to what is to done with figures of questionable virtue from the more distant past. The intensified demands in the aftermath of George Floyd's lynching that monuments honouring Cecil Rhodes, Robert F. Lee, Andrew Jackson, Leopold 11, Churchill, and all those iconic figures of the-great-white-man-theory-of-history must come down have been met with a sophistic, if predictable, response. Disingenuous sentinels of white supremacy, uncompromising enforcers of fraudulent ethical universalism and "moral clarity" only yesterday (or whenever it was convenient) now speak in the depraved accents of moral historicism. "There is no point in condemning or disqualifying what has happened through the lens of our time." Thus spoke King Willem-Alexander of the Netherlands in January 2022 on the occasion of retiring the horse-drawn golden royal carriage De Gouden Koets with its emblematic racist images of obsequious Africans and Asians adorning the vehicle's sides. Corollary of this tenet of "We can't judge things or figures of the past and their deeds by today's canons of right and wrong" is the practice of upbraiding someone for taking a stance that is "on the wrong side of history" or, alternatively, lauding someone for being "on the right side of history." Praise or blame, such is the "poverty of historicism," but perhaps not exactly what Karl Popper meant by that censure. What is the cut-off date for lawfully training the "lens of our time" upon things of the past? A more fundamental question regarding the genealogy of morals: When was it ever fine and fitting to enslave men and women and cut off their fingers for resisting torturous labour, the fate meted out to labourers in "King Leopold's Congo"? Did the victims ever think that was a faithful implementation of the labour contract, to say nothing of conformity with the most elementary idea of human requirements? Is taking another look at Andrew Jackson, Cecil Rhodes, Leopold 11 and Winston Churchill under the retroactive auspices of today's political morality an illicit anachronism? Hell no. I say: Let the stones and the rocks and the bulldozers proceed with the great demolition job in the name of unavenged ancestors, the dateless opprobrium of the world, and the immemorial idea of humanity. That is to say: not just the obscene monuments but the whole cowards' edifice of ethics with exculpatory borders of time must be demolished.

POSTSCRIPT:
FAMILY RESEMBLANCES IN METAETHICS

But was I ever gobsmacked – although I should not have been – to find that the plea not to judge things of the past "through the lens of our time," moral historicism as an exculpatory subterfuge, is not a white thing. It is by no means a device employed exclusively by descendants of Euro-American enslavers, colonialists and empire builders seeking absolution of their ancestors from sins which were not deemed to be sins in their time. It would be nice to think it is. Especially if you are a believer in the wondrous exceptionalism of the black soul and its superior way of judging things in the moral universe, calling bad things by their name irrespective of the time and place in which they occurred. Alas, that species of dodgy metaethics, it seems, is not a white thing. Contemplating the role of her great-grandfather, Nwaubani Ogogo as a slave trader in the nineteenth century, Nigerian writer Adaobi Tricia Nwaubani has this to say:

> It would be unfair to judge a 19th Century man by 21st Century principles. Assessing the people of Africa's past by today's standards would compel us to cast the majority of our heroes as villains, denying us the right to fully celebrate anyone who was not influenced by Western ideology. Igbo slave traders like my great-grandfather did not suffer any crisis of social acceptance or legality. They did not need any religious or scientific justification for their actions. They were simply living the life into which they were raised. That was all they knew.

As you can see, Adaobi Nwaubani compounds the trick of historicism with the parental sin of relativism – the implied claim that only people of the West and adherents to "Western ideology" would be opposed to the trade in human beings, a view, I suspect, not shared by those sentient beings who happened to have been enslaved. To hear Adaobi tell it, not only were her great-grandfather's actions consonant with the morality of his time and place; it is fitting that, far from being cast as a villain, he would rightly be honoured by posterity. When British anti-slavery authorities seized his slaves, he valiantly and successfully fought to get them back. That made him a revered figure in the pantheon of Igbo ethnic heroes, even a precocious anti-colonialist. Not unlike the case of Ghana's J.B. Danquah whose intrepid nationalism was inspired by his displeasure with the colonial administration's dogged and successful determination to bring to justice the "ritual" murderers of a royal from Danquah's region of Akyem Abuakwa: murderers whom Danquah vigorously defended in the name of protecting native customs from interference by foreign overlords. The nativist battle against white people and their rule of law lost, Danquah was instantly born again as a nationalist, to be canonized by his followers, flatterers and future propagandists as the "doyen of Ghanaian politics," indeed as one of the founders of the nation. From such marvellous motives spring the heroic work and reputation of many of our national demigods. That unseemly genealogy is reason enough to defenestrate the appeal to constraining historical conditions and prevailing forms of life to stop us from judging things of the past according to today's allegedly incommensurable principles.

COLLECTIVE GUILT, SELECTIVE APPLICATION

Since 9/11, from New York and London to Paris and Toronto and everywhere, "Muslim leaders" are being invited, rather hectored, to denounce terrorism and fundamentalism. (Just as "leaders of the black community" are regularly called upon to address and condemn "black" crimes, crimes, you understand, committed by individuals whose skin happens to be black.) And some of these "leaders" are anxious to oblige, ready to mouth all kinds of expiatory pieties. And how can they not, with the eyes of the "whole civilized world" censoriously fixed upon them? But nobody ever calls on "Christian leaders" to atone for crimes committed by individuals and groups who happen to be Christian. I will spare you a rehearsal of the millennial record. And let me be clear: I hold no special brief for Islamism. It's just the insufferable sophistry of it all, this selective application of the principle of collective guilt, that's what riles me. Otherwise I say, a plague on all your prison houses of organized faith.

ATO SEKYI-OTU

OF THE PASSIONS OF THE DEVOUT

Fame is no plant that grows on mortal soil,
Nor in the glistering foil
Set off to th' world, nor in broad rumour lies,
But lives and spreads aloft by those pure eyes
And perfect witness of all-judging Jove;
As he pronounces lastly on each deed,
Of so much fame in Heav'n expect thy meed.
    –John Milton, Lycidas (1637)

In the name of Allah they renounce body and earth, immolate themselves and slaughter others. Their fondest desire and anticipated reward in heaven? Seventy-two virgins. This is the hard-earned "mead" awaiting them. The cravings of the godless youth of this sinful world are arguably more restrained. Talk of deferred gratification as the promise of celestial bliss! Who says there is no life after death? But what is more odious, the overwrought but quite earthly passions of *some* hyper-devout young Muslim *men* cajoled into a perverse reading of the *Koran*? Or the orgiastic exultation of some fundamentalist Christians feeling mighty groovy at the enthralling prospect of sinners burning and writhing and shrieking – such is their religion of love – in the fires of hell? Eros and Thanatos indeed. Caveat: That some young Muslim men are goaded into violence by such passions and great expectations does not make all Muslim men, still less all Muslims, credulous murderers. Nor does the cruel thrill of some Christians aroused by the punishing fires of hell make all Christians pyromaniacs and misanthropic sadists. Contrary to the new Manicheanism preached in the aftermath of 9/11 by Pope Benedict, Richard Perle, David Fromm, Margaret Wente and Christopher Hitchens in his last years, evil is not faith specific. And neither is goodness. We should go further: neither is the product of adherence to faith, or abstention from it.

TREASON OF THE PUTATIVE LEFT

From descendants of the political movement that used to cry "Ban the bomb" came, after 9/11, the bellicose demand, "Ban the *Burka*" – a generic "mark of separation," according to the founding father of New Labour. Their contemporary ancestors were impelled to action by the real and demonstrable threat of shared annihilation and so by human solidarity. The new high-minded protestors, the cultural nationalists of the putative left, were driven by fear of human individuation. "Conform or don't come here" was Tony Blair's war cry. A vast improvement, you might say, upon the stance of yesterday's xenophobes of the extreme right who, dreading "rivers of blood," wanted the door entirely shut. But in effect old and new made common cause in a noxious traffic in fear and the demagogic desire for the enclosure of pure Britannia. What a shameful metamorphosis! Is this democracy? Yes it is, democracy of the totalitarian kind, "totalitarian democracy," the species so named by J.L. Talmon; the species of which the American republic is the quintessence; the species in danger of being cloned – this might have surprised Talmon – in other self-styled liberal democracies.

OTHER ETHNOCULTURAL CLEANSERS

Muslims in the West may be forgiven for feeling ensnared in the proverbial conundrum: you are damned if you do and you are damned if you don't. Wear the *burka* or other insignia of difference and you are criminally suspect. The enforcers of monoculturalism will order you to take it off or go back to where you came from. Whether they are shameless traitors to the official creed of democratic pluralism or primitive small-town xenophobes, they will issue their edict in the name of the necessity of common values. Holland demands proofs of adherence to Dutch life. The small Quebec town of Herouxville issues a declaration of *code de vie*, a catalogue of community values notable less for what the townsfolk cherish than what they forbid, among them, covering the face and stoning women, evidently a regular occurrence or threat on the streets of the town. This pernicious if risible specimen of primitive village communitarianism manifestly targeting Muslims got the sympathetic ear of a notorious Canadian caricaturist of multiculturalism, the Toronto *Globe and Mail*'s Margaret Wente. But let Muslims go native, so to speak, let them reveal that they laugh and cry and play just like other Canadians, just like other human beings, say, in a television sitcom such as the Canadian Broadcasting Corporation's *Little Mosque on the Prairie*. And the same Margaret the moron would find this eloquent testimony to the ordinary "way too cute." What? An imam without a menacing visage? Muslim women not enveped from head to foot in some funereal garment? Muslims speaking in comprehensible Canadian-English accents? Muslims evidently devoid of homicidal designs? Muslims with things on their minds other than suicidal jihad? In this topsy-turvy world, markers of distinctiveness offend because they are inscrutable; evidences of ordinariness disconcert because they wreck the presumption of radical separateness. Thus does a morbid fear of difference give birth to a perverse embrace of a stereotype of the different in a doomed desire to exorcise that very fear. Some years back, Lorraine Adams crafted a wonderful phrase for this phenomenon (*New York Times Book Review*, January 8, 2008). She called it the "burka effect," that "habit of mind" which sees occult and weird essences in the most ordinary *human* practices of the "other" – and demands their extirpation.

SOLIDARITY, REGARDLESS ...

Here I am, ready to defend Muslims, especially Muslims from the Arab world, against the violence of Western arms, primitive Islamophobia and the sophistic application of the principle of collective guilt. I do so in the knowledge that in recent memory Arabs were subjugating and slaughtering black Africans in Sudan. And in the land of born-again Pan-Africanist Moammar Gadhafi, black African migrants have been treated as pariahs. Presently, they will be paraded for sale at a slave labour auction. Anti-black-African racism is rife in the Arab world. And I have left off my miniaturized map of internal horrors of dehumanization, the plight of India's Dalits, a plight that makes classical apartheid look like a neighbourhood party, to say nothing of other scenes of exploitation and degradation. Criminal negligence, I confess. But you can take in only so much of this dispiriting procession of the world's odious ogres in one gulp. Hmm. At what point does the critical spirit in its uncompromising mission of divulging social evil thriving in every nook and cranny of this wretched world, but also descrying flickering glimmers of goodness on the horizon, at what point, I ask, does the critical spirit court the danger of oscillating between abject pessimism and groundless hope? What on earth is to be done? Keep hope a lie, I mean, alive albeit on desperate life support? Stay faithful to the work of solidarity in the teeth of contradictions, antagonistic or non-antagonistic contradictions – if I may disinter iconic words from yesterday's political lexicon – among and within the varied communities of subjugated humanity? I say hold tenaciously on to solidarity, not as a cushy sinecure but as a demanding task of willed kinship. Solidarity, then, with the branded and the degraded and the persecuted everywhere, regardless. Contrary to some American Afropessimists labouring under the thesis of black exceptionalism in the matter of suffering and pursuing that idea all the way down, the struggle of the Palestinian people is my struggle. How can it be otherwise?

VERBOTEN: *RERUM COGNOSCERE CAUSAS*

And it came to pass that in the early hours of the new millennium, a decree came from New Rome and its principal satrapies that the words from Virgil's *Georgics*, "*Felix, qui potuit rerum cognoscere causas.* [Happy, the one who was able to know the causes of things]," that paean to the work of reason was pronounced forbidden, anathema. After 9/11, to search for the "root causes" of the world's disorders, particularly acts of terror, was allegedly to endorse those very acts. You would think that the recurrence of these acts would make the question of causation all the more urgent. But after the London tube bombings, Tony Blair on behalf of "all those who stand in solidarity with the people of

Britain in the war on terrorism" repeated the *fatwa* against this evidently complicit and exculpatory inquiry into ultimate causes. On July 26, 2005 Tony Blair declared that to assert any causal link between the invasion of Iraq and the attacks in London was "an obscenity." In a disingenuous rhetorical move characteristic of this new interdiction on carnal knowledge of causation, Blair added: "there can be no justification for suicide bombs anywhere." Surely, the world expected from Her Majesty's Chief Minister something slightly better than this puerile Bushism – they do terror because terror is what they do – something a little more discerning than the old canard according to which to explain an act is to pardon it. Perhaps the world expected too much. You do not copulate with the mindless marauders who preside over the American Empire without being infected with their wilful ignorance. Still, it's a shame, isn't it? Virgil's line graces the emblem of the London School of Economics and Political Science, right there in Albion's capital.

But the earnest poodle was not alone. One year after he issued his America-compliant fatwa against causal knowledge, a band of empire-lighters, under the banner of the liberal democratic left, signatories to an egregiously vacuous document called the Euston Manifesto, joined the new inquisition and its interdiction against inquiring into root causes. In the vanguard of the grand inquisitors was Norman Geras, erstwhile comrade in the cause of left universalism as attested by essays of still unforgettable power, now transmogrified into a soulmate of that itinerant hustler, Michael Ignatieff (infamous apologist for American aggression under the banner of "The Lesser Evil"), parlaying a programme that could have come straight from the American Enterprise Institute. The useless manifesto. Useless because it had no distinguishable properties save those that are the common currency of the ruling powers and their all-purpose explanation of "terrorism" and their generic cure. How thoroughly and sadly Geras forgot the timeless wisdom of our erstwhile common pathfinder, Marx, who, respecting connectedness no less and no more than the specificities it gathers together, had this to say: "An explanation that does not give the *differentia specifica* is no explanation." The Euston

Manifesto exemplifies the tragic complicity of yesterday's comrades in the calculated refusal to know the specific causes of specific things and in the cruel farce of "liberal humanitarian interventionism" which results from that refusal.

CAUSE, CASE, CONNECTEDNESS

The work of the left universalist is only half done when s/he has attended to the causes of things. Of equal importance to the *left-universalist* is discerning the matter at hand, this specific predicament and the redress it invites – for all its particularity – as a *human* predicament. It is thanks to this work of explanation and re-cognition that we come to consider that predicament as being at all alterable rather than an unfathomable and so irremediable phenomenon. The African thinker Ayi Kwei Armah calls this twin labour of explanation and re-cognition *remembrance* and its defining virtue *connectedness*. Ascertaining the cause of a thing and apprehending that thing as a case of human practices and their consequences in history: such is the dual mandate of those who have renounced misanthropic fatalism together with tribalist narcissism. Here is an admirable example of that work (all the more admirable because it occurred in the same season of commanded ignorance), a sublime testimony reported in the *Toronto Star* of September 11, 2006. A number of Toronto's resident Chilean community, according to Nicholas Keung's report, gathered to remember their own 9/11, the day in 1973 when General Augusto Pinochet, with the evil genius Henry Kissinger as maestro by remote control, overthrew the Salvador Allende government. Among those at the gathering was one Helmut Sabando, son of a marine sergeant who "served for a decade under the Pinochet junta." These were Sabando's words as quoted by Keung: "Yes, our Sept. 11 happened a long time ago, at a far distance from us in Canada, but the stories of humanity are the same everywhere." "*The stories of humanity are the same everywhere.*" An utterance of such laconic beauty, at once tragic in its provenance and hopeful in its intent. I don't believe Helmut Sabando meant by that utterance to depreciate the specific gravity of the horror of the Twin Towers or that of Pinochet's reign of terror.

Two caveats: First, I hasten to add that the work of remembrance and the practice of connectedness, ascertaining the cause of a thing and its status as a case of a knowable class, is a necessary but not a sufficient condition for changing the world. There are those for whom the mission of connectedness as a way of knowing is not to change the world but to conserve it as it is. An emblematic example: For the author of *Prolegomena to Ethics*, the British Idealist philosopher Thomas Hill Green in his less progressive mood, the goal of a "self-consciousness" that rescues a succession of facts from remaining "an unconnected manifold" and brings them "into relation to each other" is that of "finding itself at home in them, of making them its own" (*Prolegomena* §132). That is not my idea and Ayi Kwei's idea of what the practice of connectedness is good for: interpreting the world not as a loveable because an intelligible whole such as it *is*, but rather as an "antagonistic totality" (Adorno), one that, precisely, demands to be changed.

And second, I do not subscribe to universalism unmodified. Not to the U.S. National Rifle Association's version according to which, beyond the manufactured constitutional guarantee in the land of the free and the craven acquiescence of its courts, there is a universal right of persons to bear arms and to engage in the homicidal "free" trade in weapons. In the age of capitalist globalization, all weapons are weapons of mass destruction. The right to sell to kill is not a universalizable right. It is an invented peculiarity of the American polity. My universalism does not honour each and every tribal rite, however wicked, as a splendid exemplar of the human commons.

OTHER RIGHTWING ACTS OF GRAND LARCENY

Postmodern cowboys, gun fetishists and armament peddlers are not alone in hijacking the universalist language of human rights in the service of nefarious ends. Our new corporate ethicists have also found that language useful and gone Kantian, pledging to treat all "stakeholders" – mostly investors – as inviolate ends in themselves. And the enemies of women's reproductive freedom have fashioned a new strategy: framing abortion as an injury to the interests and well-being of women, nay, to the human rights and dignity of women. But the most brazen of these shameless acts of grand larceny is the new rightwing conservatives' invocation of Martin Luther King's call to judge persons not by the colour of their skin but the content of their character. The rightwing translation of this injunctive dream and prophetic demand? Why, vindication of the principle of equal concern understood as treating everyone the same way irrespective of (alleged) historical privileges or disadvantages, arranged social luck or imposed encumbrances. And the inference with respect to public policy? Forget affirmative action and other "collectivist" corrective measures and illicit programmes of "social engineering," programmes instigated by calculated ignorance of unalterable facts of human character and naïve perfectionist convictions. We are all, such as we are and without exception, on our own. This is the perverse universalism of equal acquiescence to our unequal fortunes.

Are these egregious cases of pernicious appropriation of noble ideals reason enough to jettison the language of human dignity, rights and equal concern for all in its entirety as a vacuous and dangerous mystification? Hell no. Let the partisan struggle over universals begin.

DEFINITION OF THE NEW RIGHT

What is the New Right? The arranged marriage of the "free" market and the closed mind, open for business and quarantined against critical thinking. The contradiction is only apparent. The freedom of the free market is not a gift of nature. Rather it is something enforced, guess what, by the state as it shuts down, through judicial thuggery and overt force if need be, extant institutions and practices of material culture, conventions of rights and obligations, ancestral practices and idioms of community, all the cherished goods of the commons. In the process the state, at the behest of the beneficiaries of the new order, legislates the earthly and sacral virtues of the acquisitive society. It is the whip of state that, in a cruel parody of Jean-Jacques Rousseau, forces us to be free for the "free" market. This is the conundrum in which the social-conservative faction of the new right is caught. In a dance of ideological oscillations, they feign ignorance of the state's enforcement of the "free" market, in one breath demand that the state should get out of the way and, in another, gleefully ask that it intervenes in women's reproductive choices and police other private spheres of moral life. They are not in the least embarrassed by this veritable roulette; they need not be. Unwittingly, they are owning up to the coercion that is the constant companion of liberty, the paradox of forcible freedom that makes capitalist society what it is.

CONSERVATIVES AND HISTORY

Since Edmund Burke, the conservative criticism of the revolutionary imagination is that it is wilfully ignorant of history and the constraints it imposes on human action. But today it is in truth self-styled conservatives who are far more culpable of this evasion of history. For they approach contemporary social, cultural and moral debates with a serene and disingenuous amnesia with respect to the ancestry of these problems. Their hostility to any number of prominent issues of our time – women's rights, affirmative action, the claims and demands of First Nations Peoples, Critical Race Theory, multiculturalism and proposals for revising the canon of "Great Works," the demand to bring down statutes of the iconic figures of the past – all this is very much the product of this calculated amnesia. So is their response to the scepticism, sometimes the sheer irreverence, with which the dispossessed and excluded of the land greet figures and monuments of the national culture.

A case in point is the controversy surrounding Thomas Jefferson's fathering of children with one of his slaves, Sally Hemmings. In a November 1998 article published in the *National Post*, one Steven Hayward averred that the obsession with this little matter of master/slave parentage threatened to make the author of the Declaration of Independence "even more of an orphan of American political thought." What is this trivial detail, this contingent result of the body's caprice, compared to the undying majesty of the founding document of liberty and its author? In Hayward's protest we see an instance of that conservative idolatry that comes from wilfully forgetting history. The searching question we should be asking is this: What is the relation between human ideals and history? Do moral and political precepts, say freedom and natural rights, have any claim on our allegiance, when they were professed by people who practiced slavery and systematically dehumanized other human beings? I mean people who proposed these ideals with such passionate intensity precisely because they deemed the evil of unfreedom being visited upon them unimaginable? Think of the horror and revulsion with which John Locke, in the opening chapter of his *Two Treatises of Government*, sees Filmer's doctrine of royal absolutism as tantamount to a charter for slavery: "Slavery is so vile and miserable an Estate of Man, and so directly opposite the generous Temper and Courage of our Nation; that 'tis hardly to be conceived, that an *Englishman*, much less a *Gentleman*, should plead for't." Locke's horror is a knowing horror, an educated revulsion. How dare Filmer, exclaims the great philosopher and hireling of enslavers, want to do to Englishmen what Englishmen do to mere Africans? The question, once more, is this: What do we do with a philosophy of freedom, when "freedom" is so constitutively and transparently white because it is something you own in virtue of not being black, as Toni Morrison eloquently showed in *Playing in the Dark* and, more recently, Tyler Stoval in *White Freedom*? To Sartre's famous saying that we are condemned to freedom, should we not retort that "freedom" is condemned to be forever white, condemned to always being written enclosed in scare quotes. Can such a principle ever be embraced by those who were excluded from being beneficiaries of its very conception? For that matter, can social relations founded on violence, radical divisions, fearful kinship at best, leave in their wake any intimations and usable ideals of a just human association? What are the consequences of recovering memory of racial violence in the formation of the political community and the gestation of its highest ideals? Can these ideals be salvaged from their natal corruption? What do you do, for example, with South Africa's rights culture and its constitutional guarantees of equality rights, knowing that these provisions will more often than not be invoked by privileged white citizens intent on protecting their obscene wealth from distributive justice after the formal end of apartheid? Can moral artefacts of the national culture forged in blood ever become truly shared values, testaments of the common good, to say nothing of human universals? A certain radical historicism in league with fundamentalist relativism will answer "hell no" and consign these artefacts to the museum of fatally compromised and deservedly perishable things. Not so an ironic and critical attitude toward the human condition in history. Such an attitude is open to the possibility of miracle. Not divine miracle, to be sure, but the transfiguring miracle of human work. But that work has nothing in common with the indolent idolatry practiced by right-wing conservatives. It consists in salvaging the shareable promises of sublime ideals from their soiled cradle. The crucial proviso is *shareable*. That is what makes immanent criticism, even loyal opposition, possible. That is the condition of possibility of the *Jeremiad*, that species of critique predicated on acceptance of the validity of a tradition and its "original intent," denouncing and accusing today's miscreants only of betraying that tradition and the latent promises or "intimations" (Oakeshot) it harboured. But the denunciation of racial orders and their cruel legacies is *not* a form of the Jeremiad; it cannot, on pain of incoherence, appeal to the founders and architects of those very orders for inspiration, still less for vindication. Those founders and founding principles, alas, are the problem. The denunciation cannot count on historical inheritance and respect for it as a critical resource because that inheritance is not a shareable commonality. To Edmund Burke's view of the French revolutionaries – for American conservative columnist Bret Stephens, a view equally applicable to today's "far left" –, namely, that they "began by despising everything that belonged to you," to that view today's #Must Fall activists are asking: What on earth are you talking about? In what respect do these cherished monuments and cultural treasures "belong" to the descendants of those whose bodies were turned into specimens of a "strange fruit" or those who walked the terrible Trail of Tears? You are demanding piety before shrines and effigies commemorating *radical* evil? Bret Stephens' complaint is no better than Trump's reaction in September 2021 to the removal of the statue of Robert F. Lee (the general who led the Confederate Army): "Our culture is being destroyed and our history and heritage, both good and bad, are being extinguished by the Radical Left, and we can't let that happen." This is white supremacist animus whether it comes from Trump's vulgar mouth or is delivered in what Marx called "the poetry of the past," the hymnal lyrics of Burkean ancestralism. That is why today's insurgent protest seeks its warrant not from something historically shared – the bloodstained cradle of *your* heritage? – but rather from something potentially shareable, the visionary thought of common human essences the very mention of which Burke so detested: that is a certain idea of humanity, one that, as the great black bard sang, is "not yet dared," is still to be wrested through struggle by partisans. In fidelity to that agonistic idea, today's revolt against conservative ancestor worship thus enacts another kind of tradition, the tradition of possibility. How could we know and call the enslavers' idea of human life and human association skewed, self-serving, fraudulent, were it not for that tradition? An echo of a famous utterance by an ancestor of that tradition, the tradition of "insurgent universality" (Massimiliano Tomba) is apposite here: Rightwing conservatives, fetishists of the past in the service of the present order, are always suppressing the unsettling truths of history; the point, however, is to disinter them in remembrance of a justice yet to see the light of day.

"BRINGING DEMOCRACY TO INDIAN RESERVES"

Thus declaims Tom Flanagan in the time-honoured accents of the missionary intent on coercive enlightenment – *contradictio in adjecto* – of the natives. "Aboriginal leaders," hectors Father Flanagan, "would be better advised to get out in front, to cooperate with the federal government in developing a modern legislative framework for self-government to replace the Indian Act. Better that than the imposed solution that will be the eventual response to obstruction" (*Globe and Mail*, December 20, 2006). My understanding of universalism in political ethics and practice, my vision of enlarging and enriching Canadian democracy, does not include this authoritarian design of enforcing so-called liberal democratic institutions. To First Nations' thinkers and activists imagining and demanding reconfigured ethical and legal principles designed *by* their communities after conversations concerning what Patricia Monture-Angus calls "journeying forward, dreaming First Nations' independence," to them I say "right on." To the Tom Flanagans of this world sworn to "Bringing Democracy *to* Indian Reserves" and laying down "The 'Other Path' *for* Native Americans" (the tell-tale missionary prepositions in the titles of Flanagan's article and the book he co-authored with fellow Kipling-disciples), I say, in the nicest euphemism that this old anti-colonialist with an attitude can muster: back off. At this very hour the world over, fine specimens of that hubris, after wreaking unspeakable death and destruction, lie in shameful ruins.

INTERNECINE VIOLENCE OF THE VANQUISHED

No sooner was Iraq "liberated" than Sunnis and Shiites set about slaughtering one another. The enemies of "root causes" had a ready-made one of their own in this instance. The sectarian violence, they say, is the latest manifestation of a mutual hatred that goes back centuries, eons before the invading emancipators came to town. Well, not too long ago Sunnis and Shiites were seen co-existing in Iraq. Perhaps they weren't taking tea together with fraternal cordiality every single afternoon, but they were *co-existing*, within our living memory. In Gaza and the West Bank, Hamas and Fatah members have also been at each other's throats from time to time in a seemingly perverse disregard for their common predicament as Palestinians. Upon what ancient animosities are the inconstant and disingenuous purveyors of historical causes going to pin this one?

"A people united will never be defeated." So goes the reassuring chant of social and political movements in our time. But this is the tragic and disconcerting fact, call it the pathologic of existence under siege: A people besieged do not of necessity unite. They have been known to struggle till death over what is left of material and psychic space. A land under occupation need not give birth to a covenant of the insurrectionary community. On the contrary, in the words of the bard's lament, it is prone to spawn "this strange crowd that does not gather," one fatally devoid of a "common sense" (Césaire). So it is with a besieged soul; it is a territory of inner disarray and self-annihilating passions. Like the "vexations of the soul" of which Peter Tosh sang so poignantly, a conquered and tormented land breeds the collective solipsism of warring groups, a morbid species of what we used to call contradictions but couldn't quite decide whether they were "antagonistic" or "non-antagonistic" contradictions. Tragic but surprising irony, this internecine strife of the vanquished? Or nefarious mission accomplished?

SOME ICONIC NAMES AND SAYINGS OF OUR TIME IN TRANSLATION

1. **The international community** (USA and satellites, aka *allies*).

2. **CNN INTERNATIONAL.** (That we restrict our coverage and our stories almost exclusively to events in the USA, more specifically and more recently, to the engrossing drama of the 2020 presidential election and its comic aftermath, its eternal aftermath; that we had nothing to report regarding, say, the 2020 referendum on the constitution in Chile and its aftermath or on any number of notable events in other parts of the known world; that we have nothing to say about the hopes and fears of other sentient beings – they are of no intrinsic value – until we are jolted from our narcissistic slumber by events which threaten "our interests," none of that in any way gives the lie to the "international" in our self-designation. If you don't like us, you are free to tune in to *Al Jazeera*; its correspondents are all over the place, literally, promiscuously attending to anything and everything in the human world, the terrible, the tragic and the ludic alike, from

the most recent lethal Israeli assault on Palestinian "terrorists" to African football, for Christ's sake.).

3. **Stopping the proliferation of nuclear weapons.** (The only way to do it is for us to hoard our nuclear stockpiles, cancel Non-Proliferation Treaties unilaterally, build more and more, newer and newer, weapons and stop dead in their tracks all uppity nations, such as Iran and North Korea, that aspire to join the holy order of nuclear powers. Israel is naturally exempt from this proscription. Why? Because it is the only democracy in a tough neighbourhood – and democracies are never the aggressors).

4. **Free Trade.** (Of course we support free trade, open markets and rule-based economic transactions. Open your market. I retain the freedom to close mine. Abolish those tariffs; end those anti-free-market state-interventionist socialist subsidies to your farmers. *Our* farmers are special. The United States rules and that means we are free from the regular rules of human commerce. The United States rules and that means that the adverse rulings of the World Trade Organization and NAFTA are irrelevant, just as the provisions of the Geneva Convention regarding prisoners of war are quaint. In trade as in other matters, we believe in the rule of law, Immanuel Kant and Habermas's precept of universalizability, in principle, malleable principle. That's a lesson that law-abiding nations are just going to have to learn.)

5. **Humanitarian Intervention and the Responsibility to Protect.** (While we will hug our sovereignty with every fibre of our being, the principle of national sovereignty cannot be held to be universal, absolute and sacrosanct when states subject their own citizens to horrendous acts of terror and genocide, or when they fail to provide them protection from internal violence. Under such circumstances the international community (see #1 above) has the responsibility to intervene in the affairs of such failed or evil states and to protect the tormented and afflicted within their borders. Who is the moral dinosaur who will oppose this glorious revolution in international law of our time? Of course, this principle applies

only to those we designate with moral clarity as failed and wicked regimes. Saudi Arabia is ruled by a despotic, homicidal royalty, but because it buys and pays for American arms in cash, it is exempt from the application of this principle. And how dare you call for humanitarian intervention to end the regular shooting of young Americans living-while-black in the Land of the Free? Also, the principle of responsibility to protect applies only to those peoples we deem worthy of protection. Palestinians need not apply. They are manifestly undeserving. Like slaves in ante-bellum America, they cannot be accounted truthful witnesses; their testimonies and claims of suffering are by definition not worth hearing. That is why we opposed the UN Security Council draft resolution of June 1, 2018 calling for "measures to guarantee the safety and protection" of Palestinians after more than one hundred of them were slaughtered by Israeli soldiers. Although ten countries went rogue and voted in favour of the draft and four – Britain, Ethiopia, Netherlands and Poland – abstained, Nikki Hailey, our fine and valiant ambassador at the time, was absolutely right in asserting that the resolution demonstrated that the UN "is hopelessly biased" against Israel. Forget Orwell and his satiric reports on the inversion of language, truth and meaning. Forget Shakespeare too and his poignant query as to whether or not all sentient beings without exception are indeed equally susceptible to pain. Don't tell us to endorse that inclusive and sentimental view of human suffering. Don't you dare ask: But those Palestinians, if you shoot them, do they not bleed, even die on occasion? Are they not also human beings, as ordinary Ghanaians, espousing our primitive egalitarian ethics unfortunately undisturbed by the missionaries, would say?)

6. **Agreements**. (If Palestinians want peace, they must accept every one of the conditions contained in Trump's 2020 Proposals, "The Deal Of The Century," unilaterally crafted by the judicious Jared Kushner. This is the new definition of an agreement. There is no need for two or more parties to call it so. Get used to it.)

7. **We support democracy, free and fair elections.** (Yes we do, but only if and when the outcomes are acceptable. Let's not get hung up on mere fidelity to acknowledged procedures as the measure of free and fair elections, still less on (manipulated) official figures. No matter how clean the electoral process was in the estimation of international observers, Chavez's electoral victories in Venezuela were unacceptable. Ditto that of his successor, Maduro. Ditto Evo Morales. And before these more recent dictators and narco-terrorists in fake democratic costumes, Iran's Mohamed Mosaddegh's electoral victory in 1951 didn't count; a higher democratic verdict, ours, got him out of the way in August 1953 in order to make his nation safe for oil. Likewise Guatemala's Jacobo Arbenz, duly elected in 1951 and duly ejected in 1954 in order to make his land safe and fecund for United Fruit Company. And of course we follow the lead of our great ally, Israel – the only democracy in the Middle East – in scorning Hamas's fake democratic victory in the legislative elections of 2006.)

8. **Autocratic regimes.** (In the interest of semantic – and moral – clarity, we must in the first place reserve the noun "regimes" strictly and exclusively to *political* entities narrowly defined, and then solely to political entities we disapprove of. All the more reason why we must use the adjective "autocratic" if and only if the behaviour and practices of such *political* entities do not meet our standards of democratic choice and accountability. We must use the adjective, then, as a pleonasm, a superfluous expression, because falling short of, or flagrantly flouting, our standards of democratic choice and accountability is what "regimes" do as a matter of course. It is an illicit category mistake to call Elon Musk taking control of Twitter and unilaterally deciding to fire thousands of employees – half the workforce – autocratic. Why? Simple: his decision is a "purely business decision" not a political one. And although it is an entirely unilateral decree, not remotely subject to democratic deliberation, we cannot call it autocratic because Twitter is not a regime. If the noun doesn't fit, we must acquit the decision of the adjective. What after all is the

point of semantic and moral distinctions in human affairs? What would become of the meaning of meaning, what would become of the world, if we saw moral equivalence in disparate sets of practices.)

9. **China is modernizing its weapons in order to make its military power commensurate with its growing economic power and to extend its influence in the region.** (There is no reason beyond the will to conquest and dominance why China should seek this fateful correspondence of wealth and arms, or, more generally, adherence to the principle of coherence. Why can't China keep its weapons in medieval primitiveness while its economic achievements, as menacing as they are, attain postmodern heights? There is nothing odd or incongruous about that. Isn't that a healthy instance of what some Marxist folks used to call "uneven development"? As for exercising influence in the region, hell, we coming all the way from Texas and Washington DC and New York have a far more legitimate right to exert our might in that neighbourhood than the Chinese who live and breathe and shit there. "South China sea" is a misnomer, a literalist conflation of geographical accident with legitimate national rights and international law – as we see it. Geopolitics be damned, except our version, as when we claim those Latin American countries in "our very own backyard" as belonging, incontestably, to our sphere of influence. By unilateral fiat we declare our, we mean the Monroe Doctrine non-negotiable. Russia has no right to make the same claim with respect to Ukraine and Georgia. It is entirely just for those countries to be cajoled or coerced into joining NATO, in spite of their being located in Russia's backyard. A pox on Russia's manufactured and morbid historical anxieties. This land, the entire globe, is our land. Any other questions?)

10. **Concerning the right of preemptive strike and extraterritorial assassinations.** ("He [Iran's General Qusem Soleimani] was responsible for the death of countless Americans in the Middle East and was plotting many more attacks on Americans. Just like yesterday's imminent

"mushroom clouds" to be unleashed on American soil by Saddam Hussein, demonstrable evidence be damned. It is thanks to our prophetic knowledge of what Soleimani has not done but will do that we took him out on 3 January, 2020. Soleimani was not a very nice guy. Nobody regrets his elimination from the battlefield. NOBODY. Don't be fooled by the spectacle of thousands of people, palpable bodies, mourning his death in Iran and Iraq. Those are not real people; they are nobodies, you know what I'm saying. The entire international community (see #1) is with us on this one, as on other preferred understandings of evidence and idiosyncratic interpretations of the law of nations.")

REFORM REDEFINED, FREEDOM REFRAMED

Not so long ago in the history of human affairs, "reform" meant the acquisition by the people of social and political rights hitherto denied them by the ruling order. It meant, further, the expansion of such rights into larger and larger spheres of life's needs. Among the amazing transformations accomplished by neoliberalism is the semantic reversal according to which "reform" means a return to the epoch of life without these rights, worse still, withdrawal of rights and entitlements achieved through protracted struggles; the calculated confiscation of public goods; removal of regulatory measures that keep the more predatory and toxic practices of capital at bay. Neoliberal semantics cannot be accused of originalism or strict constructionism. A recent scene, right in the centre of world capitalism, of this counterrevolution in the public guarantee of life's needs and in accompanying political semantics is France, where capital has found a new Bonaparte sworn to revoke rights as the people know them, revoke and call it reform. In the Global South, India is also a recent scene in this work of conscripting the word, travestied, into the service of the reactionary deed. There, a set of new laws promulgated in September 2020 bestows the name of reform upon the termination of electricity subsidies to farmers and the withdrawal of hitherto guaranteed minimum support prices (MSP) for farm produce. The idea is that Indian farmers will be free at last to savour the liberating anarchy of the "free market," that is to say, unregulated David and Goliath transactions with the agents of agrobusiness. And indeed it is in the peripheries of capital's dominion that rights to liveable life were first attacked in the name of "reforming" labour laws and making them "friendly to investors." It is here that moves were first made to discredit, oppose and arrest the advancement of rights before they became established impediments to the dictatorship of capital's skewed freedom. Consider this disapproving report on the rights of labour construed, in Orwellian fashion, as chains and crying for their removal: "Indonesia chained by labour law." That was the heading of a *Wall Street Journal* article of 7 December, 2006. What was the writer referring to? Well, it was Indonesia's 2003 labour law which "require[d] that dismissed workers receive up to seven years in severance pay." The law, this writer reported, was "enacted as organized labour gained influence following the fall of authoritarian President Suharto in 1998" and in the aftermath of massive loss of jobs by Indonesian workers during the Asian financial crisis of the time. The law was thus a product of the struggle for the deepening of democratic rights and an answer to what Bourdieu, speaking of European workers, has called a "permanent condition of insecurity," the condition of "precarity" in today's jargon. You would think that this was a laudable achievement. In the language of human rights advocates, it united political with economic and social rights, addressing as it did conditions that vitiate the possibility of an effective exercise of citizenship by an important constituency of the Indonesian populace. A significant enlargement, then, of human liberty. But not according to the writer: Indonesia was in chains, in bondage to a legislation that made its labour environment "uncompetitive," unattractive to investors and employers, domestic and foreign alike. Capital would be constrained to take flight to more welcoming markets, markets unshackled by "inflexible labour laws." Vietnam would become the fortunate successor destination of the quest for freedom in the peculiar meaning assigned to the word by the missionaries of the new international political economy. Only yesterday China was such a favoured land for "shoe, garment and other manufacturers looking for alternative production sites." Alas, "wage costs [were] on the rise" in China. Such is the capricious nature of the market, not exactly the desired consequence of its vaunted freedom.

But what if tomorrow the sun also rises in Vietnam and in Bangladesh and in Mexico and in Botswana and in Dubai and in the Ivory Coast and in a thousand other sites of [in]human existence under capital's dominion? What if this occurs not because of the notional freedom of the market but as a result of successive and concerted acts of impertinence by the peoples of the world demanding their right to life, liberty and dignity? What if tomorrow there are fewer and fewer havens left for the lawless freedom of the free market? In dreaming this heretical version of domino theory, this fantasy of the serial extinction of antihuman "alternative production sites," I am reminded of a hilarious quip by Marx in 1850:

> When in their imminent flight across Asia our European reactionaries will ultimately arrive at the Wall of China, at the gate that leads to the stronghold of arch-reaction and arch-conservatism, who knows if they will not find there the inscription: République Chinoise, Liberté, Egalité, Fraternité.

Today, we will and we must wince a little at the manifest Eurocentrism that underwrites Marx's sardonic vision of China's democratic future and European reaction's appointed destiny. Entirely unimpeachable is his fancy that the tyrants of the world fleeing the peoples' avenging justice would soon have no place to hide. Today, we must hope against hope that this prodding prophecy of vanishing places of refuge and recovery for despots is also the fate of the new masters of the world and the word. I mean, those who after the last discomfiture and the latest revolt of the people traverse the ends of the world in a fervid search for alternative spaces of unrestricted freedom, whence to proclaim and enforce the notion that there are no alternatives, no alternatives at all to acquiescing to the globalization of plunder by the few. I mean those who in the name of freedom are bent on subjecting the destitute, the desperate and the credulous to the plea of necessity, the blackmail of arranged realism. Surely, in the inescapable commerce and conversation of humanity, another concept of liberty is possible.

TOWARDS TRUTH IN POLITICAL ECONOMY

That is no idle hope. Small yet significant victories are already at hand. In 2019, appropriately on May Day of that year, a crucial reform to Mexico's Federal Labour Law came into being. The reform enables a "legitimation vote" by workers regarding Collective Bargaining Agreements, a requirement intended, according to Canada's *The Bulletin*, "to eliminate 'protection contracts' signed by employers and unrepresentative unions without workers' knowledge or consent." Mexico's workers fought for and secured this democratic right in the teeth of threats of job termination, factory shut downs and move of production elsewhere, to the famous "alternative production sites." And in November 2021, Indian Prime Minister Narendra Modi announced the imminent repeal of the odious farm laws and in so doing bowed to the farmers' resistance to the capricious reversals of meaning in political economy. Contrary to the semantic counterrevolution, this is what reform looks like: the enlargement of "positive liberty" and the extension of rights, not their diminution. And this is a small yet crucial step towards the realization of true democracy – beyond the quadrennial ritual of choosing the most adroit among the accredited company of kleptocrats. Progress towards such true democracy includes Amazon workers around the world being able to vote to unionize without intimidation and interference by the company.

RIVAL VERSIONS OF ETHICS AND ECONOMICS

1. "There is one and only one social responsibility of business – to use its resources and engage in activities designed to increase its profits so long as it stays within the rules of the game, which is to say, engages in open and free competition without deception or fraud." (Milton Friedman)
2. "Budgets are moral documents." (Rashad Robinson)
3. "It is morally wrong and hugely costly for millions." (Nicola Sturgeon, First Minister of Scotland, describing the September 2022 UK Chancellor's mini-budget which offered huge tax cuts for the wealthy)

SOME LINGUISTIC GEMS OF OUR TIME (NOT INTENDED TO BE WITTICISMS)

1. The most unequal society in the world.
2. Humanitarian disaster.
3. Neoconservative idealists.
4. "As an instrument of resource control, bribery is..." (Peter Maass, *New York Times Magazine*, 23 December, 2007).

CHINA RISEN. NEXT?

No, I am not enamoured of despotic developmentalism, the path China's rulers have elected for their nation's gigantic leap forward. I loathe the disenfranchisement of the working class in the workers' state, the dreadful conditions of existence endured by migrant labourers in the manufacturing hubs that make Chinese products, as they say, "competitive." I look with prissy displeasure upon the shameless cross-dressing of a state-sponsored capitalism parading official socialist insignia, sworn to fashioning a "harmonious society" out of the acquisitive spirit unleashed. And I am utterly revolted by the amoral *realpolitik* that drives China's dealings with unsavoury African regimes, its indecent trafficking in tyranny in pursuit of oil, to say nothing of the less than Confucian-Kantian respect that Chinese enterprises mete out to workers in their expanding African operations.

But I cannot conceal my glee at the spectacle of a veritable Copernican revolution in the making. I mean, this twilight of a monocratic world order; the beginning of the end of an empire made heedless by uncontested force to the cries and hopes and dreams of other sentient beings on this our common earth; the glimmering dawn of a new day announcing the birth of other ways of dwelling in the world. China risen! Can it be that this signals more than a momentous increase in the wealth and might of one nation? Dare we hope that it augurs the coming efflorescence of human self-determination in all its marvellous variety and shareable incarnations, nothing less than the resurrection of possibility in what Césaire called "a form not yet dared"? Or rather, in forms yet to see the light of day? If so, then we have to say it loud: Let a hundred galaxies of power shine and a hundred constellations of freedom flourish. *Ex oriente lux*. Tomorrow my Africa, perhaps? Ah, a libation at dawn to the ancestors and our children's children.

CHINA UNDER SURVEILLANCE

With morbid delight, enemies of this auspicious transformation of the world order trumpet every crisis China faces, from the protracted pro-democracy demonstrations in Hong Kong to the initial outbreak of Covid-19 and its ominous return in 2022 after a period of successful containment. Anything that poses a challenge to China's wealth and power is good news for sentinels of the *ancien regime*. The obtuse Trump called Covi-19 "the Chinese virus." The real fear subsequently was that if indeed it was, coronavirus would end up serving as a revelation of China's world-historic homeopathic mission: the putative originating nation of the plague could well become, if not the prime source of its cure, then at the very least the exemplary school of universal health care for the rest of the world; more than that, an object lesson in what public power, contrary to neoliberal religion, can accomplish. Alas, now that the virus has returned with a vengeance, that fear of China's benign infectious example may subside, for a while. But whatever the outcome of this emblematic battle, we the struggling and searching peoples of the world should be clear-eyed regarding the stakes and what we must decidedly not do: Let us not allow ourselves to be conscripted into the *entente néfaste* of the US and its satraps, the desperate club of resentful Sinophobes bent on a manufactured contest between "democracies" and "authoritarian" regimes. Let us not be cajoled into endorsing duplicitous schemes for maintaining the global status quo in the name of human rights and China's imperfect record in that respect. And no, we need not put the term human rights in scare quotes. We can cheer China on and at the same time take rights seriously – far more seriously than what the "narrow horizon of bourgeois right" teaches. Need I add that I was not enchanted by scenes of anti-black racism in China in the first days of the virus?

TWO CONCEPTS OF POWER

The United States has only ever known and used power as an instrument for doing harm to others, power as violence. That is because in a fundamental sense, the US understands power solely as an other-directed force. Of power as first and foremost the capacity of an agent – a person or a people – for self-directed action, power as something not primarily intended for use outside the territory of the self and the community, still less as a force enlisted to bring terror to others, drag them to their knees or else slaughter them; of power as the practice of freedom, if not indeed freedom's twin, the ability of individuals or communities to design and pursue ends of their own choosing for their own good, of *that* understanding and practice of power America is ignorant. In the American mind freedom and power are bifurcated; the one is as inherently benign as the other is intrinsically maleficent, especially when wielded by others. So it is that the United States is driven by a classic mechanism of narcissistic projection to read China's "intentions" through a glass darkly. China's pursuit of empowerment can only be aimed at aggression and dominance. The fact that China, as America's very own former President Jimmy Carter noted, has attacked

PEEVES AND DREAMS, AT LARGE

absolutely no one in recent memory, that fact evidently is of no consequence whatsoever. The fact that "China is not an interventionist country," according to former President – and hapless American ally – Afghanistan's Ashraf Ghani (speaking to Fareed Zakaria on CNN, 18 April 2021), that fact too does not matter. Alternative facts, facts more consonant with the laws of nature and the destiny of nations – facts to which American realism is exceptionally privy – exist. After all, of what use is power if not conquest and dominion? The famous "rivalry" between the United States and China is not unrelated to this conflict of interpretations regarding the nature and the ends of power. The result is the manufactured dread of "Chinese aggression," a phenomenon that is entirely non-existent but transformed by constant repetition into truth: a quintessential feat of the postmodernist imagination, if ever there was one.

WHAT OF PUTIN'S RUSSIA?

Invoking witnesses of the past and truth-tellers of the present, the random observations assembled in these pages have left little doubt as to one of their central verdicts: the age of America can hardly be said to represent the triumph of the better angels of human nature – unless you take plantation slavery, Fugitive Slave Laws, the Trail of Tears, white supremacy, napalm-bombing in Indochina, Abu Ghraib, murderous sanctions against Cuba, Venezuela and Iran, the public lynching of George Floyd and the phenomenon of Donald Trump, unless you take all these historical facts as inconsequential anomalies. But that unblinkered verdict on the American enterprise does not commit its adherent to applauding every rival power and its hour of ascendancy on the world stage as an unmixed blessing. It is in that spirit of critical vigilance and educated hope that we must salute the rise of China – warts and all – as augury of a different order of things. For starters: power without empire, power in the service of native necessities, power as self-determination.

What of Russia? We did not have to wait, we cleareyed and stubborn partisans of the Global Left, for Russia's chieftain Vladimir Putin to fully unveil his dark soul before we became disenchanted with the political order over which he presides. Or, in the longer view, before we began to look with retroactive disapproval at the history of the one he inherited. Long before its final dismemberment in the closing years of the twentieth century, indeed right from its early years, we learned to see in the preceding order – the Soviet Union – as something less than the coming fulfilment of humanity's dream of earthly justice. That was the tragic wisdom shared with us by the internal Left Opposition from the inception of the Soviet adventure. So that when the end came in 1991, we lamented not the extinction of an idyll but the waste and wreckage of an epoch's opportunity to institute a new order of things, leaving in its wake the arranged and abysmal certainty that there is no alternative to the dominion of capital and a society of toxic inequities. We cursed not the external forces who aided and abetted the final dénouement, but the internal agents who from the very beginning confiscated and corrupted a prodigious promise. We lamented the egregious mishaps, grieved for what might have been, sighed in remembrance of things not done.

That is not Vladimir Putin's grief and his brief. His hatred of that very promise is second to none, as intense as that of the most zealous anti-communist from the West, as determined as that of those who presided over the dissolution of the Soviet Union. What he laments in the extinction of the Soviet Union is not the squandered promise of power to the soviets, not the possibility of what Ernst Bloch, the recalcitrant philosopher of possibility, called "real democracy," democracy beyond the quadrennial ritual of choosing the most adroit among the hustlers of the land. The death of the Soviet Union is for Putin nothing more (or less) than "the greatest geopolitical catastrophe of the century." Putin's lament is territorial, Tsarist, fuelled by Greater-Russia chauvinism and imagined primordial bonds in perfervid pursuit of the restoration. The invasion of Ukraine is the result of this belligerent nostalgia for imperial power and glory. The ends and the means placed in the service of this furious ambition are impervious even to the regular restraints dictated by realpolitik or *raison d'état*. So, it does not matter how understandable Russia's anxieties about its security and the eastward expansion of NATO in the aftermath of the collapse of the Soviet Union may be. It does not matter that the rest of the world is now victim to the vicious circle of cause and consequence: NATO's anxiogenic action which provokes Russian paranoia and aggression, which then impels NATO to further intensify its strategy of encirclement even more menacingly, which then... Even a certain wing of the US foreign policy establishment, the so-called "realist" wing – the malevolent Machiavellian Henry Kissinger among them – foresaw this prospect. No, we cannot ignore the causal logic of Russia's action. But no consistent anti-imperialist can loathe the American mayhem in Vietnam and Afghanistan and Iraq (to offer but a severely compressed précis of the story of the American enterprise abroad) and then support Putin's invasion of Ukraine. No anti-imperialist worthy of the name will fail to notice and denounce the mendacity and lethal hubris shared by the two aggressors: Dick Cheney's resolve, despite falsification of the argument for war, to go "full steam ahead" with the attack on Iraq in the belief that the invaders would be greeted with flowers; Putin's mythopoeic insistence that Ukraine and Russia are one people separated by history's caprice, and his expectation that his warriors would be welcomed by Ukrainians as liberators intent on reuniting lost siblings. We must recognize the family resemblance between these murderous delusions. We must insist on the moral equivalence, yes, moral equivalence, of the deeds they enable. We must do so fully cognizant of the fact that the template for wanton brutality with impunity was made in America. How many countries of the famous "international community," in their noble concern for the maimed and the slaughtered of Iraq, dared to impose sanctions and boycotts and embargos on the United States? Who among their leaders objected when the United States placed sanctions on the Chief Prosecutor of the International Criminal Court Fatou Bensouda for daring to initiate investigations in 2020 into alleged war crimes committed by the US in Afghanistan? Who among them for that matter ever raises a voice of outrage any time Israel, fine student of the American patent, unleashes terror upon the Palestinians? We are fully cognizant of this history of criminal silence and duplicity. We cannot fall prey to one unfortunate result of Russia's invasion: instant historical amnesia regarding America's crimes. All the same, we must oppose Russia's aggression in spite of our living and livid memory of those crimes, the hypocrisy of Western powers, and the legitimacy of Putin's geostrategic concerns. Why? Because our anti-imperialism is not a matter of strategy or of choosing the greater or lesser evil among the ogres of the world. Our anti-imperialism rests on an ethical principle: the right of persons and peoples to self-determination. That principle cannot be any more accommodating towards today's invaders than towards yesterday's aggressors turned lovers of peace and a "rule-based" global order. Above all, that principle cannot be held hostage to geopolitical fears and claims; thanks to its adamant universalism, it does not bend or bow before what the early Marx called "the sophistry of interests." Still less does it defer to putative debts incurred by yesterday's alliances and allegiances. That is why South African Julius Malema's vow of unwavering loyalty to Russia – "We will never denounce Russia because Russia was with us during difficult times" – is seriously mistaken. Not only does it conflate Russia, Putin's Russia, with the Soviet Union warts and all, among them, support for the anti-apartheid struggle and anti-colonial movements, whether driven by *realpolitik* or by noble and disinterested commitment. More egregiously, Malema's oath of allegiance betrays that principle of self-determination sacred to any anti-imperialist worthy of the name.

TESTING THE CATEGORICAL IMPERATIVE

Sadly, not all of the brave people of Ukraine in whose behalf we uphold and must uphold the principle of self-determination are Kantians in their treatment of other sentient beings, especially other "others," in particular, visible quintessential specimens of *the* Other. African students fleeing death and destruction at the hands of the Russian invaders have been subjected to racist insults, cruelty and even violence at border crossings; they have been told that if you are black you need not apply. It took egregiously horrendous outbreaks of the congenital disease of

American anti-black racism in recent years to spark Black Lives Matter. It took one week's revelation of Ukrainian anti-black racism to provoke a fleeing medical student into forming an organization of Black Women for Black Lives, thereby contributing to the material (and not just symbolic and supportive) globalization of Black Lives Matter. Hmm. How easy to forget that "you were once slaves in Egypt?" What am I saying? "Once," as in some remote past? I mean to say, how easy to forget that you were just a moment ago, more precisely, that you are right at this very moment, facing damnation at the hands of another people, a people who are convinced that they belong to a superior species of humanity and are endowed with superior rights than you and your compatriots? BBC Africa's Peter Okwoche may be forgiven for his visceral astonishment at the spectacle of mistreatment of African students by some Ukrainian border officials: "You are being bombed and still you have time for racism?" But can it be that the hunted and the endangered of the earth are no zealous harbingers of the Kingdom of Ends? Hmm. We cannot afford naivety. Neither can we afford the slippery slope into abject misanthropy. That is much too easy. Our only option? Keep on testing the categorical imperative, regardless.

THE LURE OF MISANTHROPY

Keep holding on to the categorical imperative even as you murmur "testing, testing, testing... ." Easier said than done, isn't it? The lure of misanthropy is indeed powerful. What with those on the receiving end of iniquity today becoming copycats tomorrow, a place of infamy close by looking uncannily like a faithful replica of a place of the self-same infamy elsewhere: evil as a macabre travelling circus. What with each of us forfeiting by our deeds the moral credibility to sit in judgement of the other. "Is that then the whole truth?" Thus spoke Teacher of *The Beautyful Ones Are Not Yet Born* as he tethered on the precipice of "cosmic pessimism," as one critic characterized the overwhelming gloom. "It ain't necessarily so," retorts our stubborn adherent of educated hope. Perhaps. But consider these facts on the ground. Donald Trump and his followers call migrants from Mexico criminals and rapists who must be sent back to where they came from, or barred from crossing the border in the first place. While we look down with condescension on these followers and smirk at the unintended witticism that refers to them as "the base" – as in the basest specimens of our species because bereft of all human decency – permit me to transport you to Alexandra, South Africa. There, native black South Africans are on a warpath against African immigrants and migrants whom they blame for crime and violence and stealing their jobs. A movement with the guileless name "Dudula" (force out or knock down in Zulu, slightly more direct than Trumpian "send them back") orchestrates the xenophobic violence. As the BBC's Rimza Fihlani reports: "from [their] shacks, residents [of Alexandra] can easily see the towering skyscrapers of Sandton [Johannesburg], one of the richest districts on the whole of the continent, just a few kilometres away." So close in physical distance and yet too logistically remote as a target, too abstract an object of the people's resentment, their "look of envy" (Fanon). Far more concrete and visible are African interlopers. Nevertheless, the South African case, for what it is worth, is not one of state-sponsored "Afrophobia." Cameroonian migrants in Equatorial Guinea are not so fortunate. Here also their youth in search of jobs are accused, in an all too familiar bill of indictments, of harassment, theft and armed robberies. But in this instance they are expelled as a matter of official state policy. We can try exculpatory explanations for these unpleasant proceedings: The unhealed injuries of apartheid, the wretched conditions of existence in which people are mired, these are not conducive to making the inhabitants of Alexandra or for that matter denizens of any African postcolony sentimental Pan-Africanists, native Kantians and votaries of ubuntu without borders. These people have their own problems, tons of them, damn it. True. But the more compelling and less complicated inference we are tempted to draw from these ghastly facts on the ground is this: Xenophobia is transracial and transcultural, a human universal, just not the kind we love to glorify in verse. That inference dissipates the quandaries, banishes idyllic fantasies of human solidarity, brings a certain equanimity, doesn't it? Such is the lure of misanthropy, moral psychology kept simple. All the same...

BEAUTIFUL BONDS

I was deeply moved, as I am sure you were, by the way ordinary citizens of neighbouring countries, particularly Poland, opened their hearts and homes to Ukrainians fleeing Russian terror. Simply beautiful. This had nothing to do with consanguinity, aka white privilege and solidarity without borders, does it? Was this but the covenant of those blessed with blue eyes at work? Just wondering. Would that such touching solicitude were extended to what Martin Luther King memorably called "all of God's children." I take that to be MLK's way of affirming the earthly holiness of every single one of us.

TRAITOROUS TIES

A rather less praiseworthy form and show of kinship: How come Israel's Naftali Bennett – bless his anti-colonialist soul – was palling around with Putin, offering his services as mediator? Could it be because of their shared knowledge of how to spit on international law, annex other peoples' lands and reduce their homes to rubble? Was this the dastardly beginning of a pact of silence concerning their respective atrocities? Should we prepare ourselves for Russia's abstention in the next United Nations Security Council vote on the condition of the Palestinians, after yet another brutal assault on Gaza, in exchange for Israel staying mum or mumbling concerning Russian aggression? And what a weird web of not very funny ironies, utterly indecent ironies designed to make you cry: Leader of the Jewish State lending a helping hand to the brutal invader of a country whose leader happens to be Jewish and has traumatic memory of the Nazi holocaust, but whom the invader accuses of presiding over a den of neo-Nazis. And at that very hour, while Ukraine was under horrific assault and Palestine under ruthless occupation, chieftains of the Arab world, in callous contempt for the court of analogy, heedless to the cries of "our Palestinian brothers," were holding a confab with Israeli leaders intended to forge a new *entente cordiale* between their countries with an eye to encircling Iran. If there is a lesson here, it is surely that the enabling foundation of solidarity is ethical, not consanguinity, not the inconsequential accident of so-called blood ties. That is another way of saying that the perfidy of the Arab overlords, to echo Fanon's indictment of the treason of the postcolonial "national bourgeoisie," is *not* racial; it is political.

TREACHEROUS OATHS

Beware of binding commitments undertaken today in the service of realpolitik or even daring principle. They may come back to haunt you tomorrow. See how NATO is hamstrung by the famous Article 5 of its Treaty – the Article that says that an attack on one member state constitutes as an attack on all. That would seem to mean, *mutatis mutandis*, that a military engagement by a NATO member state against any non-member state may be construed as a collective action on the part of all NATO member states and so will invite a response by that non-NATO state against any NATO member state. The fear that Russia will construe enforcement of a no-fly zone over Ukrainian skies by any NATO member precisely in that manner and undertake retaliatory measures accordingly, that fear is what is deterring NATO from acceding to Ukraine's insistent demand for a no-fly zone. A commitment made in the spirit of gallant solidarity has resulted in timid calculation of unsavoury consequences on the part of its architects, now hopelessly hoisted by their own petard. As they rush to admit Sweden, Finland and other countries into the ALLIANCE OF THE FREE AND THE JUST, the rulers of Europe and the United States might want to ponder the irony of such knowable consequences.

THE GRATEFUL DEAD

The horrible news that the Russians were deliberately targeting civilians in their "special military operations" in Ukraine elicited from US Col. Cedric Leighton (Ret.) this proud assertion of American exceptionalism, even in the arts of war: "That shows the difference between how the Russians wage war and how we wage war." All future enemies of the United States must find that mooted *differentia specifica* most reassuring. Kinsfolk of their fallen warriors will lay them to rest with equanimity, content to count them among the grateful dead, random casualties of war's wanton cruelty, no undeserving victims of targeted violence. Where is Orwell to mock this macabre tomfoolery? Where is Wilfred Owen to paint in vivid colours the gruesome gore that gushed from lacerated bodies bearing no tell-tale traces of the killers' fine distinctions?

XII

PERSISTENT POLEMICS, COUNTERVAILING MUSINGS

TWO UNPUBLISHED LETTERS TO THE EDITOR, OR FAILED EXPERIMENTS IN CONVERSATION WITH THE FREE PRESS

To the Editor, *National Post*, Re: Andy Lamey "White lies about Indians," Saturday November 20, 1999.

What a propitious time to debunk two myths about "Indians." Just when Canadian courts and some provincial governments, in the tyrannizing grip of white guilt, are busy giving away unearned rights and special privileges to those people, two truths are told, as the bard would put it: The natives, the generic natives everywhere, have no special virtues. Nor was some extraordinary violence visited upon their soil and soul, upon the ways they allegedly invented to relate to their surroundings, to one another and to the extended family of other beings. No need to heed knee-jerk calls for material and moral reparations. Absolutely no need to listen to voices vindicating a "politics of recognition" for cultures and communities supposedly disrespected or destroyed by white people. I have gained a deeper understanding of the intent of Andy Lamey's earlier piece in your newspaper lambasting one such leading voice, philosopher Charles Taylor. So, walk into the new millennium, white man, head held high, as always with Kipling as tutelary spirit, from guilt and shame – to say nothing of higher taxes – set free.

★★★

PERSISTENT POLEMICS, COUNTERVAILING MUSINGS

To the Editor, *National Post*, Re: Robert Fulford, "Fanon had a real talent for hate." February 2, 2002.

No, Frantz Fanon would not have been a soulmate of today's pathetic band of grovelling vassals of white supremacy who go by the name of black conservatives. Condoleezza would be no sister of his. Unlike those seriously afflicted with historical amnesia, Fanon hated what one of our writers calls the "fearful holocaust" that Europe visited upon the African world: the capture and brutal enslavement of our people, the seizure of our lands and the maiming of our souls. Fanon hated that ghastly history and its enduring consequences. That hatred, Robert Fulford may be shocked to know, is as old and as unimpeachable as the spirit of the captives who first plunged headlong into the menacing sea from the slave ships in order to avoid a nameless fate. That hatred, when regular people practice it, is commonly called love of liberty. And it is not the product of a "talent," as David Macey's stupid characterization in his biography of Fanon would have it. Fanon came by that hatred the hard way, through bitter experience and deep reflection. Fanon learned to hate racial injustice, indeed "all forms of exploitation," with a passion. All that is true.

What is not true is the idea that Fanon's "approach to truth was purely political" or, as the cardinal item in the current catalogue of deadly sins would have it, "moral relativist." The frequency with which this charge is being made of late in the rightwing press, to say nothing of the truncated citation of Fanon's text used to support it, leads me to suspect that the prosecutors have never read Fanon himself. They simply cite one another and so reproduce the same malicious lie without blushing. Fulford's verdict echoes that of Anthony Daniels in The New Criterion of 19 May 2001 and Adam Shatz in The New York Times Book Review of 12 September 2001 (by uncanny coincidence the day after the event, Fulford hints, that had Fanon's name as tutelary spirit written all over it!). All three cite, in truncated form as I said, the passage in The Wretched of the Earth *in which Fanon dramatizes "the problem of truth" in the context of the colonial order and the enterprise of dismantling it. All three seem unaware of or simply ignore the fact that the famous offending line – "Truth is that which hurries on the break-up of the colonial regime" – is followed by this utterance: "In the colonial context there is no common standard of truth. And the good is quite simply that which is evil for them [the colonizers]." And all three ignore a sentence that comes earlier in the paragraph and contains Fanon's preemptive verdict on the apartheid vision of the world that produces this interests-relative notion of the true and the good. That sentence says: "To the lie of the colonial situation the colonized replies with an equal lie." Nor is that all. The succeeding paragraph characterizes this strategic reciprocation of "lies" as follows: "Thus we see that the primary Manicheism which governed colonial society is preserved intact during the period of decolonization." In Fanon's Dialectic of Experience, I argue that in the ensuing sections of The Wretched of the Earth Fanon dramatizes how this reactive and avenging Manicheism of the anticolonial rebel comes to be challenged and eventually revised in light of resurrected and new forms of social division and solidarity. In the end, Fanon envisions the transcendence of what he calls "the racial and racist frame of judgment." Trained to hate racial oppression and racist culture with a passion, Fanon was determined to see that they would not provide the final vocabulary for our moral reasoning and our understanding of the human condition in history. A brave and intricate vision of one who lived such a short life. But to begin to appreciate the measure of that audacity and that complexity, you will have to entertain the possibility that Fanon was a thinker. And that means first of all reading him, and reading him with the same assiduousness as you would the texts of "real," aka white, people. Ultimately, it means entertaining the possibility that Africans and people of African ancestry can think. Beyond ritual respect for the ineffable thoughts of a Clarence Thomas, that is a task which rightwing commentators like Fulford and his mentors, whether because of wilful ignorance or just plain illiteracy, seem utterly incapable of undertaking.*

POSTSCRIPT: STILL FRAMING FANON

It is an appropriate time, isn't it, to take Fanon down a notch or two on this the sixtieth anniversary of the 1961 publication of the English translation of Les damnés de la terre by Grove Press. Just in case the commemorative celebrations get out of hand and Fanon is in danger of being taken really seriously as a thinker, a thinker of prophetic relevance for our time. An ideal candidate for this task of deflation is eminent philosopher Kwame Anthony Appiah who, since the 1994 publication of his famed In *My Father's House*, should know a thing or two about having your views not just misunderstood and caricatured, but falsified outright. Who better to bring up to date the work of "framing Fanon," particularly in the matter of his putative views on truth enacted in that notorious passage in his book than the illustrious Kwame Appiah on the occasion of the Grove Press' new edition of the disreputable "campus classic," as he calls *The Wretched of the Earth* with sneering condescension? Who better to revive the task initiated by Hannah Arendt and pursued by Anthony Daniels, Adam Shatz, the unlettered Robert Fulford, the obscurantist Homi Bhabha and a succession of misreaders, uncomprehending and wilful misreaders, than the inimitable analytic liberal philosopher with a postmodernist attitude? You have to read Appiah's calumny of a review of that new edition in the New York Review of Books, 24 February 2022. Et tu Kwame?

PERVERSE CONSISTENCY: THE CASE OF ARENDT

Speaking of Hannah Arendt, trailblazer among Fanon's detractors and distorters. At the height of the embattled demands in the United States for Black Studies in the 1960s and 70s, Arendt vented her disdain in *On Violence* for Swahili and other "non-existent languages." That disdain was prefigured in *The Origins of Totalitarianism*. There, Arendt wondered aloud about the very humanity of Africans and, under the auspices of phenomenological ontology, scripted this disgusting apology for genocidal violence against Africans:

> This fright of something like oneself that still under no circumstances ought to be like oneself remained at the basis of slavery and became the basis for a race society... What made them [Africans] different from other human beings was not at all the color of their skin but the fact that they behaved like a part of nature, that they treated nature as their undisputed master, that they had not created a human world, a human reality, and that therefore nature had remained, in all its majesty, the only overwhelming reality compared to which they appeared to be phantoms, unreal and ghostlike. They were, as it were, "natural" human beings who lacked the specifically human character, the specifically human reality, so that when European men massacred them they somehow were not aware that they had committed murder.

"Critic of Boers or Africans?" That is the question Gail Presbey asks regarding Arendt in an essay of that title. The answer: We have here an unmistakable, revolting testimony of the banality of vulgar white supremacist evil. To counter it Presbey would proffer evidences of African cultural accomplishments. Lost cause. Worse still, complicit cause. Lost and complicit because predicated on white supremacy as court of adjudication regarding what is a human accomplishment, indeed what constitutes "the specifically human reality," owners of the criterion before which we African supplicants must prove our worth. Here is my question: Is there more than a fortuitous affinity between Arendt's mouthing of white supremacist antiblack racist *volk*lore in 1951 and her contemptuous dismissal of Swahili two decades later? From the subhuman you could hardly expect the capacity for language, the hallmark of civilization or more profoundly, "the house of Being," according to

Arendt's teacher Martin Heidegger. It would be even more absurd to attribute to Africans the capacity for philosophical rumination on human existence, death and finitude, wouldn't it? Thus decrees vulgar racism voiced in the authoritative accents of philosophy. All the same, I am intrigued by the following two utterances, one from darkest Africa, the other from "the West," before it became "the West". The first comes from the lyrics of a Ghanaian popular song:

> "Had I known that I was destined to die, I would never have come into this world."

The second, cited by Arendt in the closing paragraph of *On Revolution*, is from Sophocles:

> "Not to be born prevails over all meaning uttered in words; by far the second-best for life, once it has appeared, is to go as swiftly as possible whence it came."

What? An extended family resemblance between ancient Greek thinking and an emanation of the savage mind as archetypes of a tragic metaphysics of human existence? An invitation to listen to cogitations by the accredited progenitors of Reason together with effusions from ancestral spirits of the Rastaman's Vibrations? Is that possible? Philosophical investigations – call them scenes of the proverb contest – featuring African and Western conceptual specimens? What follows is an invitation to share the challenge and the thrill of a proverb contest offered in the belief that our eyes and ears have not been rendered irremediably incurious by the din and the blinkers designed to keep our senses imprisoned in windowless enclosures.

ATO SEKYI-OTU

SOME TRANSCULTURAL CURIOSITIES

The ways of fortune are obscure whither they go.
–Euripides, Alcestis.

I judge that it might be true that fortune is arbiter of half our actions, but that it leaves the other half, or close to it, for us to govern.
–Machiavelli, The Prince.

When a man says yes his chi says yes also.
–An Igbo saying made famous by Chinua Achebe in *Things Fall Apart*.

Man proposes, God disposes.
–A favourite Christian Ghanaian saying.

*i found god in myself
& i loved her/i loved her fiercely.*
–Ntozake Shange

The mighty God is a living [wo]man...In the kingdom of Jah [wo]man shall reign.
–Bob Marley and the Wailers (with necessary amendments)

Which of these countervailing sayings leaves a larger space for human freedom? We primitive Africans are said to believe in the existence and power of devils. Pure superstition, they say. Christians, being civilized, believe in the existence and the power of *the* devil. Poly-demonology versus mono-demonology. Big difference, no doubt. But which one is less restrictive: a belief that, in postmodernist jargon, "decentres" the source and symbolism of evil (and by implication the provenance and possibility of goodness); or one that assigns it all to one figure, one agent? Can it be that the former has the virtue of nesting a certain metaphysical pluralism and thereby fostering the prospect of human self-determination in all its rich and shareable forms, variegated idioms of what it means to belong to this peculiar community of earthlings called humanity?

THE POVERTY OF MONOCULTURALISM

Harold Bloom might have sneered at the very thought of such a possibility, the reciprocal intelligibility of African and Western philosophies of existence. Bloom devoted a lifetime to studying the work of the man, Shakespeare, who dramatized the luxuriant shapes in which human universals come. And what did he come up with? The idolatry of monoculturalism, the idolatry which *is* monoculturalism, the worship of one finite story of the human enterprise, the self-blinding ritual Chimamanda Ngozi Adichie warns us against. Pity. Had he been liberated from that imprisoning monopoly, Bloom might have been intrigued by the following contrasting utterances concerning the posthumous fate of human reputations: "It is only after it dies that we can tell the [true] size of a frog" – An Akan saying. "The evil that men do lives after them/Their good is oft interred with their bones" – Shakespeare (of course), *Julius Caesar*. Two versions of meditation on death, memory and the true measure of a human life. But in Bloom's judgment Shakespeare is the one and only true god contemplation of whose majesty would save the West from destruction by the barbarians – feminists, Marxists, Black Studies types, all the sorry inmates of "the school of resentment." Shakespeare single-handedly "invented the human." Just like other one-man acts of world transformation such as: "Ronald Reagan single-handedly defeated the Soviet Union and ended the Cold War." Let's confine matters to the realm of worldly things and say absolutely nothing about truly wondrous solo cosmic works of *creatio ex nihilo* accomplished by the divinity, a divinity who bears a suspiciously striking resemblance to our African potentates. No wonder our potentates are all ardent men of faith, faith in a god made in their own image, all powerful just like them – monumental narcissism masquerading as fearful piety.

ATO SEKYI-OTU

WRONGFUL CONVICTION

Bloom, the zealous sentinel of Western civilization, should have looked closer home before pinning responsibility for the threat to cultural treasures on those resentful barbarians: emblematic instance of mistaken identity and wrongful conviction, if ever there was one. Bloom should have listened to the chief ministers of the "special relationship" as they deployed their verbal arsenal in the grand enterprise of "subduing the proud and protecting the weak" as Virgil, griot laureate of empire, would have put it. These were their terms of art: "collateral damage," "degrading his weapons of mass destruction," "regime change" and the like, grotesque euphemisms for ghastly acts. These phrases will no doubt enrich the linguistic legacy bequeathed to the "civilized world" from theatres of slaughter since the aggression against Vietnam, aggression misnamed, in a characteristic act of verbal trickery, as the "Vietnam War" – precursor as brutal fact and duplicitous language to the "Iraq War" some five decades later. It was, you will recall, in the vortex of that earlier heroic undertaking that killing was given the lyrical moniker, "terminating with extreme prejudice." John F. Kennedy, New Rome's iconic charmer, famously said of Winston Churchill – bless his anti-imperialist soul – that "he marshalled the English language and sent it forth into battle." In the prelude to the Mesopotamian mayhem and even as its unspeakable horror unfolded, Churchill's progeny, the wretched Tony Blair, would join in the degradation of the language of *the* bard – the only one – enlisting it in the service of sophistry, adorning the unjustifiable with specious reasoning, as he savoured the vicarious thrill of imperial power now that Britannia no longer ruled the waves and pillaged the earth. But such were the debased standards of intelligible speech in New Rome that the pedestrian Blair was held up as a paragon of eloquence, peerless surrogate for the crudities of the voice of America and its mumbling chieftain, George Bush. Why indeed wouldn't the US rush to adopt Blair as surrogate spokesman after the world was subjected to the leaden prose of Colin Powell's lying testimony before the United Nations Security Council on the eve of the American aggression against Iraq? Why wouldn't aphasiac America in desperation conscript Tony Blair after France's Foreign Minister Dominique de Villepin delivered a memorable rebuttal in the elegant poetry of Gallic reason – "In this temple of the United Nations, we are the guardians of an ideal."? Blair as the true leader of the "free world" when it badly needed one, true leader for being inimitably obsequious. Where is Orwell, again, when we really need him?

"SINGING TRUTH"

Wicked deeds are always accompanied, if not presaged, by the degradation of language and the elevation of its artful manipulator to a place of honour. The work of justice is inseparable from the felicity of words, words of "singing truth," as it is said of the speech of Isanusi, the seditious seer in Ayi Kwei's tale of the African condition, according to him "the most profoundly human condition": speech of radiant beauty even as the truth it tells sears the innermost depths of our being.

EPILOGUE

While I Am Still Old Enough To Dream

Concerning "Home," the last of the triad of places named in the title of these reflections, I have said little, envisioning it as the undiscovered country of our unending yearning and preferring to evoke the prodigal variety of places and people, events and acts, ways of being and seeing, which have conspired to render that yearning seem doomed to remain perpetually incapable of consummation. It is as if we are only ever permitted glimpses and intimations of home from dismal knowledge of what it is not, the blighted tapestry of places where at one point in time or another, by choice or happenstance, we lay our heads and dwell, the contingent homesteads of our fraught existence, beginning, alas, with the land of our birth. In the foregoing considerations, then, unvarnished pictures of unwholesome conditions, cruel social orders, horrendous events set afoot by terrible desires, demonic deeds committed by wicked powers and principalities – these things would seem to have all but overruled imagination of another world and remembrance of future times, eclipsing the faintest glimmers of the lodestar whose name is home. Nevertheless, that lodestar *as* lodestar endures. It can be descried in stubborn spaces of refusal the world over, gleaned from the people's murmurs and outbursts of discontent, prefigured in the aspirations and ends made manifest in their curses and demands, in so many insurgent practices presaging "this Africa to come," one local vision of the universal affirmation that another world is possible. But is it not odd for an aged soul to hold on to the dream of home, hold on with such tenacity to the very principle of hope, always the special province and natural right of youth? Not when the young, foresaken by gluttonous and visionless elders, overwhelmed by what the poet calls "the industry of survival," their temporal horizon shrunken to artful coping, one day at a time, with the exigencies of bare life, not when the young are thus in danger of utterly abjuring that natural right of cultivating seedlings of a better tomorrow. Under these circumstances, we are constrained to question received wisdom regarding the rightful age for representing that regenerative organ of time's body called possibility. Then we are led to reconsider the things we can do with words foretelling human prospects in accordance with life's cycle.

"When I grow too old to dream": so wails the famous Sigmund Romberg and Oscar Hammerstein II song. But by the time Stanley Turrentine, with a little help from Jimmy Smith, puts his saxophone to work on that tune, the soaring exultation of its cadences gives the lie to those very words, utters a sublime rebuttal to the canard according to which the will to dream is doomed to decay even as the body's energies wither with inexorable finality. It is as though the only way to endure bearing witness to the world's sour truths is to savor without end the invincible power of the song; to heed in so doing Bob's call to "Chant Down Babylon"; to proclaim, in defiance of time's vaunted dominion, the ageless possibility of the dream. Nothing less will do justice to the ills that stirred an old soul to echo the voices of the furies in this concert of peeves. Nothing will more fittingly honour the task the ancestors keep asking of us: to strive after a home worthy of our humanity.

About the author

Ato Sekyi-Otu is a Ghanaian political philosopher. He was born at Saltpond, Ghana in 1941 and until 1971 was known as Daniel Sackey Walker. He went to Harvard and received an A.B. in Government in 1966. He pursued graduate studies at the University of Toronto where he worked with the renowned Canadian political theorist C.B. Macpherson and received his PhD in 1971. He taught in the Department of Social Science and the Graduate Program in Social and Political Thought at York University, Toronto until he retired in 2006 as Emeritus Professor. He is best known for his work on Frantz Fanon and Ayi Kwei Armah. In 1996 he wrote an acknowledged classic in the literature on Fanon entitled *Fanon's Dialectic of Experience* published by Harvard University Press. His most recent book is *Left Universalism, Africacentric Essays* published by Routledge in 2018, which won the 2019 Caribbean Philosophical Association Frantz Fanon Outstanding Book Award.

Partisan Universalism. Essays in honour of Ato Sekyi-Otu. Edited by Gamal Abdel Shahid & Sofia Noori. Daraja Press, 2021. https://darajapress.com/publication/partisan-universalism-essays-in-honour-of-ato-sekyi-otu

www.ingramcontent.com/pod-product-compliance
Lightning Source LLC
Chambersburg PA
CBHW070838160426
43192CB00012B/2237